THIS IS ETHICS

THIS IS PHILOSOPHY

Series editor: Steven D. Hales

Reading philosophy can be like trying to ride a bucking bronco – you hold on for dear life while "transcendental deduction" twists you to one side, "causa sui" throws you to the other, and a 300-word, 300-year-old sentence comes down on you like an iron-shod hoof the size of a dinner plate. *This Is Philosophy* is the riding academy that solves these problems. Each book in the series is written by an expert who knows how to gently guide students into the subject regardless of the reader's ability or previous level of knowledge. Their reader-friendly prose is designed to help students find their way into the fascinating, challenging ideas that compose philosophy without simply sticking the hapless novice on the back of the bronco, as so many texts do. All the books in the series provide ample pedagogical aids, including links to free online primary sources. When students are ready to take the next step in their philosophical education, *This Is Philosophy* is right there with them to help them along the way.

This Is Philosophy: An Introduction
Steven D. Hales

This Is Philosophy of Mind: An Introduction
Pete Mandik

This Is Ethics: An Introduction
Jussi Suikkanen

Forthcoming:

This Is Metaphysics: An Introduction
Kristopher McDaniel

This Is Epistemology: An Introduction
Clayton Littlejohn

This Is Philosophy of Religion: An Introduction
Neil Manson

This Is Modern Philosophy: An Introduction
Kurt Smith

This Is Political Philosophy: An Introduction
Alex Tuckness and Clark Wolf

This Is Bioethics: An Introduction
Udo Schuklenk

THIS IS ETHICS

AN INTRODUCTION

JUSSI SUIKKANEN

WILEY Blackwell

This edition first published 2015

Registered Office
John Wiley & Sons Ltd, The Atrium, Southern Gate, Chichester, West Sussex, PO19 8SQ, UK

Editorial Offices
350 Main Street, Malden, MA 02148-5020, USA
9600 Garsington Road, Oxford, OX4 2DQ, UK
The Atrium, Southern Gate, Chichester, West Sussex, PO19 8SQ, UK

For details of our global editorial offices, for customer services, and for information about how to apply for permission to reuse the copyright material in this book please see our website at www.wiley.com/wiley-blackwell.

Library of Congress Cataloging-in-Publication Data is available for this title

hbk: 9781118479407
pbk: 9781118479858

A catalogue record for this book is available from the British Library.

Cover design by Cyan Design

Set in 10.5/13 pt MinionPro by Toppan Best-set Premedia Limited

Printed and bound in Singapore by Markono Print Media Pte Ltd

1 2015

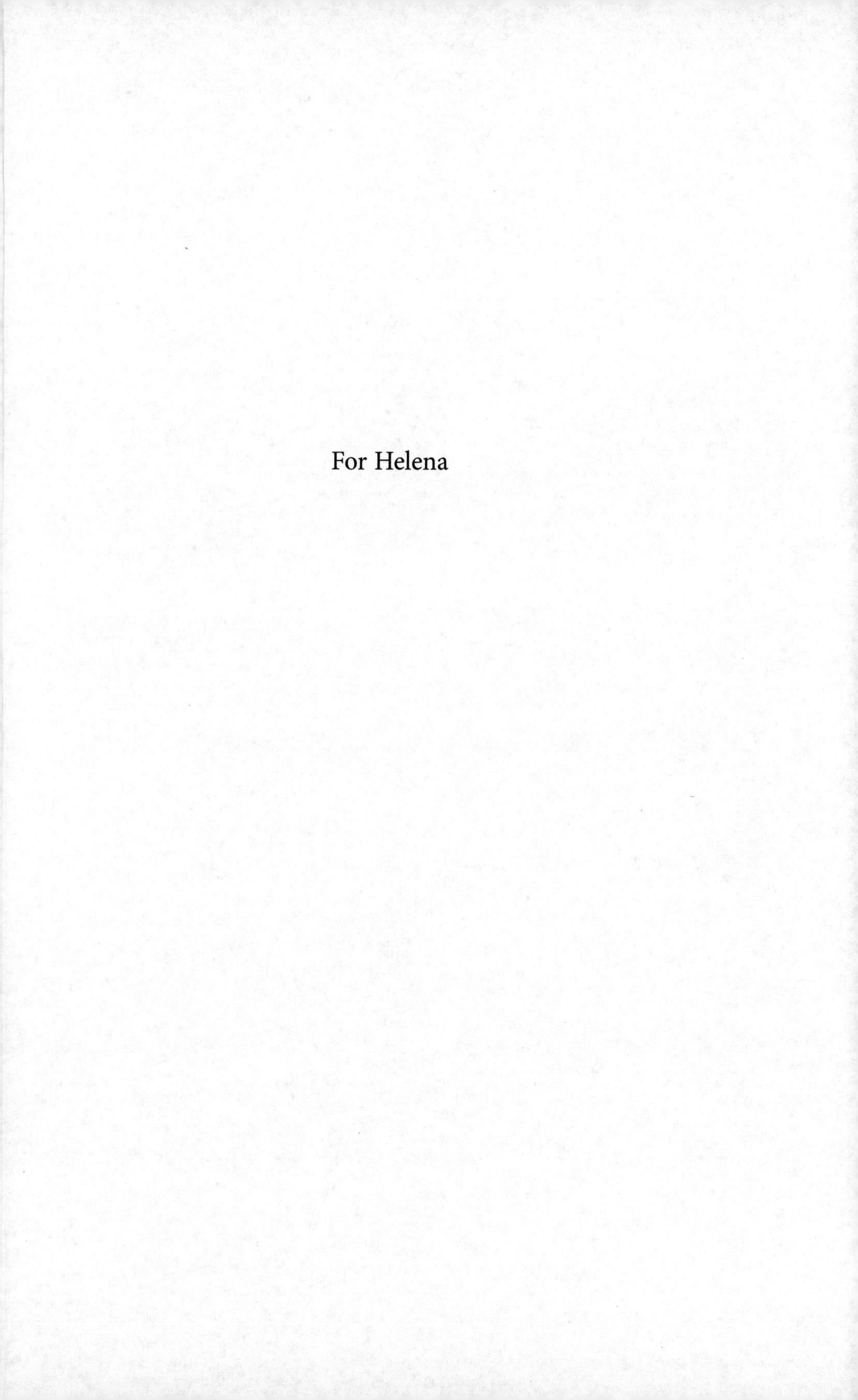

For Helena

For Helena

CONTENTS

PREFACE

This book is an introduction to philosophical investigation of morality. If this were an introduction to the philosophy of quantum mechanics, the first part of this book would need to tell you what quantum mechanics is. Fortunately, when it comes to morality, we can start philosophizing more directly. You already have your own views about what is right and wrong. Hopefully, you think that burning newborn babies just for the sake of it would be wrong and that it is right to help your friends when they are in need. Like most people, you also care about doing the right thing and you blame other people for acting wrongly. You have had moral disagreements with other people: you have perhaps debated the rights and wrongs of practices such as abortion, suicide, torture, using drugs, and eating meat. This means that you already know quite a lot about the subject matter of this book. This book is not intended to preach to you on these issues, which you have probably figured out yourself.

If you already understand so much about ethics, why should you spend even more time reading about it from this book? As mentioned, it's not even going to give you all the right answers. Fortunately, there are plenty of good reasons for reading this introduction to moral philosophy. Here are the main ones. First of all, the subject matter of moral philosophy matters to each one of us in a very personal and concrete way. A large part of moral philosophy tries to understand how you can live a good life and how you should treat other people. Even if philosophy might not be able to give you conclusive answers to these questions in the new situations you face, it can definitely help you to investigate them more clearly and thoroughly. If you study ethics carefully, you will have better conceptual resources and argumentative skills for thinking about how you ought to live. In this way, studying ethics can make a real difference to your life.

There are also other good reasons for studying ethics. If you read moral philosophy with an open mind, this can alleviate at least some of the worries you might have about whether anything really matters in the first place. Many people today are skeptical about morality. It is fashionable to say that it's all just a matter of opinion and that "might makes right." Philosophers have recognized how hard defending these skeptical views really is. Philosophy can thus also make you more confident about moral standards. Hopefully, by the end of this book you will also grant that there is reason to study ethics just for its own sake. Moral philosophy has attracted some of the greatest minds throughout human history and the work done in this area is often fascinating and brilliant. Yet much of the best research in moral philosophy is also fairly difficult due to the complex nature of the subject matter. One aim of this book is to give you the tools you will need for studying academic moral philosophy further.

This book is divided into four parts. Each part will consider a set of basic questions in moral philosophy. The first part is about what makes your life go better. Consider important life choices such as whether to raise a family or pursue a career in media or health care. When we make these kinds of choices, we often think about what we enjoy and what makes us happy. We might also think about how we could live a good or a meaningful life. The first part of this book is about these basic concepts (pleasure, happiness, well-being, and the meaning of life) which we all use to make important decisions in our lives. It asks what these things are and how important they are ultimately.

The second part of this book is about how we should treat other people. The area of moral philosophy which investigates this question is called "normative ethics." In normative ethics, philosophers investigate ethical theories which attempt to capture systematically what is right and wrong. Should you do what is best for you, or what is best for everyone? Should you do what a virtuous person would do in your situation, or act in a way you could want everyone to act in it? These are some of the questions that will be investigated. This part will also consider how complicated morality is. Is what is right and wrong so messy that it can't be captured with a simple set of basic principles?

The third part of this book will focus on more theoretical questions about morality. It considers whether what is right and wrong depends on what moral principles we accept or on what God commands us to do. It also investigates whether actions can be objectively right and wrong and whether right and wrong can be investigated scientifically. The last chapter of this part will also attempt to understand how morality moves us. Why is it that when someone sincerely says that eating meat is wrong, you would expect them not to eat meat? This question leads us to examine a theory according to which moral claims express our personal attitudes.

The concluding part of this book explores two more concrete ethical questions. The first of these concerns moral responsibility: when is it appropriate to praise and blame other people for what they do? For example, if everything we do is determined by the laws of nature, is it still all right to be angry if someone cheats on you? After all, in this case they couldn't help it. The very last chapter describes how philosophers have approached one of the most pressing ethical problems of our times. At the moment, the number of people living in the world is increasing rapidly and we also know that the world is getting warmer because we continue to emit greenhouse gases. Many people are worried that because of this the lives of future people will be much worse than ours. What are our obligations toward future generations in this situation? Should we make any sacrifices to help them?

The most important ideas covered in each chapter will be summarized at the end of the chapter. These summaries will also include study questions, which will both test how well you have understood the philosophical ideas and ask you to evaluate the discussed views and arguments. Hopefully you will also get a chance to discuss these questions with other people at a seminar or a reading group. Furthermore, each chapter contains an annotated bibliography, which should help you to find further material to read on the topics you are interested in.

The text also contains hyperlinks. They mainly guide you to online sources which explain the basic concepts and theories in more detail. They also link to podcasts and videos in which famous philosophers talk about the discussed views. Some links contain more information about the examples used in this book and some are just for entertainment (please do not let these links distract you when you go through the material for the first time).

A few words are needed about notation. **Bold letters** are used for two purposes. All hyperlinks are in bold. If you are using a paper copy of the book, there is always an endnote in the text after these links that gives you the address of the linked web site. In addition, all technical terms are in bold. These terms are explained within the text, but you can also find them in the glossary which is at the end of this book. *Italics* are used for emphasis and book titles. Finally, quotation marks (" ") are used for two purposes. They are used for both ordinary quotations and for when words are mentioned but not used (this latter use of the quotation marks will be explained in Chapter 7).

This book has been divided into core material and additional material. If you are reading the book for the first time and you have not studied any philosophy before, you should read the core materials first. They constitute the main bulk of the book. The additional material can be found in the sections marked with an asterisk (*) both in the bibliography and the book itself. These sections will introduce you to more sophisticated views, arguments, and objections in the given area. They are both important and much discussed in contemporary moral philosophy, but also often are slightly more technical and not always absolutely necessary for understanding the basic crux of the topic in question. These additional materials are explained in a way that should still be accessible if you use a bit more time and effort on the arguments.

The order in which the main elements of moral philosophy have been presented in this book is natural. It is easiest to start from thinking about your own life since the question of how to live well is a reasonably simple one. After you have thought about this question it is much easier to consider other people and how you should treat them. Once you have considered these basic questions in moral philosophy, you will tend to start to think about the status of morality from a more general, theoretical perspective. You should then finally be able to use all the new resources you have acquired throughout the book for thinking about some of the most important concrete ethical problems we face.

Some people will prefer a different route around moral philosophy, because they think that we must tackle the theoretical worries about morality first. If you are worried about the possibility of moral knowledge, you could equally well start from the metaethical material in Part Three. It should address some of the fundamental worries you might have. If these chapters convince you that it makes sense to talk and think about moral questions, then you could go on to study normative ethics (Part Two) and questions about the good life (Part One) next. This would allow you to leave the more concrete questions about moral responsibility, population growth, and climate change to last. If you are building a lecture course around this book, you should split each chapter into at least two lectures. Just to take few examples: you could spend one lecture on happiness and one on well-being (Chapter 2), one on consequentialism and one on Kantian ethics (Chapter 4), and so on. This should allow you to go into a bit more detail regarding the basic material presented in this book.

ACKNOWLEDGMENTS

I first want to thank Kirk Surgener and three anonymous referees from Wiley-Blackwell for valuable comments and corrections on earlier drafts of this manuscript. Much of this book is based on discussions I've had with other philosophers. For this reason, I would like to thank the following people:

- at the **University of Helsinki** (http://www.helsinki.fi/philosophy/), Antti Kauppinen, Teemu Toppinen, Pilvi Toppinen, Pekka Mäkelä, Mikko Salmela, Jaakko Kuorikoski, Raimo Tuomela, Timo Airaksinen, Gabriel Sandu, Panu Raatikainen, Maria Lasonen-Aarnio, Petri Ylikoski, Al Mele, Piers Rawling, Jens Timmermann, and many others;
- at the **University of Reading** (http://www.reading.ac.uk/phil/), Brad Hooker, Philip Stratton-Lake, Jonathan Dancy, Bart Streumer, John Cottingham, Max de Gaynesford, David Oderberg, Emma Borg, Galen Strawson, Alex Gregory, Guy Fletcher, Debbie Roberts, Fiona Woollard, Bryan Weaver, Jeppe Andersen, Constantine Sandis, Daniel Whiting, Anna Bergqvist, and many others;
- at **UNC, Chapel Hill** (http://philosophy.unc.edu/), Geoffrey Sayre-McCord, Sven Nyholm, Caj Strandberg, Joshua Knobe, Ben Bramble, Susan Wolf, Dorit Bar-On, Thomas Hill Jr., and many others;
- at **Oxford** (http://www.philosophy.ox.ac.uk/), Jonas Olson, Krister Bykvist, John Broome, Daniel Star, Ralph Wedgwood, Joseph Raz, Roger Crisp, Nicholas Southwood, Matthew Liao, Simon Rippon, and many others;
- at the **University of Leeds** (http://www.leeds.ac.uk/arts/info/20048/philosophy/), Pekka Väyrynen, Gerald Lang, Daniel Elstein, John Divers, Robbie Williams, Chris Megone, Ulrike Heuer, Rob Lawlor, Jamie Dow, Georgia Testa, and many others;

- at the **University of Birmingham** (www.birmingham.ac.uk/philosophy/), Alex Miller, Nikk Effingham, Al Wilson, Darragh Byrne, Iain Law, Heather Widdows, Joss Walker, Jeremy Williams, Kirk Surgener, Lisa Bortolotti, Tom Sorell, and many others;
- and finally, at the **Pea Soup blog** (http://peasoup.typepad.com/), Doug Portmore, Ben Bradley, Campbell Brown, Chris Heathwood, Dan Boisvert, David Shoemaker, David Sobel, Jamie Dreier, Jimmy Lenman, Mark Schroeder, Mark van Roojen, Robert Johnson, and many, many others.

Without talking to you and learning from you, this book could not have been written. I'd also like to thank everyone else who has philosophized with me at various conferences and talks, and finally my mother and father for all their support.

Part One

WHAT'S IN OUR INTERESTS?

1
PLEASURE

Even if some people (usually parents and administrators) seem to think so, studying ethics doesn't *necessarily* improve the quality of your life or make you a better person. It will, however, give you useful resources for thinking about some of the most important things in life more clearly. If you get your head around these tools and apply them in real life, this can make a real difference to how you will live. Philosophical tools can help you to make important decisions in life and even sometimes to become a better person. In this sense, ethics isn't just an abstract and theoretical academic discipline. It isn't just about talking a lot about nothing. 1.1

The two main practical questions philosophers have thought about are how you should treat other people and what goals you should have in order to live well yourself. It is easier to begin from the second question, which concerns your own life only. When you think about how to live well, you don't have to take other people into account, at least to begin with. All you need to ask yourself is: how can I make my own life go better? This will be the main focus of Part One of this book. The second part will then consider what kind of constraints morality sets on you when you pursue your own good. What are the things that it would be wrong to do when you consider not only your own life but also the lives of others? 1.2

So let's start from the question of how you can make your life go better. Consider the following kinds of concrete questions: 1.3

- Should you pursue a career in journalism or health care?
- Should you practice an instrument or play computer games?

This Is Ethics: An Introduction, First Edition. Jussi Suikkanen.

- Should you study hard or hang out with friends?
- Should you have passionate affairs or a stable relationship?
- Should you travel or volunteer?

How you answer these questions will, in many ways, decide what your life will turn out to be like. Get the answers right and you will prosper. Approaching these questions can be daunting because it's not immediately obvious how you could even begin to tackle them. What is it that you should be thinking about when you are trying to decide?

1.4 The first two chapters of this book will offer you philosophical tools for finding answers to these basic questions about how you should live. They are some of the first philosophical questions which philosophers started to think about thousands of years ago. The main ethical works of **Plato** and **Aristotle**, the founding fathers of philosophy who lived in Ancient Greece, are entitled ***The Republic*** and ***Nicomachean Ethics*** respectively.[1] These famous books, which were written about 2500 years ago, both consider the question of how to live a good life. Following Plato and Aristotle, it is natural to approach the previous questions by considering the following kinds of things:

- what you would enjoy;
- what would make you happy;
- what would improve your life; and
- what would make your life more meaningful.

Studying philosophy can clarify what you should be focusing on when you make important life choices by using these natural standards. It can also help you to weigh how important pleasure, happiness, well-being, and a meaningful life are. This chapter will focus on **pleasure** and how important it is. The next chapter will then discuss **happiness**, **well-being**, and **the meaning of life**.[2] The topics of these chapters are then directly relevant for how we are to live.

Three Questions about Pleasure

1.5 When you consider the connection between pleasure and living a good life, you should **follow Aristotle**[3] and distinguish between three sets of different questions. These are:

1. What are the sources of pleasures? What gives you pleasure?
2. What is it to experience pleasure? What does pleasure consist of?
3. How important is pleasure? Should you pursue pleasure?

These questions can be illustrated with a simple example. Ann is suffering from the common cold. In this case, we also can ask the previous three questions. How did Ann get the cold? This is a question about the causal origin of her cold. An answer to it might tell a story about how Ann met people who were already suffering from the cold or a story about how viruses move from one body to another.

The second question would in this case focus on what it is for Ann to 1.6
suffer from the cold. In virtue of what does Ann count as a person who is suffering from the cold? This question is not about Ann's symptoms. It is rather about the nature of her disease. The correct answer to it would tell a story about upper respiratory tract infections which are usually caused by hundreds of different species of viruses.

The final question about Ann's cold is about how bad it is for Ann 1.7
to have the disease. This is an evaluative question about **good and bad.**[4] The answers to it should tell Ann how much effort she should use to try to avoid getting the cold. You can then ask exactly the same questions about pleasure. What are the things that give you pleasure? What constitutes experiencing pleasure? And, how important is it to experience pleasure?

The correct answers to these questions might well depend on one 1.8
another. Views about the nature of pleasure have significant consequences for how valuable pleasure is. However, we should at least attempt to treat these questions separately. **As Descartes advised us, we should pursue clarity in philosophy by dividing philosophical problems into smaller parts that can be considered separately.**[5]

Philosophers are rarely interested in the sources of pleasure because you 1.9
don't need philosophy to tell you what gives you or other people pleasure. We all know what gives us pleasure personally. You probably get pleasure from eating ice cream, seeing friends, sunbathing, and so on. You are also aware that other people do not enjoy the same things as you. They might get pleasure from lifting weights or dancing samba. Different people thus get pleasure from different things.

The best way to tell what gives other people pleasure is to ask them. This 1.10
is why it is the job of the psychologists and social scientists rather than philosophers to tell us what the sources of pleasure are. **The empirical**

study of the sources of pleasure has already revealed many interesting facts[6] Scientists now know that about 25% of people have tongues with a higher density of receptors (Bloom, 2010, pp. 27–29). Because of this, they are called **supertasters**.[7] If you are a supertaster, then everything will taste more intense to you. There are things that many other people find pleasant (such as whiskey, beer, black coffee, hot spices, sprouts, cabbage, and grapefruit) which the supertasters find unpleasant. So, if you don't like these things, then you probably are a supertaster.

1.11 It is not news that different people find different foods pleasant. We have always known this. However, that different foods systematically taste unpleasant for people who have more receptors in their tongues is interesting and something you can't know from the armchair. You need science to reveal this interesting fact about the sources of pleasure.

1.12 There are also many interesting questions about how you should investigate what the sources of pleasure are. Should you ask people or scan their brains when they are engaged in various activities? Moral philosophers should at least be aware of what the causal origins of pleasure are. Such information will be relevant when you try to answer questions about the nature of pleasure and its importance.

What Is Pleasure?

1.13 Sometimes the simplest questions are the most difficult to answer. One such question is: What is pleasure? Many philosophers have assumed that this question has an obvious answer. This has led them to state their answers too rashly. More recently, this question has become a focus of intense philosophical speculation (**Katz, 2006**[8]; Crisp, 2006, pp. 103–111). This section will consider three basic views about what pleasure is.

1.14 You have already experienced pleasure. You have hugged your parents, eaten ice cream, and taken a bubbly bath. You are therefore personally acquainted with pleasure in the same way as you are also acquainted with your friends. This matters because whatever this chapter ends up saying about pleasure should fit what you all already know about positive experiences.

1.15 We also use many other words such as "joy," "enjoyment," and "delight" for pleasure. All these words refer to the experiences which you have when you feel good and happy. The flip side of these pleasant experiences are the negative experiences of pain and suffering. We have them when we feel sad and unhappy. Psychologists use the terms **positive affect and negative affect**[9] for pleasures and pains in this broad sense. In virtue of what, then, does an experience count as a pleasure?

The sensation view

According to the sensation view, pleasure is a simple sensation of its own 1.16
kind. This answer was defended by **David Hume** and **Jeremy Bentham (Hume, 1739–1740, book II, I.i; Bentham, 1789, ch. 4)**.[10] Consider other simple experiences like hearing the C note played on piano. There is something it is like to have this experience. This experience is unique, because it doesn't feel like any other experience. It is also difficult say how this experience is different.

The sensation view says the same thing about pleasure. According to this 1.17
view, all you can say about pleasure is that it is a **warm fuzzy feeling**.[11] People who accept this view therefore think that pleasure is a simple and unanalyzable experience which doesn't feel like any other experience.

This view fits with the idea that there are different sources of pleasure. 1.18
You can have the sensation of pleasure because you are eating chocolate, whereas perhaps your friend gets that same sensation from playing with dogs instead. This view also leaves room for important differences between different experiences of pleasure. The pleasure you get from eating chocolate can be shorter and be more intense than the pleasure your friend gets from playing with dogs. More intense and long-lasting pleasures are presumably more valuable than shorter and less intense pleasures.

The attitude view

The previous view has an obvious problem, which has led many people to 1.19
adopt a more complex theory called the attitude view (**Brentano**,[12] 1981 [1929]). The motivation for this view is that many pleasures are not simple sensations but rather more complex attitudes.

You can be pleased about your friend's new job or take pleasure in using 1.20
your new phone. The main distinguishing feature of these more complex pleasures is that they are not merely bodily sensations but rather experiences that have complex content. They are pleasures *about* how things are. The previous simple view is unable to make sense of these pleasures.

1.21 If you like the simple view, you could respond that when we talk about these more complex pleasures we really are talking about the causes of the relevant, simple, pleasure sensations. When you are pleased about your friend getting a job, this would only mean that her getting the job is causing you to have the simple sensation of pleasure. This idea does not work, though. What causes you to experience pleasure is not always the same thing as what you are pleased about. That something bad happens to someone you know can cause you to be pleased about how things are in your own life. If your neighbor hadn't lost his job, you perhaps would not be so pleased about your own job. Despite this, it is not true that what causes you to experience the pleasure (your neighbor's misfortune) is what your pleasure is about (your own job).

1.22 A better theory of pleasure needs to make sense of the fact that you can be pleased about things and take pleasure in doing things. The attitude view does this by saying that an experience of pleasure is a special attitude toward thoughts, objects, and activities. The attitude represents the relevant thoughts and objects in a certain positive way. When you are pleased about your team winning, you represent the thought that your team has won in a way that feels a certain good way.

1.23 Consider the attitude of fear. Instead of just being afraid, you are usually afraid of things. You can be afraid of snakes or that you will lose your job. Feeling fear consists in part of having a certain sensation – there is something it is like to be afraid. Despite this, fear is not just a sensation. It is an attitude toward things that are the objects of fear. Having this attitude toward things represents them in a way that feels a certain negative way.

1.24 According to this model, pleasure is likewise an attitude that represents things in a way that feels good. It is possible for different people to have different attitudes toward the same thing – you can be afraid of a horror film while you friend takes pleasure in it. These are different attitudes because they do not feel the same.

The desire view

1.25 The previous two views are problematic in the same way (**Sidgwick, 1907, p. 127**).[13] Consider different pleasures: the pleasure of having sex, the pleasure of eating a nice meal, the pleasure of dancing, and the pleasure of talking to friends. The previous views assume that all these pleasures feel the same.

The sensation view assumes that different things cause us to have a unique positive sensation which always feels the same. The attitude view claims that different pleasures are attitudes toward different things and that these attitudes always feel the same. There is always a unified positive tone to what it feels like to represent the relevant objects in the relevant way. 1.26

You might wonder why the previous two views need to assume that pleasures are either sensations or attitudes that feel in a certain unique positive way. The reason for this assumption is that both these views use how pleasures feel to explain what makes a certain state of mind a pleasure. They use the distinct positive tone of pleasures to explain what is supposed to make a pleasure a pleasure. 1.27

The main problem of these views, then, is that not all pleasures feel the same. When you consider what it feels like to have sex and what it feels like to talk to your friends, these experiences feel very different and yet both these experiences are pleasures. 1.28

According to the desire view, in all cases of pleasure there is first some more basic experience of its own, be it the experience of having sex or talking to your friends. These experiences are not pleasures as such, but they are experiences which you desire to have for their own sake when you have them (**Sidgwick, 1907, p. 127**;[14] Kagan, 1992, p. 170; Sumner, 1996, p. 90; Feldman, 2004 (Feldman calls his theory "attitudinal theory" of pleasure and his view combines the elements of the attitudinal and desire theories as described here). This desire toward the relevant experience makes all these experiences pleasures. In other words, the fact that you desire to have an experience when you are having it explains why this experience is a pleasure. 1.29

This view avoids the problems of the previous views. It can explain what is common to all pleasures without assuming that all pleasures feel the same. This is because it does not feel the same to desire different experiences. It can also tell us why we want to have pleasant experiences. If to experience pleasure is to have an experience you want to have, how could you fail to want to experience pleasure? So, the fact that you want to have pleasant experiences is just a trivial truth based on the nature of pleasure on this view. 1.30

The defenders of the other two views have used an analogy for responding to the objection that not all pleasures feel the same (Kagan, 1992, 172–175). Consider the **loudness**[15] of sounds. We can rank sounds by how loud they are. Yet you can compare how loud different sounds are even when these sounds have nothing else in common. They can have 1.31

different timbre, pitch, and so forth. In addition to loudness itself, there is nothing in common between the sound of a guitar and the sound of a saxophone.

1.32 Pleasantness might likewise be a dimension on which experiences vary. Like the case of loudness, perhaps there is nothing in common between equally pleasant experiences of sex and talking to your friends other than their pleasantness. Do you think that this analogy works? Here's just one reason to worry that it doesn't. When it comes to different sounds like the sound of a guitar and the sound of a saxophone, there is a genuine single dimension of loudness in experience on which they vary and you can put a finger on what that dimension is. It is hard to put into words, but if you think about it, there is a genuine similarity between loud sounds. In contrast, it is more difficult to find a genuine similarity in very different kinds of pleasant experiences. For example, not all very pleasant experiences are very intense experiences. Because of this difference, trying to understand pleasantness of experiences using the analogy of loudness of sounds doesn't seem to be very illuminating. It's not easy to put a finger on what that unique dimension of pleasantness would be like in all your experiences.

1.33 We should recognize, however, that the desire view also has its own problems. There are experiences which you desire to have for their own sake even if they are not pleasant. Imagine **a person who has never experienced pain**[16] (Crisp, 2006, p. 107). She could desire to continue to have her first experience of pain for its own sake just because it is a new experience. According to the desire view, this experience of pain would therefore be a pleasure. This must be wrong.

Physiology of pleasure*

1.34 The previous views are three ways to understand what pleasure is. Which one of these theories is correct is a controversial and interesting philosophical question. At this point, you might wonder why this question about what pleasure is can't simply be answered by considering what is going on in our brains when we experience pleasure. Why can't the philosophical question about the nature of pleasure be answered by considering the **physiology**[17] of pleasure?

1.35 **The physiology of pleasure**[18] can be summed up like this. When you experience pleasure, your body releases chemicals called **endorphins and enkephalins.**[19] They belong to the opioids group, which also includes heroin. Your brain has receptor cells that are sensitive to these chemicals. These receptor cells are located in a region deep in your brain called the **ventral pallidum**.[20] Some of the receptor cells are also in an area just behind your eyes called the **orbitofrontal cortex**.[21] When you experience pleasure, there are a lot neurons firing in these areas of your brain.

You could suggest that pleasure is just the physical event of neurons 1.36
firing in the relevant regions of the brain. This simple view used to be popular in the philosophy of mind.[22] The problem is that views like this seem unable to capture the fact that experiencing a pleasure *feels* like something. Even if we knew everything there was to know about what happens in the brain of a person who is having a pleasant experience, it seems that this doesn't amount to understanding very much about pleasure. For that, you have to experience pleasure yourself and you have to know what role pleasure plays in people's lives.

This is why many philosophers believe that there must be something 1.37
more to pleasure than merely certain neurons firing in your brain. The previous views about pleasure attempt to capture what this additional element is. Of course, they too face similar challenges. If a crucial element of pleasure is the way it feels, then in understanding pleasure it may not be very helpful just to know that pleasures are the experiences we want to have. This means that the philosophical views, too, need to have a more informative story to tell about how pleasures feel.

Value of Pleasure

Let us then consider how good pleasure is. Is pleasure so important that 1.38
you need to think about the amount of pleasure you will experience when you make important decisions in your life? When you ask this question, you must first decide what kind of value you are interested in. A single joke can be both funny and insulting. Such a joke has a lot of comedy value but little moral value.

This section is only interested in the **prudential value** of pleasure. 1.39
Prudential value is a technical term. When philosophers consider the prudential value of pleasure, they are interested in whether having pleasant experiences makes your life go better. Is having these experiences in your interests and good for you? It is also important to keep in mind that some things have **intrinsic** prudential value whereas other things have only **instrumental** prudential value (and some have both).[23]

1.40 The things that have merely instrumental value do not make your life go better in themselves. They only help you to get other things that improve your life. Money is like this. Having it in itself is not that great, but it does help you to get other things that are good for you.

1.41 Intrinsic prudential goods are, in contrast, fundamental elements of living a good life. Many people, for example, think that having close personal relationships is a constituent of a good life in itself. You do not want to have such relationships merely because having them enables you to have some other goods. Having close personal relationships itself improves your life.

1.42 The question then is whether pleasure has intrinsic prudential value. Does having pleasant experiences make your life go better in itself? There are three answers to this question. **Hedonism**[24] claims that only pleasure is good for you. Pluralism agrees that pleasures make your life go better, but it adds that other things can do so too. Pessimism, in contrast, argues that pleasure cannot make your life go better at all.

Hedonism

1.43 As we saw above, pleasures are either attitudes that feel a certain positive way or experiences which you desire to have when you have them. It seems plausible that such attitudes and experiences are an important element of living a good life. Likewise, all pains either feel a certain negative way or they are experiences which you do not want to have. Having these experiences obviously makes your life go worse.

1.44 However, hedonists add that *only* pleasures can make your life go better and *only* pains can make your life worse. Nothing else matters. Consider having friends and family, being healthy, knowing things, and seeing beautiful works of art. According to hedonists, these goods cannot make your life go better as such. They can only improve your life insofar as you can get pleasure from them.

1.45 Hedonism has a number of advantages (Shafer-Landau, 2010, ch. 1). It can explain why there are many different kinds of good lives. According to hedonism, this is because different things give different people pleasurable experiences. Hedonism also fits the idea that you know best what would improve your life. Hedonists argue that this is because you know best what gives you pleasure. There are, in addition, two even stronger reasons to accept hedonism.

Argument in favor of hedonism 1: Discernible differences Many people believe that only things that you can notice can make your life go better. Whatever improves your life must make a discernible difference to your life from your own perspective. 1.46

Derek Parfit[25] invented a famous example to illustrate this (Parfit, 1984, p. 494). Imagine that you meet a stranger on the train. He tells you that he is seriously ill. Naturally, you want this stranger to get better, but, sadly, you will never hear what happens to him. The stranger will either get better or he won't, but you will never know which. What happens to the stranger after you leave the train makes no difference to what your life will look like from your own perspective. 1.47

Many people think that in this situation, what happens to the stranger later on cannot influence how well your life is going. According to them, only things that affect how things seem to you can make your life go better or worse. Hedonism nicely fits this idea. It says that only pleasures and pains can make your life go better or worse. These clearly are things that you can notice. Hedonism does not, therefore, leave room for things that could improve your life without you noticing them. Many people find hedonism convincing for this reason. 1.48

Argument in favor of hedonism 2: Motivation Many philosophers believe that nothing can make your life go better unless it is something that motivates you. If you then also think that we are all biologically hardwired to pursue pleasure, we get a powerful argument for hedonism. We can find traces of parts of this argument again from Bentham: "Nature has placed mankind under the governance of two sovereign masters, *pain* and *pleasure*. It is for them alone to point out what we ought to do, as well as to determine what we shall do" (**Bentham, 1789, ch. 1**).[26] 1.49

This quote nicely illustrates the popular view that pleasures and pains motivate you to pursue the sources of pleasure and to avoid the sources of pain. If you then also believe both that (i) what makes your life go better must be able to motive you and that (ii) nothing else than pleasures and pains moves you, you are forced to accept that only pleasures and pains have prudential value. 1.50

Higher pleasures There are thus many good arguments for hedonism. Before we move on, we need to discuss a famous objection to it and John Stuart Mill's equally famous response to this objection. 1.51

1.52 As mentioned above, hedonists used to believe that there are differences between pleasures only on two dimensions: length of duration and intensity. This leads to a problem that can be illustrated by a choice between the life of **Joseph Haydn** and the life of **an oyster** (Crisp, 1997, p. 24).[27] Haydn lived for 72 years and his life contained many intense pleasures. The oyster can only experience the most primitive mild pleasures. Imagine, then, a magic oyster whose life lasts for a million years. Would its life be better than Haydn's?

1.53 According to the simple hedonist view, the life of this oyster would be better than Haydn's even though Haydn's pleasures are more intense than the oyster's. At some point, the length of the oyster's pleasures will compensate for the fact that its pleasures are less intense. So if the intensity and duration of the pleasures are the only dimensions on which pleasures vary, if you make the mild pleasures last long enough they will always outweigh short intense pleasures in value. Many people find this consequence unintuitive. They think that Haydn's life must be better than the oyster's life no matter how long the oyster lives. For this reason, we must find another dimension on which pleasures vary such that no matter how long the mild and trivial pleasures last they will never be as good as Haydn's pleasures.

1.54 **John Stuart Mill** suggested that the previous problem can be avoided if you think that pleasures can be evaluated on a third qualitative dimension (**Mill, 1861, ch. 2, paras 4–8**).[28] Thus, according to him, some pleasures are qualitatively higher than others, just as some pleasures are more intense than others. For example, you might think that the pleasure of reading a novel is qualitatively higher than the low pleasure of watching reality television. The higher a pleasure is qualitatively, the better it makes your life. This helped Mill to claim that the oyster's life will never be as good as Haydn's because Haydn's pleasures are qualitatively so much higher than the oyster's trivial lower pleasures.

1.55 How do you know which experiences are higher pleasures? According to Mill, we must consider an experienced, competent, and sensitive person who is familiar with both types of pleasures and able to attain them both. If she "calmly and knowingly" chooses to have one pleasure over another, then that pleasure is a higher, more valuable pleasure. So, if this type of a special judge really chooses, after careful consideration, to compose music instead of just staying in the jacuzzi, then the former pleasure is qualitatively higher.

1.56 Does this response solve the problem? Many people worry that it either fails to deal with the Haydn/oyster case or it gives up on hedonism.

Remember that hedonism is the view that only pleasures can make your life go better. According to Mill, pleasures now vary on three dimensions: duration, intensity, and quality. The more an experience scores on these dimensions, the more pleasantness it has and thus the more value it also has. Haydn's pleasures are intense and qualitatively high but they last for only a short time. The oyster's pleasures are mild and qualitatively low but they last for a very long time. If we make the oyster's pleasures long enough, then it seems that the length of these pleasures should compensate for both their low intensity and their low quality so that the oyster's life once again becomes better than Haydn's.

In this situation, Mill seems to have to admit that something other than mere pleasantness makes Haydn's life better than the oyster's life. Mill himself sometimes wrote about how noble certain experiences are. This would allow him to say that Haydn's life is better because even if his life is less pleasant than the oyster's, it is better because it is a nobler life. The problem is that if you are a hedonist you can't say this, because, according to hedonism, only the pleasantness of our lives counts. 1.57

Pluralism about prudential value

You probably agree that having pleasures and avoiding pains makes your life go better. If you are **a pluralist**, you think that other things can improve your life too. In addition to pleasures, getting what you want, having friends, and achieving things can make your life go better. **Pluralism about prudential value**[29] is the view that many different things are good for you in themselves. 1.58

Different versions of pluralism will be discussed in more detail in the next chapter. This section focuses on one influential argument in favor of pluralism, which is supposed to show that pleasures and pains can't be the only things that affect how good your life is. This argument was first presented by **Robert Nozick** in his book *Anarchy, State, and Utopia* (Nozick, 1974).[30] It is based on a thought experiment of an **experience machine**.[31] 1.59

Nozick's experience machine argument Here is Nozick's influential argument in full: 1.60

> Suppose there were an experience machine that would give you any experience you desired. Superduper neurophysiologists could stimulate your brain so that you would think and feel you were writing a great novel, or making

a friend, or reading an interesting book. All the time you would be floating in a tank, with electrodes attached to your brain. Should you plug into this machine for life, preprogramming your life's experiences? ... Would you plug in? *What else can matter to us, other than how would lives feel from the inside?* (Nozick, 1974, pp. 42–43)

If you have seen ***The Matrix***,[32] you'll know what Nozick is imagining. If you haven't, you should, as it's a great sci-fi film (but skip the sequels that aren't as good).

1.61 Here is the crux of Nozick's argument. In real life, you experience a mix of pleasures and pains. You are then promised a life which would contain more pleasant experiences. The only downside is that you would have to live this life in a computer simulation. Nozick claims that you would not want to plug yourself into the machine, because this wouldn't improve your life.

1.62 According to hedonism, if you have more pleasant experiences in the machine, then your life will be better in it. Hedonists, after all, think that only pleasures and pains affect how good your life is, and yet most people say that they prefer to live in the real world. If you agree with this intuition, you should conclude that hedonism is mistaken. There are other things besides pleasures and pains that make a difference to how good your life is.

1.63 Nozick himself concluded from this case that there are at least three other things that must matter as well. Firstly, he thought that we want to do things and not merely have the experiences of doing them. In the experience machine you can only have the experience of swimming, whereas in the real world you can actually swim.

1.64 Secondly, Nozick believed that we want to be certain kinds of persons. Your life goes better the more courageous, kind, intelligent, witty, and loving you are. You can't realize these character traits in the machine. Finally, Nozick claimed that it matters to us that we are in actual contact with a deeper reality. You can have this contact in the real world. You can talk to real people and admire genuine works of art. In the experience machine you can only have simulated experiences, which are not the same.

1.65 *Two responses to Nozick* Although many people agree with Nozick's argument, it also has its problems. The first problem of the argument is that it assumes that our intuitions about the case are a reliable indication of what is good for us. There are empirical reasons to doubt this (**De Brigard, 2010**).[33] One reason is that we have been shown to suffer from **status quo bias.**[34] People have a strong preference for keeping things the way they are used to even if a change would be an improvement for them. The suggestion then is that this prevents you from seeing how good things would be for you in the experience machine.

This first response has a serious problem. De Brigard is saying that our intuitions about what kind of life is good – and, more importantly, our intuitions about the experience machine – are flawed because they reflect the fact that we just happen to like the way things are now. Unfortunately, if this were true then we would be more generally prevented from knowing what things are good for us, including whether pleasures themselves make our lives go better. The worry is that if the hedonist uses the status quo bias to respond to the experience machine objection then she has no way left for arguing for her own view either. Anything she might say for hedonism too would be based on her flawed intuitions. Fortunately, the hedonist has a better response to the experience machine objection. 1.66

Nozick's argument assumes that you could have equally pleasant experiences in the machine. This is the reason why hedonists have to accept that experientially slightly superior lives in the machine are better than lives in the real world. The problem for Nozick is that hedonists do not need to accept this idea (Feldman, 2004, p. 111). 1.67

Take the desire theory of pleasure. According to this theory, an experience is a pleasure if you desire to have the experience when you are having it. Assume that you want to have genuine experiences rather than simulated experiences in the machine. You have this desire even if you can't tell the two types of experiences apart from the inside. 1.68

According to the desire theory of pleasure, you could not in this situation have pleasures in the experience machine. You would probably believe in the machine that you were having pleasant experiences. This belief would be false, because you would not be having the genuine experiences that you want to have. This theory of pleasure thus enables the hedonists to explain why you would have fewer pleasures in the machine and why your life would therefore be worse in it. 1.69

Pessimism about the value of pleasure*

If you agree with Nozick, then you think that both pleasures and other things can make your life go better. Pessimists about pleasure argue that this view is false because pleasures have no value at all. The best argument for this was offered by a fairly cryptic and strongly pessimistic German philosopher, **Arthur Schopenhauer (Schopenhauer, 1844, book IV, sections 56–57)**.[35] 1.70

1.71 The starting point of Schopenhauer's argument is that you only want things because you experience a lack in your life. According to Schopenhauer, such experiences amount to suffering and when you suffer you want to do something about it. For example, hunger is an experience of lack of food. It is an unpleasant experience which makes you want to eat food. So initially, when you start to want things, you are suffering and thus your life is not going well. The question then is: is there any way in which your life could get better?

1.72 In some cases of suffering you fail to get what you want. In these cases the lack in your life continues and you thus continue to suffer. In other cases you manage to get what you want and this removes the deficiency in question. On these occasions you experience a brief moment of pleasure and satisfaction and so momentarily you might think that your life can go better. Yet Schopenhauer's most striking claim is that pleasure and satisfaction in these cases is simply a removal of an absence and for this reason it doesn't get you to the positive side of the scale of making your life good. You have returned to the neutral baseline state that existed before you started to experience the given lack, and so you are not any better off than you were at the beginning.

1.73 If this is what pleasure and satisfaction is, then it is easier to believe that these experiences do not have at least very much prudential value. Experiencing pleasure only means that you are in the same neutral state as before, which doesn't sound all that great. According to Schopenhauer, pleasure also tends to lead quickly to boredom. It is not thrilling merely to have what you previously lacked. This is why we continuously think of new things that we lack. This only makes us suffer in new ways. Despite this pessimism, Schopenhauer thought that most people can find a balance: "This is the life of almost all men; they will, they know what they will, and they strive after this with enough success to protect them from despair, and enough failure to preserve them from boredom and its consequences" (**Schopenhauer, 1844, sect. 60, para. 3**).[36]

1.74 Schopenhauer's argument is important in at least three ways. Firstly, it gives you a genuine reason to think about what matters in your life. We often too easily assume that our life is going well if we just enjoy it. Schopenhauer challenges this complacency and also directs us to consider what things other than pleasure can make our lives better. Secondly, Schopenhauer's argument asks you to consider whether your life will really be made better by all the latest gadgets and other consumer goods you might want. He warns that you'll be quickly bored of these too.

Finally, Schopenhauer's argument is also good target practice for critical philosophical thinking. The argument has several weak spots, which you should consider. For example, you might ask why removing an absence from your life that is making you suffer could not be very good for you. Or, is it really true that we always get bored of having the things in life that we want to have? Do you get bored of your friends and family, for example? By considering these questions you can better understand both Schopenhauer's philosophy and what matters in your own life. 1.75

Summary and Questions

This chapter started with three questions about pleasure. You can first ask what gives you pleasure. This is a question about the causal origins of pleasure. You can then ask what makes a given experience a pleasure. This is a question about the nature of pleasure. You can furthermore ask how important it is to experience pleasure. This is a question about the prudential value of pleasure. 1.76

The rest of the chapter focused on the most important philosophical answers to these questions. There are three views about what pleasure is. According to the sensation view, pleasure is a simple positive sensation of its own kind. According to the attitude view, pleasure is an attitude that represents thoughts, objects, and activities in a positive light. Finally, according to the desire view, pleasure is any experience you want to have when you are having it. 1.77

The remainder of this chapter considered the prudential value of pleasures. Do pleasurable experiences make your life go better? According to hedonism, pleasurable experiences, and only those, are in your interests. Nozick's experience machine argument is often used to argue that there must be other things that matter to us too, such as a genuine connection to the world. This has led many people to accept pluralism about prudential value. This last section of the chapter then explained Schopenhauer's pessimist argument, to the conclusion that pleasures have very little value in themselves. 1.78

Based on the philosophical resources introduced in this chapter, consider the following questions: 1.79

1. In the first section, we distinguished between three types of question about pleasure. How would you pose and answer similar questions about (i) breakfasts, (ii) family, and (iii) religion?

2. What are the main differences between (i) the sensation view, (ii) the attitude view, and (iii) the desire view of pleasure? Which one of these views is most plausible and why?
3. Can the loudness of sounds analogy be used to defend the sensation and attitude views of pleasure against the objection that not all pleasures feel the same?
4. Would you plug yourself into the experience machine? Why? Why not?
5. Where does Schopenhauer's pessimist argument go wrong? Why?

Annotated Bibliography

Aristotle (circa 350 BC) *Nicomachean Ethics*, full text available at http://classics.mit.edu/Aristotle/nicomachaen.html, accessed February 19, 2014. Aristotle's main work in ethics, which has had a profound influence on how many philosophers understand happiness, virtues, voluntary actions, friendship, pleasure, and other central notions in moral philosophy.

Bentham, Jeremy (1789) *An Introduction to the Principles of Morals and Legislation*, full text available at http://www.efm.bris.ac.uk/het/bentham/morals.pdf, accessed February 19, 2014. In this classic work, Bentham argued that governments should make laws in order to promote the happiness of their citizens. He also devised the hedonic calculus for the purpose of estimating how valuable different pleasures are.

Bloom, Paul (2010) *How Pleasure Works* (London: The Bodley Head). In this fascinating book, psychologist Paul Bloom uses the tools of psychology, neuroscience, philosophy, economics, and child development studies to investigate why we experience pleasure from the things we do.

Brentano, Franz (1981 [1921]) *Sensory and Noetic Consciousness: Psychology from an Empirical Standpoint III*, ed. Linda MacAlister (London: Routledge & Kegan Paul). A collection of posthumously published works by the German philosopher Franz Brentano.

Crisp, Roger (1997) *Mill on Utilitarianism* (London: Routledge). This book is both a brilliant introduction to Mill's moral philosophy (including his views about pleasure) and a thoughtful and original work of moral philosophy in its own right.

Crisp, Roger (2006) *Reasons & the Good* (Oxford: Oxford University Press). In this book Crisp argues that all our reasons are based on well-being, which he understands in the hedonist way. The section on enjoyment is helpful.

De Brigard, Felipe (2010) "If You Really Like It, Does It Matter If It's Real?," *Philosophical Psychology*, *23*(1), 43–57, full text available at http://www.unc.edu/~brigard/Xmach.pdf, accessed February 19, 2014. An attempt to use the new methods of experimental philosophy to respond to the experience machine objection to hedonism.

Descartes, René (1637) *Discourse on the Method of Rightly Conducting One's Reason and of Seeking Truth in the Sciences*, full text available at http://www.gutenberg.org/files/59/59-h/59-h.htm, accessed February 19, 2014. Descartes' early work in which he argues that you should use the model of mathematical investigation also in science and philosophy. This book contains early formulations of the Cogito argument (I think, therefore I am) and Descartes' arguments for the existence of God and mind–body dualism.

Feldman, Fred (2004) *Pleasure and the Good Life: Concerning the Nature, Varieties, and Plausibility of Hedonism* (New York: Oxford University Press). The best recent attempt to defend hedonism. Feldman explains clearly his attitudinal view of pleasure and responds to all traditional objections to hedonism.

Hume, David (1739–1740) *A Treatise of Human Nature*, full text available at http://www.gutenberg.org/ebooks/4705, accessed February 19, 2014. Hume's radical empiricist masterpiece in which he uses Newton's physics as a model in the study of us as humans. The main focus is on the psychological mechanisms through which we come to have our ideas. Books II and III contain classic discussions on emotions, desires, moral judgments, and virtues.

Kagan, Shelly (1992) "The Limits of Well-Being," *Social Philosophy and Policy*, *9*(2), 169–189. The beginning of this paper on well-being contains an illuminating discussion of pleasure.

Katz, Leonard (2009) "Pleasure," in *The Stanford Encyclopedia of Philosophy* (Fall 2009 edition), Edward N. Zalta, full text available at http://plato.stanford.edu/entries/pleasure/, accessed February 19, 2014. Very thorough overview of philosophical discussions of pleasure.

Mill, John Stuart (1861) *Utilitarianism*, full text available at http://www.gutenberg.org/files/11224/11224-h/11224-h.htm, accessed February 19, 2014. One of the classics in moral philosophy. Chapter 2 is the clearest formulation of utilitarianism.

Nozick, Robert (1974) *Anarchy, State, and Utopia* (Oxford: Blackwell). A famous work in political philosophy, which defends strong property rights and a minimal state. You can also find the experience machine in this book.

Parfit, Derek (1984) *Reasons and Persons* (Oxford: Oxford University Press). One of the modern classics in moral philosophy, which made significant contributions to philosophical thinking about populations, personal identity, well-being, prudence, and rationality.

Phillips, Helen (2003) "The Pleasure Seekers," *New Scientist*, *2416*, 36–40, full text available at http://www.wireheading.com/pleasure.html, accessed May 29, 2013. An accessible overview of the recent science of pleasure.

Plato (circa 370 BC) *The Republic*, full text available at http://www.gutenberg.org/ebooks/1497, accessed February 19, 2014. A book-length discussion of the question "Why be just?" In answering this question, Plato also explores the nature of the human mind, the structure of societies, good governance, art, education, value, virtues, and the nature of reality.

Russell, James and Carroll, James (1999) "On the Bipolarity of Positive and Negative Affect," *Psychological Bulletin*, *125*(1), 3–30, full text available at https://www2.bc.edu/~russeljm/publications/psyc-bull1999.pdf, accessed February 19, 2014. A very dense paper on how psychologists understand positive and negative affect. It also argues that these states should be understood as polar opposites.

Schopenhauer, Arthur (1844) *The World as Will and Representation*, full text available at http://www.naderlibrary.com/lit.schopenwill.toc.htm, accessed February 19, 2014. Schopenhauer's main work, which develops a comprehensive worldview in epistemology, ontology, aesthetics, and ethics. The pessimist arguments in Book IV are relevant for this chapter.

Shafer-Landau, Russ (2010) *The Fundamentals of Ethics* (Oxford: Oxford University Press). Very clear, accessible, and up-to-date textbook, which covers many of the same topics as this book. Highly recommended to be used alongside this book.

Sidgwick, Henry (1907) *The Methods of Ethics*, full text available at http://archive.org/details/methodsofethics00sidguoft, accessed February 19, 2014. A groundbreaking work in ethics in which Sidgwick compares egoism, intuitive moral principles, and utilitarianism as ways of arriving at moral judgments.

Smart, J.J.C. (1959) "Sensations and Brain Processes," *The Philosophical Review*, *68*, 141–156, full text available at https://mywebspace.wisc.edu/lshapiro/web/Phil554_files/SmartIDTheory.pdf, accessed February 19, 2014. A classic defense of materialist monism in philosophy of mind. This is the view that different types of mental states are identical with specific brain processes.

Sumner, Wayne (1996) *Welfare, Happiness, and Ethics* (Oxford: Oxford University Press). This book is a classic philosophical discussion of well-being and happiness. Sumner also says many interesting things about pleasure too.

Online Resources

1 For the life and works of Plato and Aristotle, see http://plato.stanford.edu/entries/plato/ and http://plato.stanford.edu/entries/aristotle/. For information about *The Republic* and *The Nicomachean Ethics*, see http://en.wikipedia.org/wiki/The_Republic_(Plato) and https://en.wikipedia.org/wiki/Nicomachean_Ethics.

2 For overviews of how these concepts are understood in philosophy, see http://plato.stanford.edu/entries/pleasure/, http://plato.stanford.edu/entries/happiness/, http://plato.stanford.edu/entries/well-being/, and http://plato.stanford.edu/entries/life-meaning/.

3 For a quick explanation of Aristotle's notion of four causes, see http://en.wikipedia.org/wiki/Four_causes.

4 Evaluative questions are investigated in value theory. See http://plato.stanford.edu/entries/value-theory/.

5 Descartes gave this advice in the second section of his *Discourse on the Method*. See http://www.gutenberg.org/files/59/59-h/59-h.htm#part2.

6 Paul Bloom's lecture "How Pleasure Works": http://www.youtube.com/watch?v=lWOfP-Lubuw.

7 A nice article on supertasters: http://www.guardian.co.uk/lifeandstyle/wordofmouth/2013/feb/12/are-you-a-supertaster.

8 Katz's incredibly detailed overview article on philosophy of pleasure: http://plato.stanford.edu/entries/pleasure/.

9 Russell and Carroll's 1999 article, "On the Bipolarity of Positive and Negative Affect": https://www2.bc.edu/~russeljm/publications/psyc-bull1999.pdf.

10 For the lives and works of Hume and Bentham, see http://plato.stanford.edu/entries/hume/ and http://en.wikipedia.org/wiki/Jeremy_Bentham. For the relevant sections of the *Treatise* and *Introduction to the Principles of Morals and Legislation*, see http://www.gutenberg.org/files/4705/4705-h/4705-h.htm#link2H_4_0047 and http://www.efm.bris.ac.uk/het/bentham/morals.pdf.

11 See the student smiling on the background: http://www.youtube.com/watch?v=GXMy7S-azYA.

12 The life and works of Franz Brentano: http://plato.stanford.edu/entries/brentano/ and Fred Feldman's homepage: http://people.umass.edu/ffeldman/.

13 For the relevant page from the *Methods of Ethics*, see http://archive.org/stream/methodsofethics00sidguoft#page/126/mode/2up.

14 For the relevant page from the *Methods of Ethics*, see again http://archive.org/stream/methodsofethics00sidguoft#page/126/mode/2up.

15 This is a rare jazz recording that was originally done for testing sound on different levels of loudness: http://www.youtube.com/watch?v=sMvUipwABzU.

16 There is a rare disorder that can make people insensitive to pain: http://en.wikipedia.org/wiki/Congenital_insensitivity_to_pain.

17 Explanation of physiology: https://en.wikipedia.org/wiki/Physiology.

18 Helen Phillips' 2003 article "The Pleasure Seekers": http://www.wireheading.com/pleasure.html.

19 Wikipedia article on endorphins and enkephalins: http://en.wikipedia.org/wiki/Endorphins.

20 Information about the ventral pallidum's roles in reward and motivation: http://www.ncbi.nlm.nih.gov/pmc/articles/PMC2606924/.

21 Explanation of orbitofrontal cortex: http://en.wikipedia.org/wiki/Orbitofrontal_cortex.

22 J.J.C. Smart's 1959 famous article defending the type-identity version of physicalist monism: https://mywebspace.wisc.edu/lshapiro/web/Phil554_files/SmartIDTheory.pdf.

23 Thorough explanations of intrinsic value and instrumental value: http://plato.stanford.edu/entries/value-intrinsic-extrinsic/ and http://www.colorado.edu/philosophy/center/rome/RoME_2009_full_papers/Dale_Dorsey_What%20is%20Instrumental%20Value_.pdf.

24 A useful encyclopedia entry on hedonism: http://plato.stanford.edu/entries/hedonism/.

25 The exciting life and works of Derek Parfit: http://www.cas.umt.edu/phil/documents/HOW_TO_BE_GOOD-PARFIT.pdf.

26 Bentham's *Introduction to the Principles of Morals and Legislation*: http://www.efm.bris.ac.uk/het/bentham/morals.pdf.

27 The life and works of Joseph Haydn and oysters: http://en.wikipedia.org/wiki/Joseph_Haydn and http://en.wikipedia.org/wiki/Oyster.

28 The life and philosophy of John Stuart Mill and the second chapter from *Utilitarianism*: http://plato.stanford.edu/entries/mill/ and http://www.gutenberg.org/files/11224/11224-h/11224-h.htm#CHAPTER_II.

29 Overview of pluralism in value theory: http://plato.stanford.edu/entries/value-pluralism/.

30 Robert Nozick's life and works: http://en.wikipedia.org/wiki/Robert_Nozick.

31 Shelly Kagan explains the experience machine argument: http://www.youtube.com/watch?v=kSs5waj3h2Y.

32 IMDb on *The Matrix*: http://www.imdb.com/title/tt0133093/.

33 De Brigard's article "If You Like It, Does It Matter If It's Real?": http://www.unc.edu/~brigard/Xmach.pdf.

34 Information about status quo bias: http://en.wikipedia.org/wiki/Status_quo_bias.

35 The life and works of Schopenhauer and the fourth book of *The World as Will and Representation*: http://plato.stanford.edu/entries/schopenhauer/ and http://www.naderlibrary.com/lit.schopenwill.4.htm.

36 See http://www.naderlibrary.com/lit.schopenwill.4.htm.

2

HAPPINESS, WELL-BEING, AND THE MEANING OF LIFE

The previous chapter began to explore how you should live. It focused on the nature of pleasure and its prudential value. Prudential value was understood in terms of what makes your life go better. Prudentially valuable things are the things that are in your interests. We then considered whether having pleasant experiences is in your interests in this sense. 2.1

This chapter expands the focus by concentrating on the notions of **happiness** and **well-being**, which are some of the most fundamental concepts in ethics.[1] These notions are also important for us as individuals in real life because they are what we think about when we make important decisions in our lives. When you consider what career to pursue, you will probably think about how happy different options would make you. You might also think about which option would be the best for the quality of your life. For this reason it is important to think about what happiness and well-being consist of. 2.2

When philosophers talk about **well-being**, they are talking about prudential value.[2] Things in your life have prudential value if they make your life go better. Having friends and a job thus has prudential value because they improve your life. Imagine then that you have all the things in your life that have prudential value. In this case your life has, by definition, a high level of well-being. Conversely, if you lack the things that have prudential value, then your life has a low level of well-being. 2.3

This means that different goods, such as friends or employment, can have prudential value, whereas your life itself has a level of well-being. Conversely, if your life goes well, then your level of well-being is high. This 2.4

This Is Ethics: An Introduction, First Edition. Jussi Suikkanen.

is how the notions of prudential value (of objects) and the level of well-being (of lives) define one another.

2.5 Happiness is an easier concept to understand. This is because you probably have been happy at some point yourself. You have thus personally experienced happiness and therefore know what it is. We also often discuss with our friends whether we are happy. Well-being, in contrast, is a more technical word which is mainly used by philosophers. You might at this point ask what the connection between happiness and well-being is. One way to think about this is to think that happiness is an important part of well-being, but not one and the same thing. If you are happy, then certainly your life is going at least somewhat well and you have at least a decent level of well-being. However, it is important to recognize that other things than happiness can make your life go better. Your life might, for example, go better if you have friends, family, and an interesting job even if these things don't add to your happiness as such.

2.6 But even if we've all been happy and know what it's like, the concept of happiness has its philosophical complications. First of all, we use the idea of happiness in three different senses (Tatarkiewicz, 1976, p. 1). Imagine that you agree that Ben is happy. What are the different things you could mean by this?

2.7 You could, first, be thinking that Ben is *feeling happy*. Here you are using the word "happy" to describe Ben's experiences. You would be claiming that he has a certain positive sensation which can also be described by using words such as "joy," "contentment," "euphoria," and the like. When we talk about happiness in this sense, nothing more is required for being happy than feeling happy.

2.8 Sometimes, when you think that Ben is happy, you mean more than that he is just having certain positive sensations. This is illustrated by the fact that **you can use drugs to get sensations of euphoria**,[3] but arguably by doing so you cannot make yourself genuinely happy. Many people similarly report that they have felt miserable during the happy periods of their lives. Athletes often say that the grueling periods of intense practice are some of the happiest times of their lives. This means that we talk about happiness in some deeper sense. You do this, for example, when you make an overall evaluation of how happy a person has been during a longer period of time.

2.9 Finally, sometimes when you think that a person is happy, all you mean is that they are living a life with a high level of well-being (**Aristotle, book I, sect. 4**).[4] Here, happiness just means well-being. We do not always talk about happiness in this most demanding sense. On some occasions, it makes sense to say that someone lived a happy life even if their life had a fairly low level of well-being. **The living standards in the developed world have improved dramatically over the previous hundred years or so,**[5] which means that the average level of well-being has gone up. However, it is not true that most people are therefore happier now.

The rest of this chapter will focus on the most interesting philosophical theories about well-being and happiness and what they consist of. Some of these views are more naturally read as views about either well-being or happiness. At the end of the chapter we will consider the question of the meaning of life. 2.10

Hedonism, Again

You are already familiar with one traditional theory of both happiness and well-being. The previous chapter explored pleasures and pains. **Hedonism** was the view that your level of well-being (how well your life is going) is determined solely by how many of these experiences and attitudes it contains. The more pleasures you have in your life, the higher your level of well-being is; and the more your life contains pains and suffering, the lower it is. 2.11

There is no reason to repeat the arguments for and against this view here. If you accept the experience machine argument, then you will agree that your level of well-being will also be affected by other things than pleasures. But would it make more sense to accept hedonism as a theory of happiness? This view was put forward by **John Stuart Mill**: "By happiness is intended pleasure, and the absence of pain; by unhappiness, pain, and the privation of pleasure" **(Mill, 1861, ch. 2, para. 2)**.[6] 2.12

There is one sense of happiness which Mill surely captures. As I mentioned above, sometimes when you say that Ben is happy, all you mean is that he is feeling happy. To think this is to think that he is experiencing pleasure. Therefore, if by saying that someone is happy you mean that they are feeling happy, happiness *in this sense* has to consist of pleasant experiences. 2.13

However, sometimes when you think about happiness, you have something deeper in mind than merely fleeting sensations of happiness. When you think about happiness in this sense you are making a broader evaluation of the person's life during a longer stretch of time. We use the 2.14

notion of happiness in this sense when we say that Ben was happy in his twenties.

2.15 Can Mill's theory be used to capture this deeper sense happiness? Does whether Ben was happy in his twenties depend only on the balance of the pleasures and pains? There are two good reasons to doubt this (Haybron, 2008, ch. 4).[7]

Objection 1: Trivial pleasures

2.16 Consider the pleasant experiences Ben had when he was in his twenties. They might have included "eating crackers, hearing a song, sexual intercourse, scratching an itch, solving a puzzle, playing football and so forth" (Haybron, 2008, p. 63). According to hedonism, these pleasures make Ben's life happier. This sounds absurd. If you take a trivial pleasant experience such as eating a cracker, this experience in itself can't make Ben's life happier in the deeper sense.

2.17 This problem becomes clearer if we consider Ben's life as a whole. Imagine that it consists of nothing but eating crackers. Every time he eats one he experiences a minor pleasure. When you consider one individual case, it feels funny to say that Ben's life is made happier by the given minor pleasure. This might just be because the increase in Ben's happiness is so trivial and tiny. The real problem, however, is that if we add a lot of these trivial pleasures together, we should get a Ben whose life is a lot happier. This conflicts with most people's intuitions. No matter how many crackers Ben eats, you would not want to say that this makes Ben very happy.

2.18 There is a similar problem if we consider intense pleasures such as sex and delicious meals. According to hedonism, these pleasures would give a huge boost to how happy you are. However, a person who indulged in these pleasures all the time would not live a much happier life than other people.

Objection 2: The role of happiness in deliberation

2.19 The second problem with hedonism is based on the role which happiness plays in our lives. You want to be friends with people who are generally happy because you expect them to be better company, most of the time, than those who are very unhappy (even if admittedly happy people too can be bores). Likewise, when you make important life choices, you consider how happy your alternatives would make you. Both of these considerations show that happiness is important – we use it to make important decisions in our lives. Yet making these choices in this way would not make sense if happiness just consisted of pleasure. A person who is experiencing intense pleasures is tiresome company. Likewise, it would be odd to make decisions about your career merely on the basis of how many pleasures you would experience. The problem then is that pleasures seem too trivial to play the important role which happiness plays in our lives.

Satisfaction Theories

The next family of views about well-being and happiness are called satisfac- 2.20
tion theories. In the debates about well-being, these views are called **desire satisfaction theories.**[8] Corresponding views of happiness are called **life satisfaction theories.**[9] Let's look at desire satisfaction views of well-being first, and then life satisfaction views of happiness.

Desire satisfaction theories of well-being

Desire satisfaction theories of well-being are easy to understand (see Parfit, 2.21
1984, pp. 494–495; Griffin, 1986, part 1; Murphy, 1999; **Heathwood, 2005**).[10] You have goals, which are the things you want, plan for, and intend to have in your life. Desire satisfaction theories of well-being say that your level of well-being is then determined by how many of your goals are satisfied. If you get what you want, this makes your life go better; if not, you will suffer from a low level of well-being.

This is a plausible way to understand well-being. You might want to 2.22
live in a nice house, have good friends and a meaningful job. It seems plausible to think that your level of well-being depends on whether you get these things that you want. This theory of well-being has also played a fundamental part in the development of modern economics and **decision theory.**[11] This is because well-being understood as desire satisfaction offers an easy way to evaluate the consequences of different public policies.

Desire satisfaction theories can also explain how there are many differ- 2.23
ent kinds of good lives. This is because people have different goals; thus different things will satisfy their desires and hence improve their lives. It likewise explains why you are the top expert on what would improve your life. You know best what you want.

2.24 Desire satisfaction theories also fit the idea that the things which make your life go better must be able to motivate you to pursue them. After all, you want to get the things you desire to have and, according to the desire satisfaction view, well-being is about getting what you desire.

2.25 Finally, these theories can also deal with the experience machine. Because you want to have real interaction with other people, the life in the experience machine will not satisfy your desires. According to the desire satisfaction views, a life in the simulation machine will therefore have a low level of well-being. Desire satisfaction theories of well-being therefore have many important advantages.

Objections to desire satisfaction theories

2.26 Desire satisfaction theories of well-being have two main problems. The first problem is that it is difficult to formulate a satisfactory version of the theory (Hooker, 2000, pp. 39–41). The second problem is related to expensive tastes (**Dworkin, 1981**).[12]

2.27 *Objection 1: Which desires count?* Thinking that the satisfaction of all your desires makes your life go better has implausible consequences. We all have impersonal, uninformed, trivial, and bizarre desires. Consider the earlier example of meeting an ill stranger in the train and wanting them to get better. If he does get better, would this increase your well-being even if you will never learn that this happened? What if you want there to be life on the other side of the universe? Does the satisfaction of this desire affect your level of well-being?

2.28 In response, the defenders of the desire satisfaction theory often claim that only the satisfaction of the desires that are closely connected to your own life affects your well-being (Overvold, 1980). What happens to the stranger, or whether there is life on the other side of the universe, does not satisfy this condition. However, spelling out which desires are closely connected to your own life in the right way is a difficult task.

2.29 Uninformed desires are equally problematic. You might want to drink from the glass in front of you even if, when you went out 15 minutes ago, someone replaced the water in your glass with a deadly poison. It is hard to see how the satisfaction of your desire could in this case increase your well-being. In order to avoid this problem we could think that only the satisfaction of fully informed desires improves your life (Brandt, 1979, pp. 126–129). The problem with this suggestion is that you would not want to eat your lunch if you knew in detail what happens to it in your stomach. According to the new proposal, eating wouldn't be good for you!

Trivial and bizarre desires pose similar problems. Sometimes you 2.30
just want to whistle. Does the satisfaction of this trivial desire make your life go better just as much as the satisfaction of your desire to have friends? Other people want **to count the blades of grass on their lawn** (**Rawls, 1971, p. 432**).[13] Does the satisfaction of this bizarre desire make their lives go better?

The point of all these examples is to illustrate the idea that it is not 2.31
plausible that the satisfaction of just any old desires makes your life go better. This means that the desire satisfaction theorist must be able to offer a principled constraint on which desires count such that it rules out just the right amount of impersonal, uninformed, and bizarre desires. This isn't meant to be a knock-down argument against the theory. It's just a reminder that if you want to defend a desire satisfaction theory of well-being then you have a lot of hard work to do when formulating your theory.

Objection 2: Expensive tastes Expensive tastes pose another interesting 2.32
problem for desire satisfaction theories (**Dworkin, 1981, pp. 229–240**).[14] Consider **Louis**. He is satisfied with his life but currently he lacks ambition to develop himself.[15] Louis just wants to work every day and then have dinner with his family. After this, Louis likes to watch television and have a beer. This is all he wants and he gets it every day. Because of this, Louis's life is going extremely well according to the desire satisfaction views.

When Louis is watching television he sees people living in a different 2.33
way. People go to the **opera** and enjoy **caviar** and **champagne**.[16] As a consequence, Louis decides to develop new tastes in order to improve his life. He too wants to live like the stars. As a result, he develops new expensive tastes and desires. He also becomes more ambitious. He works really hard to acquire the new objects of his desires and as a result he does achieve some of his goals, but not all of them. The problem is that according to desire satisfaction theories, this whole process has made Louis's life worse. Before, all his desires were satisfied, whereas now only some of his desires are satisfied. Yet many of us would want to say that Louis's life has improved.

Something like this happens to all of us. We want to become better 2.34
people by acquiring new tastes, interests, and projects. As Schopenhauer

observed, we do this in order to avoid boredom. The problem is that acquiring new tastes would not make sense if the desire satisfaction theories were true. By acquiring new desires we could only make our lives go worse if we start from a situation in which all our desires are satisfied, and so in that situation there would be no reason to acquire new desires. Again, this isn't a knock-down argument against desire satisfaction views. The point is just that desire satisfaction theorists should offer us some rationale for why it is good for us to develop new desires even if on their view this seems to make our lives go worse eventually by the lights of the desire satisfaction theory itself.

Life satisfaction theories of happiness

2.35 If you don't think that desire satisfaction theories of well-being are plausible, perhaps you might think that we should instead try to understand happiness in terms of desire satisfaction. You probably have a rough life plan. This plan consists of how you intend to achieve a nice combination of all the things you want to have in your life. A simple **desire satisfaction theory of happiness** would claim that you are happy to the degree your life plan is satisfied.

2.36 This theory of happiness has never been very popular. The main problem is that how happy you are presumably makes a difference to what life looks like for you. Happiness makes a difference to you. It's like the rose-tinted glasses that make everything seem so much better. Sadly, desire satisfaction isn't like this. Very often we don't even know that our desires are being satisfied, and when they are this doesn't always make much of a difference to us.

2.37 For this reason, the so-called **life satisfaction theory of happiness** has always been more popular (see Sumner, 1996, pp. 145–147; for critical evaluations, see Haybron, 2008, ch. 5; Feldman, 2010, ch. 5). This theory begins from the desire satisfaction theory of happiness, but it then tries to adapt that view so as to make happiness more connected to what life looks like to you from your own first-person perspective. The life satisfaction theory of happiness claims that the fulfillment of your life plan itself doesn't determine how happy you are. Rather, once you have a life plan, you can form beliefs about whether your life is going according to your plan. The life satisfaction theory claims that you are happy to the degree that *you think* your life satisfies your life plans. According to this view, to be happy is to be satisfied in your own mind with how well your life matches up to your life plan. In this way, life satisfaction theory enables you reflect about your own life: What is your life plan? Do you think that your life is going according to your plan? Are you happy, then? Trying to answer these questions is often helpful for us.

The life satisfaction theory is a plausible theory of happiness. One of its central advantages is that it makes happiness easily measurable. You can ask people how satisfied they are with their lives and the different aspects of their lives. This is precisely what many social scientists do (**Veenhoven, 1984**).[17] **The findings of these studies are extremely interesting.**[18] 2.38

For example, we now roughly know whether **money makes you happy**.[19] It does in one way but not in another. Your absolute level of income and wealth does not make you happy. If all of us in society were made richer, we would not be much more satisfied with our lives. In contrast, getting more money than the other people around you can make you happier. Being happy thus correlates with comparative wealth but not with your absolute level of wealth. 2.39

Another interesting empirical finding is that **we adjust well to change**.[20] Even if bad things happen to people, usually after three months they claim to be just as satisfied with their lives as before. One of the few exceptions to this rule is unemployment. No matter how long you are unemployed you will be less satisfied with your life. It has been suggested that employment is an important source of self-esteem, which is a crucial element of life satisfaction. 2.40

An objection to life satisfaction theories

Fred Feldman has recently raised an interesting objection to life satisfaction theories of happiness (Feldman, 2010, pp. 70–89). It starts from the insight that some spontaneous people are happy. You probably know people who do not plan their lives in advance. What people like this want to do can change every day, but they can still always enjoy what they are doing. These people don't even need to be planning to take things as they come. The problem is that according to life satisfaction theories of happiness, these people aren't happy. 2.41

According to the theory, in order to be happy you must form a life plan and then consider whether your life is going according to that plan. But your spontaneous friend never does this – she just takes each day as it comes (without even planning to do so). Thus, according to the theory, people like this fail to count as happy. But surely this is wrong. 2.42

2.43 For the life satisfaction theories, the only way to avoid this problem is to give up the idea that you have to form a plan and compare your life to it in order to be happy. Perhaps it would be enough that if you were to form a life plan and compare your life to it you would be satisfied with your life. This proposal doesn't work either. Many spontaneous happy people would find their lives unsatisfying if they had to spend time forming life plans and thinking whether their lives match those plans. The problem is the same: life satisfaction theories fall down because they end up claiming that only reflective people can be happy.

Objective List Theories

2.44 The previous two sections explored two theories of well-being. According to these views, well-being consists of either pleasures or the satisfaction of your desires. Both these views assume that your level of well-being depends in some way on your mental states, either pleasures or desires.

2.45 One lesson to draw from the problems with these views is that they allow too many different kinds of lives to have a high level of well-being. A life in the experience machine or one in which bizarre, trivial, and misinformed desires are satisfied can't be a good life, no matter what the person who lives it thinks. One way to avoid these problems is to deny that your level of well-being depends on what you want or find pleasant. This is what the **objective list theories of well-being**[21] do. These views are discussed often, but they have not been defended by that many people (for discussions, see Sumner, 1996, ch. 3 and Parfit, 1984, pp. 499–502; and for defenses, see Finnis, 1980, chs 3–4, Hurka, 1993, chs 7–10, and **Rice, 2013**).[22]

2.46 Objective list theories are based on the idea that there is a set of goods that make your life go better whether you want them or whether they give you pleasure. The listed goods increase your well-being independently of what you think of them.

2.47 Different sets of goods have been proposed for the list, but they tend to include health, housing, food and drink, knowledge, human interaction and close personal relationships, friends and family, meaningful employment, self-esteem, political participation, art, achievements, diverse natural environments, security, autonomy, and so on. You could also include pleasure and avoidance of pains on the list. Whenever a person has these things in their life their life has a high level of well-being. This is true even if the person does not care about these goods.

Objections to the objective list theories

Many people think that the defenders of this view are telling you how you should live your life. They also worry that these philosophers want to force you to live according to their conception of a good life. This would be objectionably arrogant and **paternalistic**.[23] Who are they to tell you how to live? 2.48

The defenders of the objective list theories are puzzled by this reaction. They know that even if you knew what well-being is this would not justify you in coercing other people. After all, there are many reasonable (but perhaps mistaken) conceptions of a good life (Rawls, 1971, pp. 92–94). Because other people accept such reasonable alternatives, you can't force them to live in the way you want. 2.49

The defenders of the objective list views also openly admit that they could be mistaken about what belongs to the list of objectively good things. Because of this they rarely push their own views about well-being on others. The objective list views do not therefore lead to objectionable forms of paternalism. 2.50

Notice also that one of the items on the standard list is **autonomy**.[24] This means that deciding yourself how to live your life is also supposed to increase your level of well-being. As a result it would be inconsistent for the defenders of these views to impose their views of well-being on you. This would only make you less able to live your life autonomously. 2.51

Despite all this, the original reaction to the objective list theories is on to something. The defenders of the objective list theories have to answer the following questions: 2.52

- What determines which items belong to the correct list?
- How do we know what belongs to this list?

Some people insist that it is a brute fact that some goods belong on the list. According to this view, there is no further explanation for this, in the same way as there is no a further explanation for what the **gravitational constant**[25] is. How then do you know which things should be on the list? Many defenders of this view argue that you know what should belong to 2.53

the list in the same way as you know many other things: through a combination of experience, critical reflection, and rational debate. Opponents of the objective list view often find answers like this unsatisfactory. For this reason, the next section will discuss a version of the objective list theories called **the capability approach**,[26] which attempts to give more informative answers to these questions.

2.54 The objective list theories also face other challenges. For one, these theories seem to lack some of the advantages of hedonism and desire satisfaction views. Objective list views will find it more difficult to explain:

i. how there can be many different types of good lives;
ii. how you are an expert on whether your life is going well; and
iii. why you tend to be motivated by what you think is good for you.

It's not that objective list views can't say anything in response to these questions. They might say in response to (i) that there just are so many different objective goods that individuals can create different kinds of good lives by combining these goods in different ways. In response to (ii) and (iii), objective list theorists can likewise say that perhaps the objective goods make your life go better only on the condition that you accept that they do so. If you have to endorse the items on the list as a part of your well-being then you would know what improves your life and you would be motivated to pursue them.

2.55 These responses alleviate some of the worries you might have about the objective list theories. Yet, it is important to note that all these responses seem problematic. Against the first response to (i), we can ask: Wouldn't getting all the many different objective goods make your life even better than some smaller combination of them? Doesn't this mean that ultimately there is then just one very best kind of life? Similarly, the previous answer to questions (ii) and (iii) seems to undermine the original motivation for the objective list theories. That idea was that we shouldn't let what people want determine how well their lives are going because people can have all kinds of funny desires. Yet now the objective list theorist seems to return to the idea that our desires play an important role in determining when our lives go well. In any case, the aim wasn't here to offer a knock-down argument against the objective list theories by posing unanswerable questions for the defenders of that view. Rather, the aim was to raise some interesting questions which you should think about if you find objective list views appealing.

The Capability Approach*

This section will discuss **Martha Nussbaum**'s[27] **capability approach** and 2.56
see how it deals with some of the problems with an objective list theory raised above (Nussbaum, 2000, ch. 1). It combines elements of Aristotle's ethics and **Amartya Sen**'s[28] capability theory (Aristotle, circa 350 BC; Sen, 1985). **Nussbaum**[29] starts from the idea that the members of different species naturally act in different ways. For example, two activities are essential for living a human life: living together with other people in social and political communities and using theoretical and practical reason. You use your theoretical reason to investigate the world and your practical reason to plan how to live with other people.

Sometimes Aristotelians make two further claims about these two activi- 2.57
ties. According to them, these activities are both unique to human beings and what human beings are for (**Aristotle, circa 350 BC, book I, sect. 7**).[30] These claims are probably not true. Other higher animals also seem to live in communities and use their reason. Furthermore, our modern scientific worldview does not support the idea that we have a purpose as human beings. Despite this, it is plausible that when human beings successfully live with other people, and use their reason, they live a good life.

Nussbaum calls the central human activities **functionings**.[31] She thinks 2.58
that certain capabilities are objectively required for successfully carrying out these functionings. Your level of well-being is then determined by whether you have the capabilities that are needed for the central human functionings.

At this point, you might ask why we should think that well-being con- 2.59
sists of having the capabilities for the important human functionings instead of achieving the functionings themselves? Why, for a high level of well-being, you only need the capabilities to certain things rather than doing those things themselves? Nussbaum's answer to this question is simple. One important typical human functioning is eating nourishing and tasty food. Consider then a deeply religious person, whose religion requires her to fast. If well-being consisted of the important functionings themselves, then you would have to think that there is an element of well-being which this person is missing out on. This seems counterintuitive. If the person in question has the resources and capabilities to eat nourishing and tasty food but decides not to do so for religious reasons, then we want to say that she still has an equally high level of well-being. This is why

Nussbaum thinks that when you think about well-being you should focus on the capabilities for functionings rather than the functionings themselves.

2.60 Nussbaum's objective list, therefore, is created by what is needed for the activities that constitute living a typical human life. Her list includes the following items (Nussbaum, 2000, pp. 78–80):

1. Life (being able to live to the end of the normal length of a human life).
2. Bodily health (including reproductive health).
3. Bodily integrity (being able to move freely, being able to be secure against assault and rape, autonomy in sexual matters).
4. Senses, imagination, and thought (being able to use senses and to imagine, being able to think and reason, having an education, taking part in art and religion, freedom of speech, being able to have pleasurable experiences and to avoid pains).
5. Emotions (being able to have attachments to things and people, to love and to grieve, not needing to fear or experience anxiety).
6. Practical reason (being able to form a conception of a good life and to plan one's life critically).
7. Affiliation (being able to live together with others, to show concern for them, take part in social interaction, to have compassion, having social bases of self-respect, freedom from humiliation, having protection against discrimination).
8. Other species (being able to live in relation to animals, plants, and the world of nature).
9. Play (being able to laugh and play, and to enjoy hobbies).
10. Control over one's activities (being able to participate in political decision making, being able to hold property, having fair opportunities and freedom from search and seizure).

Nussbaum admits that she may be wrong about some of the items on her list. Perhaps you do not need all of them for the central functionings, and maybe you also need some other capabilities that are not on the list.

2.61 Nussbaum's view, however, solves the most serious problems of the standard objective list theories. First, she can tell you what determines which items belong to the list of the objective goods. What belongs to the correct list is determined by which activities are essential for living a typically human life. Secondly, she can also tell you how we know what belongs to the list. You first need to observe the ways in which human beings live and you then need to consider what capabilities are required for living in that way.

Like all philosophical theories, this view has its problems. You could 2.62
argue that the notions of typically human activities and functionings are not determinate enough to tell us what is needed for well-being. When you go more deeply into the details there is less agreement about what human beings typically do and what is required for pursuing these activities successfully.

You could also argue against the previous claim that merely having the 2.63
capabilities for taking part in the relevant activities is enough for well-being. What if you always decide not to use the capabilities? What if you have all the necessary skills for having friends and a family but you choose not to use them? Do you still have a high level of well-being?

Happiness and the Meaning of Life

The rest of this chapter will discuss one new attractive theory of happiness 2.64
and then it will turn to the question of the meaning of life. If you accept an objective list theory of well-being, what should you then think about happiness? One alternative you would have in this situation would be to try to use your list also to make sense of happiness.

In that case you would think that well-being and happiness are one and 2.65
the same thing. This would mean that you are happy when you have the things on the list like friends, meaningful work, knowledge, and so on. What life is like from your own perspective would make no difference to how happy you are. This view has never been popular because, as we saw, whether you are happy or not must make some difference to what your life looks like from your own perspective. Even if you had all the items on the list, your life could still seem pretty grim.

More sophisticated Aristotelian versions of the objective list view of 2.66
happiness can avoid this problem. As we saw above, this tradition understands happiness in terms of successfully taking part in typically human activities. Aristotle used the word "**eudaimonia**"[32] for this fundamental human goal. This Greek word has been translated both as "flourishing" and as "happiness." It could then be argued that successful participation in

typically human activities requires also experiencing the activities in a certain way. If you do not feel certain sensations and emotions when you live with other people and take part in the important human activities, you are not doing these things in the right way. This view would mean that a person who is feeling grim from her own perspective just could not have the things that belong to the objective list of the things that constitute happiness. You only successfully have the items on the list (living with other people, using practical and theoretical reason, and so on) when you experience your life in a certain way.

2.67 The second alternative is to use the objective list for understanding well-being and to give a different account of happiness. In this case, you could accept either hedonism as a theory of happiness or the whole life satisfaction theory. However, you also have a third alternative.

Emotional state theory of happiness*

2.68 According to **Daniel Haybron's emotional state theory of happiness,**[33] your level of happiness consists of your overall emotional condition (Haybron, 2008, chs 6–7). In order to be happy it is not enough that you have individual experiences of pleasure, but instead your deeper psychological makeup must be in a certain stable state.

2.69 According to Haybron, if you are happy you must have a number of positive emotions and moods, which include things like being cheerful and joyful, feeling happy at times, experiencing joy, and being inclined to feel pleasure. However, happiness does not on this view merely consist of having these fairly superficial cheery attitudes. It is in addition, and more importantly, also requires having deeper and more important positive emotions such as feeling confident, safe, optimistic, tranquil, fulfilled, and being in good spirits and untroubled. Many of these deeper emotions also dispose us to have other positive experiences. Furthermore, you must also be strongly disposed to have these emotions and moods.

2.70 Haybron believes that to be happy in this deeper emotional sense is to react to your life favorably: it requires responding to your life emotionally as if things were going well for you. This fits the saying that happy people see their lives through rose-tinted glasses. A happy person is at home with their life, and they are enthusiastic about what they do. Happy people also endorse the kind of life they have chosen to live.

2.71 Haybron's proposal has many significant advantages. Even if it doesn't claim that happiness is any particular experience, it still argues that your happiness makes a difference to what your life looks like from the inside. Haybron's view also explains why experiencing trivial pleasures isn't enough for happiness. These experiences just aren't a deep enough part of our emotional state to make a difference to how happy we are.

Haybron's view furthermore makes sense of why you generally want to be with happy people and why you consider your happiness when you make important life choices. Your – and other people's – psychological well-being, in the relevant deep and important sense, matter to us. You want to be with people who are in a positive mood and you want to live in the way you can feel emotionally at home with. 2.72

The question of the meaning of life

Now you have an idea of what happiness and well-being are. You might still want to know **whether your life has any meaning.**[34] Consider Carl. By the standards of the views discussed so far he is happy and his life has a high level of well-being. His experiences are pleasant and most of his desires are satisfied. Carl also has all the capabilities for the central human functionings, and his emotions and moods are positive. Many people worry that Carl's life might still turn out to be meaningless. According to them, a meaningful life needs to contain more than just happiness and well-being. 2.73

Some philosophers believe that the people who worry about the meaning of life are confused (see Wiggins, 1988, pp. 127–128 for a description of this worry). They think that only elements of language can have meaning. The word "vixen" has a certain meaning, the same meaning as the words "female fox." The meaning of a linguistic expression can be understood in terms of what a speaker must know to be able to use that expression. Looked at this way, words and sentences can have meanings, but objects like trees or frogs cannot. Given that a life is not a linguistic expression but rather a long process, it would be **a category mistake**[35] to think that lives have a meaning. 2.74

This fails to satisfy those of us who worry about whether our lives are meaningful. No matter how much we analyze language, this worry just refuses to go away. Because of this, the question about the meaning of life is once again a respectable topic in philosophy in which progress is being made. To illustrate this, let us look at one illuminating new philosophical theory about the meaning of life. 2.75

Susan Wolf's fitting fulfillment theory

2.76 The previous views of happiness and well-being can be classified into **subjective and objective**[36] views. The subjective views begin from your mental life and then make sense of happiness and well-being in terms of it. The objective views, in contrast, begin from a set of objective goods. We can also approach the meaning of life from these directions.

2.77 The subjective views of the meaning of life begin with your passions, which include what you enjoy, love, care about, and find satisfying and meaningful (**Taylor, 1970, ch. 15**).[37] These views then claim that you live a meaningful life if you pursue your passions. This means that all you need for a meaningful life is that you find it fulfilling.

2.78 This theory enables lives to be meaningful too easily. People who have bizarre passions can still pursue them. They can experience deep fulfillment from counting blades of grass, **participating in lawn-mower racing**, **taking care of their pet fish**, and **pressing the levers at the factory**.[38] Yet most of us want to say that if you spend your whole life doing these things your life still lacks meaning.

2.79 We can also approach the meaning of life from the other direction of objective goods and objectively good activities (Singer, 2011, ch. 12). Consider raising a family, learning to play an instrument, excelling in sciences, being able to build well-functioning buildings, helping poor and sick people, and taking care of children. A simple objective view would claim that if you take part in these valuable activities, or others like them, this is enough to make your life meaningful. It doesn't matter what *you* think of your life.

2.80 The problem is that lives like this can still miss something. Consider Kate. She is a doctor who helps sick people for living. She also spends a lot of time with her family and friends. When she has time she even practices the violin. Does this mean that Kate's life must be meaningful? If Kate feels that her life does not truly belong to her, you would want to say that her life can still lack meaning. In this situation Kate would be unable to enjoy what she does. Kate would not find her life meaningful; and you would agree with her.

2.81 **Susan Wolf**'s theory avoids these problems by combining the best elements of the subjective and objective views (**Wolf, 2007**).[39] She calls the resulting view **the fitting fulfillment theory** of the meaning of life. According to Wolf's theory, in order to live a meaningful life you must love, and be positively engaged with, objectively worthwhile projects. This theory thus sets both subjective and objective requirements for living a meaningful life. You must have certain passionate attitudes toward your projects and you need also to find pursuing these projects fulfilling. This is the subjective requirement for living a meaningful life. Your projects must also be good and worthwhile, which is the objective requirement for living a meaningful life.

This view can avoid the problems of the subjective and objective theories. Bizarre projects do not give your life meaning because they lack objective worth. Yet in order to live a meaningful life you must also care about pursuing these projects. Because of this, if, like Kate, you find your life alien, you are not living a meaningful life. 2.82

Imagine then that you are taking part in objectively worthwhile projects and you are passionate about this. Is it still an open question whether your life is meaningful? You might deny that this question makes sense anymore at this point. Some people might still worry that even these kinds of lives might not have meaning. They might think that **meaningful lives would need to be a part of God's great scheme or, at the very least, require having religious beliefs** (Cottingham, 2003).[40] 2.83

Summary and Questions

This chapter has explored the notions of happiness, well-being, and the meaning of life. We started by clarifying the distinction between happiness and well-being. Well-being is a theoretical standard which you can use to evaluate how good a given life is. In contrast, the concept of happiness is used more in our everyday lives. Happiness is also more closely connected to how your life appears to you from your own perspective. 2.84

Can you make sense of what happiness is in terms of pleasures and pains? The problem with this proposal is that trivial pleasures don't seem to be relevant to how happy you are. After hedonism, we considered desire satisfaction theories of well-being and life satisfaction theories of happiness, which understand well-being and happiness in terms of whether we get what we want. These views can explain why you want to pursue well-being and happiness, but one downside of these views is that they would allow even bizarre desires to affect your happiness and well-being. 2.85

The next sections discussed objective list theories of well-being and happiness. We focused on Martha Nussbaum's capability approach because it 2.86

bravely attempts to explain which goods increase well-being objectively. Even if Nussbaum's view is a plausible theory of well-being, it is less likely to work as a theory of happiness. A better account is given by Daniel Haybron's emotional state theory of happiness, according to which happiness is a deep positive emotional condition. Then we took on the question of the meaning of life. Susan Wolf attempts to answer this question with her fitting fulfillment view, according to which you must passionately pursue worthwhile projects.

2.87 Based on the philosophical resources introduced in this chapter, consider the following questions:

1. Which one of the different uses of the word "happiness" seems most natural and widespread to you? Why?
2. Is there anything which the defenders of hedonism as a view of happiness could say in response to Haybron's objections?
3. If we accept a desire satisfaction theory of well-being, does the satisfaction of all our desires make a difference to our well-being? If not, which desires matter?
4. Can the capability approach solve the problems of the traditional objective list theories?
5. If you passionately pursue worthwhile things in your life, can your life still lack meaning?

Annotated Bibliography

Aristotle (circa 350 BC) *Nicomachean Ethics*. See the bibliography of Chapter 1 above.

Brandt, Richard (1979) *A Theory of the Good and the Right* (Oxford: Oxford University Press). A classic defense of rule-utilitarianism. Brandt also defends a view of well-being according to which well-being consists in the satisfaction of the desires which we would have after cognitive psychotherapy.

Cottingham, John (2003) *On the Meaning of Life* (London: Routledge). A wonderful short historical tour of thinking about the meaning of life. Cottingham argues that a part of human nature is to yearn for the infinite and that religious spirituality can often satisfy this longing.

Dworkin, Ronald (1981) "What is Equality? Part 1: Equality of Welfare," *Philosophy and Public Affairs*, *10*(3), 185–246, full text available at http://strongwindpress.com/pdfs/TuiJian/DworkinEquality.pdf, accessed February 20, 2014. In this article Dworkin argues that equal treatment of citizens cannot mean guaranteeing them an equal amount of well-being. This article also contains an insightful critical examination of the traditional theories of well-being.

Feldman, Fred (2010) *What Is This Thing Called Happiness?* (Oxford: Oxford University Press). In this wonderfully thorough book Feldman argues against traditional versions of hedonism, whole life satisfaction theories, and eudaimonist theories of happiness. He also defends his own attitudinal hedonism.

Finnis, John (1980) *Natural Law and Natural Rights* (Oxford: Oxford University Press). An important book in philosophy of law and rights. Chapters 3 and 4 formulate and defend an objective list theory of basic value.

Griffin, James (1986) *Well-Being: Its Meaning, Measurement, and Moral Importance* (Oxford: Oxford University Press). Griffin considers what well-being is, how it can be measured, and what its role is in ethical and political thought. The first four chapters offer an illuminating investigation of different views of well-being.

Haybron, Daniel (2008) *The Pursuit of Unhappiness* (Oxford: Oxford University Press). A groundbreaking work on happiness. This book contains clear explanation of what we want from a theory of happiness, thorough arguments against the traditional views, and a clear defense of the emotional state view.

Heathwood, Chris (2005) "Desire-Satisfaction Theories of Welfare," full text available at http://spot.colorado.edu/~heathwoo/DSTW.pdf, accessed February 20, 2014. A PhD thesis in which Heathwood defends desire satisfaction theories against many traditional objections.

Hooker, Brad (2000) *Ideal Code, Real World* (Oxford: Oxford University Press). One of the clearest defenses of rule-consequentialism which also contains a diplomatic overview of the different views of well-being.

Hsee, Christopher, Yang, Yang, Li, Naihe, and Shen, Luxi (2009) "Wealth, Warmth, and Well-Being: Whether Happiness Is Relative or Absolute Depends on Whether It Is About Money, Acquisition, or Consumption," *Journal of Marketing Research*, *46*, 296–409, full text available at http://home.uchicago.edu/~/luxishen/papers/2009_HseeYangLiShen_WWW_JMR.pdf, accessed February 20, 2014. Gives an overview of literature on how absolute and relative wealth affects our happiness.

Hurka, Tom (1993) *Perfectionism* (Oxford: Oxford University Press). In this book Hurka argues that the development of human nature is the fundamental good. He then uses this as a central element of a consequentialist ethical theory.

Mill, John Stuart (1861) *Utilitarianism*. See the bibliography of Chapter 1 above.

Murphy, Mark (1999) "Simple Desire-Fulfillment Theory," *Noûs*, *33*(2), 247–272. A brave defense of the view that the satisfaction of your actual desires is more important than the satisfaction of some idealized set of hypothetical desires.

Nussbaum, Martha (2000) *Women and Human Development: The Capabilities Approach* (Cambridge: Cambridge University Press). A clear defense of the

Aristotelian capability approach. Nussbaum also masterfully applies her framework to women in developing countries.

Overvold, Mark (1980) "Self-Interest and the Concept of Self-Sacrifice," *Canadian Journal of Philosophy*, *10*, 105–118. Overvold argues that well-being cannot consist of the satisfaction of all of our desires as this would make self-sacrifice impossible.

Parfit, Derek (1984) *Reasons and Persons* (Oxford: Oxford University Press). See the bibliography of Chapter 1 above.

Rawls, John (1971) *A Theory of Justice* (Cambridge, MA: Harvard University Press). A modern classic in political philosophy. On Rawls's view, well-being consists of satisfaction of rational life plans. He also argues that there are many different reasonable conceptions of the good and that the state should be neutral between them.

Sen, Amartya (1985) *Commodities and Capabilities* (Oxford: Oxford University Press). An influential book in which Sen argues that we should understand how well a person is doing not in terms of what they have, but rather in terms of what they can do.

Singer, Peter (2011) *Practical Ethics*, 3rd ed. (Cambridge: Cambridge University Press). A classic textbook in applied ethics. Singer covers treatment of animals, abortion, global poverty, and climate change.

Sumner, Wayne (1996) *Welfare, Happiness, and Ethics* (Oxford: Oxford University Press). See the bibliography of Chapter 1 above.

Tatarkiewicz, Wladyslaw (1976) *Analysis of Happiness* (The Hague: Martinus Nijhoff). Remarkably detailed philosophical investigation of all aspects of happiness. Very thorough on the history of philosophical thinking about happiness.

Taylor, Richard (1970) *Good and Evil* (New York: Macmillan). An attack against the idea that moral values are based on objective features of the world. On Taylor's view we confer value to the world by desiring. In the last chapter he applies this theory to the meaning of life.

Veenhoven, Ruut (1984) *Conditions of Happiness* (Dordrecht: Reidel), full text available at http://www2.eur.nl/fsw/research/veenhoven/Pub1980s/84a-full.pdf, accessed February 20, 2014. An extensive overview of the science of happiness, which goes through different conceptions and measures of happiness and much of the research results on the topic.

Wiggins, David (1988) "Truth, Invention, and Meaning of Life," in *Essays on Moral Realism*, ed. Geoffrey Sayre-McCord (Ithaca: Cornell University Press), pp. 127–165. A classic paper in which Wiggins argues that non-cognitivism (see Chapter 8) leads to an inconsistent view about the meaning of life.

Wolf, Susan (2007) "Meaning in Life and Why It Matters," full text available at http://www.philosophy.northwestern.edu/conferences/moralpolitical/08/

papers/Wolf.pdf, accessed February 20, 2014. A brilliantly insightful investigation of one of the oldest and most intriguing philosophical questions.

Online Resources

1 Encyclopedia articles on happiness and well-being: http://plato.stanford.edu/entries/happiness/ and http://plato.stanford.edu/entries/well-being/.
2 A discussion on well-being: http://www.philostv.com/ben-bradley-and-dale-dorsey/.
3 Wikipedia entry on euphoriants: http://en.wikipedia.org/wiki/Euphoriant.
4 Book I of the *Nicomachean Ethics*: http://classics.mit.edu/Aristotle/nicomachaen.1.i.html.
5 Richard's Easterlin's article on the standard of living since 1800: http://jamesgoulding.com/Data%20(Historical)/Economic/Standard%20of%20Living%20(World).pdf.
6 The life and works of John Stuart Mill and Chapter 2 of his *Utilitarianism*: http://plato.stanford.edu/entries/mill/ and http://www.gutenberg.org/files/11224/11224-h/11224-h.htm#CHAPTER_II.
7 Dan Haybron's homepage: https://sites.google.com/site/danhaybron/.
8 Overview of desire satisfaction theories: http://plato.stanford.edu/entries/well-being/#DesThe.
9 Haybron's explanation of the view: http://plato.stanford.edu/entries/happiness/#TheHap.
10 Chris Heathwood's doctoral thesis on desire satisfaction theories of well-being; http://spot.colorado.edu/~heathwoo/DSTW.pdf.
11 Decision theory: http://lesswrong.com/lw/gu1/decision_theory_faq/.
12 Ronald Dworkin's article "What Is Equality? Part 1: Equality of Welfare": http://strongwindpress.com/pdfs/TuiJian/DworkinEquality.pdf.
13 Image of a creature counting blades of grass and a summary of Rawls's *A Theory of Justice*: http://images.wikia.com/mlp/images/8/83/Spike_counting_blades_of_grass_S03E09.png and http://en.wikipedia.org/wiki/A_Theory_of_Justice.
14 Dworkin's "What Is Equality? Part 1: Equality of Welfare": http://strongwindpress.com/pdfs/TuiJian/DworkinEquality.pdf.
15 Louis is named after Louis XIV of France: http://en.wikipedia.org/wiki/Louis_XIV_of_France.
16 Verdi's Aida and information about caviar and champagne: http://www.youtube.com/watch?v=b8rsOzPzYr8, http://en.wikipedia.org/wiki/Caviar, and http://en.wikipedia.org/wiki/Champagne.

17 Ruut Veenhoven's *Conditions of Happiness*: http://www2.eur.nl/fsw/research/veenhoven/Pub1980s/84a-full.pdf.
18 An interesting discussion on well-being and empirical research: http://www.philostv.com/simon-keller-and-valerie-tiberius/.
19 Hsee, Yang, Li, and Shen's article "Wealth, Warmth, and Well-Being: Whether Happiness Is Relative or Absolute Depends on Whether It Is About Money, Acquisition, or Consumption": http://home.uchicago.edu/~/luxishen/papers/2009_HseeYangLiShen_WWW_JMR.pdf.
20 A meta-analysis: http://europepmc.org/articles/PMC3289759/reload=0;jsessionid=yT5UYgMOAY67pAigdxQ0.10.
21 An overview of objective list theories: http://plato.stanford.edu/entries/well-being/#ObjLisThe.
22 Christopher Rice's article "Defending the Objective List Theory of Well-Being": http://christopherrice.weebly.com/uploads/1/0/3/1/10317856/defending_the_objective_list_theory_of_well-being.pdf.
23 Clear overview of philosophical questions related to paternalism: http://plato.stanford.edu/entries/paternalism/.
24 An overview article on autonomy: http://plato.stanford.edu/entries/autonomy-moral/.
25 Wikipedia on gravitational constant: http://en.wikipedia.org/wiki/Gravitational_constant.
26 Overview of the capability approach: http://plato.stanford.edu/entries/capability-approach/.
27 Martha Nussbaum's homepage: http://www.law.uchicago.edu/faculty/nussbaum/.
28 Amartya Sen's homepage: http://scholar.harvard.edu/sen.
29 An interview with Martha Nussbaum in which she explains the capability approach (starting at 18 minutes from beginning): https://www.youtube.com/watch?v=Qy3YTzYjut4.
30 Book I of the *Nicomachean Ethics*: http://classics.mit.edu/Aristotle/nicomachaen.1.i.html.
31 Explanation of functionings: http://plato.stanford.edu/entries/capability-approach/#FunCap.
32 Wikipedia on "eudaimonia": https://en.wikipedia.org/wiki/Eudaimonia.
33 Dan Haybron uses a simple example to explain his theory of happiness (starting from 7 minutes in): http://www.youtube.com/watch?v=iqRl1MBZXyM.
34 Clear overview of philosophical work on the meaning of life: http://plato.stanford.edu/entries/life-meaning/.
35 Definition of category mistakes: http://en.wikipedia.org/wiki/Category_mistake.
36 How these terms are understood in philosophy: http://www.iep.utm.edu/objectiv/.

37 Taylor's chapter on the meaning of life: http://www.calstatela.edu/faculty/tbettch/Taylor%20Meaning%20of%20Life.pdf.

38 Film-footage of these activities: http://www.youtube.com/watch?v=oEgwfQypnlM, http://www.youtube.com/watch?v=cYU_dhrmvyU, and http://www.youtube.com/watch?v=DfGs2Y5WJ14.

39 Susan Wolf's homepage: http://philosophy.unc.edu/people/faculty/susan-wolf and her article "Meaning in Life and Why It Matters": http://www.philosophy.northwestern.edu/conferences/moralpolitical/08/papers/Wolf.pdf.

40 A podcast in which John Cottingham explains his views: http://philosophybites.libsyn.com/category/John%20Cottingham.

Part Two
NORMATIVE ETHICS

3

EGOISM AND ALTRUISM

The previous two chapters were about how you could live a good life. This 3.1
discussion was purely about you, and it led us to explore pleasure, happiness, well-being, and the meaning of life. We now turn to the area of ethics that covers how we should interact with other people and animals. Consider the following questions:

- Is it ever right to lie to your friends?
- Is it wrong to eat meat?
- If you hear your professors discussing the answers to a forthcoming exam, is it wrong to use this information to your advantage?
- Is it wrong to have an abortion?
- Is it wrong not to tip if you receive bad service?

These questions are not answered by just considering what is good for you. Betraying your friend might make you better off but this leaves it open whether you should do so. In answering these questions, you must also consider other people and what happens to them.

The area of moral philosophy which investigates these questions is 3.2
called **normative ethics**.[1] In it, the most fundamental question is not "How should I live?" but rather "Which acts are right and which acts are wrong?" This area of philosophy tends to focus on **ethical theories**.[2] They are systematic attempts to determine where the line between right and wrong actions is. These theories put forward general moral principles that are supposed to tell us what is right and wrong. In this chapter, I will

This Is Ethics: An Introduction, First Edition. Jussi Suikkanen.

consider two competing ethical theories: egoism and altruism. Chapter 4 will then consider Kantian and consequentialist theories. Chapter 5, finally, will ask a wider question: do we need moral principles in normative ethics in the first place?

3.3 But what do we mean when we say that something is morally right or wrong? Sadly, there is no uncontroversial way of answering this question. We have all discussed ethical questions such as the ones listed above. On these occasions, we understand what we are talking about. We all also have some shared basic beliefs about what is morally right and wrong: you probably share my intuition that it is morally right to keep your promises and morally wrong to rape other people.

3.4 When we use the words "right" and "wrong" we are not always talking about what is morally right and wrong. When I say that your answer to a math problem is wrong, I do not mean that it is morally wrong. I only mean that it is incorrect – that it is mathematically wrong. What then distinguishes morally right and wrong from the other types of right and wrong?

3.5 One answer to this question relies on the reasons you have. The idea is that whenever an act is morally wrong you have decisive reasons not to do it (Smith, 1994, pp. 62–65; Joyce, 2001, ch. 2). If it is wrong to steal, then you have decisive reasons not to do so. Likewise, whenever an act is morally right you have decisive reasons to do that act. If it is right to help your friends, then you have decisive reasons for doing so. Of course, this way of explaining right and wrong is not helpful if we do not understand what reasons are. Very roughly, the idea is that whenever an act is morally wrong something important can be said against doing that act.

3.6 The second way to characterize moral right and wrong connects these notions to how we react to what others do (Gibbard, 1990, pp. 41–48). When someone does something that is morally wrong it is usually appropriate to blame them for acting in this way. If I act morally wrongly myself, I tend to feel guilty, or at least I should do so. People who act in the morally right way also often deserve praise and admiration.

3.7 In contrast, if your answer to a math question is wrong, you do not deserve to be blamed for this. On this view, then, moral rightness and wrongness are uniquely tied to our relationships to other people and how we are to treat one another in these relationships (Scanlon, 1998, chs 4–5). Rightness and wrongness have to do with what we can expect from other people and with what we can criticize them for failing to do. That we have the previous kind of moral emotions toward right-doing and wrong-doing is an illustration of this. Such emotional reactions to what others do are constitutive of the important moral relationships we have with others.

Different Forms of Egoism and Altruism

Chapters 1 and 2 gave you tools to compare the levels of well-being of dif- 3.8
ferent lives. As we saw in Chapter 2, some lives contain more satisfaction of desires or more objective goods than others. This makes these former lives better than others. We can then use this idea to explain egoism and altruism as ethical theories.

Psychological egoism[3] is the view that, as a matter of fact, there is only 3.9
one thing that can motivate you to act as a human being: namely, what you perceive to increase your well-being. This thesis attempts to describe generally what all of us are motivated to do all of the time. **Psychological altruism**, in contrast, is the view that we all only pursue other people's well-being all the time. The third alternative is to think that we sometimes pursue our own well-being and sometimes the well-being of others.

Ethical egoism[4] makes a different kind of a claim. Instead of saying that 3.10
you already pursue your own well-being, it claims that it is morally right for you to do so. Instead of *describing* what you are already doing, this theory *prescribes* what you should do. On this view it is morally right for you to pursue your own well-being, and morally wrong for you not to do so. It is therefore morally wrong for you to promote the well-being of others if this diminishes your own well-being.

Ethical altruism, in contrast, claims that morally right acts are those 3.11
that promote the well-being of other people, and morally wrong acts are those that fail to do so. According to this view, it would be wrong for you to pursue your own well-being if this diminished the well-being of others. There are different versions of this view, depending on what the relevant group of others is taken to be. Impartial versions of ethical altruism claim that you should promote the well-being of everyone else equally. More restricted versions claim that morality only requires us to promote the well-being of other people in some smaller group around us where this group could be our own family or the citizens of our country.

Feldman's objection to ethical egoism

3.12 Many people assume that ethical egoism is the doctrine of selfishness and that it therefore can't tell us what is right and wrong. Ethical egoism is certainly deeply unintuitive. Consider a case described by philosopher **Fred Feldman** (Feldman, 1978, p. 95): **the treasurer** of a workers' pension fund discovers that he can use the money deposited in the fund for promoting his own well-being without getting caught.[5] He could steal the money, buy a huge yacht, and sail away to a South Sea island. His life would be improved as a consequence while at the same time the well-being of other people would be diminished.

3.13 According to ethical egoism, it would be morally wrong for the treasurer not to commit the fraud. Because most people reject this conclusion, they reject ethical egoism as well. However, it would be a mistake to conclude from this case that ethical altruism must therefore be correct. For one thing, both ethical egoism and ethical altruism might be mistaken. Morality might require you to pursue your own well-being on some occasions and to promote the well-being of others on other occasions (**Sidgwick, 1907, pp. 496–506**).[6]

3.14 Another consideration is that acting rightly can't merely require *aiming* to promote the well-being of others, as many altruists assume. Even **the most evil dictators**[7] claim to aim at improving the lives of others. **Mao Zedong** started the **Great Leap Forward** in order to modernize China and to provide well-being for its citizens.[8] This good intention produced the most deadly mass killing in history. We have reasons for doubting Mao's sincerity, but what if he sincerely aimed at the well-being of his followers? Would this excuse his actions? Surely not. Even if you aim at promoting the well-being of others, you can act wrongly when you fail to achieve this goal. One reason why people with good intentions fail to improve lives is that they have mistaken beliefs about how to do so. Acting rightly must at the very least actually promote the well-being of others.

3.15 Despite these issues ethical egoism deserves to be taken seriously. In the following two sections we will consider two compelling arguments in favor of ethical egoism and one flawed argument against it. Next, we will consider an ethical theory called **contractarianism**, which attempts to show that ethical egoism leads to more plausible views about right and wrong than is often assumed. The chapter concludes with a discussion of the problems that arise from this view. If you want to learn more about the problems of ethical egoism, I can recommend the work of Russ Shafer-Landau (2010, ch. 8), James Rachels (**2003, ch. 6**), and Robert Shaver (**2010, sect. 2**).[9]

Two Arguments for Ethical Egoism

Most arguments for ethical egoism begin from the thesis that psychological 3.16
egoism is the correct way to understand human behavior. They start from the claim that the only thing that can motivate us to act is the prospect of our own well-being. On this view we are all hardwired to pursue what is in our selfish interests.

There have always been people who accept this premise. We often 3.17
observe people behaving selfishly. We see a waiter pocketing too large a share of the tips, mothers neglecting their children to go clubbing, or students cheating on tests. We also pursue what is good for us ourselves.

There is, then, some evidence that we often act selfishly. It is natural to 3.18
conclude from these everyday experiences that people always do what is good for them. This is because we all tend to **make generalizations too quickly**.[10] From seeing a few bad episodes of a TV show we jump to the conclusion that the whole series must be no good. In the same way, from seeing a few instances of selfish actions we jump to the pessimistic conclusion that everyone always behaves selfishly.

Could selfish motives be used to explain all actions in a uniform way? 3.19
Consider the famous case of **Raoul Wallenberg**.[11] Wallenberg served as a Swedish diplomat in Budapest at the end of World War II. During this time, he saved thousands of Jews from the Nazi concentration camps by issuing them protective passports and by hiding them in buildings belonging to the Swedish. By doing so, Wallenberg saved other people's lives by making huge personal sacrifices. He even risked his own life on many occasions. Were his actions too motivated by his selfish interests?

The psychological egoist's answer is that, even in these cases, there is 3.20
always something present that is in the lifesaver's interests. Wallenberg's actions only *seemed* to be altruistic. Deep down he was moved by the pleasure he got from helping others or by the fame or rewards which he expected to get later on. And all these are selfish motivations. Because such alternative explanations are always available, psychological egoism is difficult to refute.

Psychological egoism itself does not directly entail that ethical egoism is 3.21
the correct ethical theory. That we always pursue our own well-being does

not mean that it is always morally right to do so. We therefore need some way of getting from psychological egoism to ethical egoism. The following sections provide two different routes.

The "ought implies can" argument

3.22 The first route relies on the famous **ought implies can** principle (**Stern, 2004**).[12] This is the idea that you can be morally required to act in some way only if you can act in that way. You can't be required to do make the Earth spin backwards like **Superman**[13] for the simple reason that you cannot do so.

3.23 Recall that according to the doctrine of psychological egoism you can only pursue what you think is going to make your life go better – you are never motivated to do anything else. This idea – together with the "ought implies can" principle – suggests that morality can't require you to sacrifice your own perceived well-being in order to promote the well-being of others. It is always right for you to pursue what you think is in your interests, because it would be impossible for you to do anything else. In contrast, you can't be motivated to pursue what you think is in the interests of others, and for this reason morality can't require you to do so either.

3.24 As you have surely noticed, there is an awkward gap in this argument. The conclusion of this argument doesn't quite match ethical egoism as it was defined above. What you get from this argument is that it is right to do what you perceive will improve your own well-being (after all, there isn't anything else you could be motivated to do). This isn't quite the version of egoism which was introduced above. That said that right actions are the ones which really make your life go better. The problem is that the actions which you think increase your own well-being needn't be the ones that really do so. After all, you might have false beliefs about what is good for you. This is why only the egoists who accept this slightly different form of egoism can rely on the "ought implies can" argument.

The practical reasons argument

3.25 The second argument relies on a certain view about practical reasons (Shafer-Landau, 2010, pp. 106–108). It goes like this: in order for some act to be morally right for you to do, you must have sufficient reasons for doing that act. Therefore, it would not be right for you to keep a promise you have made unless you had good reasons for keeping that promise.

But when do you have good reasons to act? One suggestion is that you have good reasons to act in some way only if this serves your selfish interests. According to this view, you do not have a good reason to keep your promise unless it is in your interests. This view makes what you have reasons to do relative to what is in your interests. 3.26

It then follows from these premises that right acts must always be in your selfish interests. After all, no act is right unless you have good reasons to do it, and you only have good reasons to do something if it is in your selfish interests. One worry about this argument is that it seems to help itself to a premise, which pretty much just looks like ethical egoism itself. The argument assumes as a premise that you only have reasons to do what serves your selfish interests. This is something which the opponents of egoism already deny, which is why this argument probably will not convince people who don't already accept egoism. 3.27

Two Objections to Psychological Egoism

Do the previous two arguments sound correct to you? If you don't like them, you have a couple of options. You could show that the conclusion – ethical egoism – does not follow from the premises or you could argue that the premises are not true. Both of the previous arguments rely on the premise that psychological egoism is true and that you therefore always pursue what you think is in your own selfish interests. It is therefore easiest to challenge these arguments by criticizing this basic premise. Note that even if the previous arguments for ethical egoism don't work, there might still be some other good reasons for accepting that theory. The previous two arguments are just two that are fairly often mentioned and discussed. 3.28

Let us look at two objections to psychological egoism. The first is based on the everyday, practical way most people look at life – we'll call this the everyday objection. The second objection is based on **evolutionary biology**.[14] We'll call it the evolutionary objection. 3.29

The everyday objection

Consider Diana, who is a traditional housewife (see **Jean Hampton's Terry example**).[15] She is severely depressed. Her whole life consists of taking care of her husband and four children. She has no time for herself; her sense of 3.30

duty compels her to put her family first. Because of this Diana is deeply unhappy.

3.31 Because of her depression, Diana consults a psychiatrist. As you would expect, the psychiatrist advises Diana to put herself first at least some of the time – to occasionally forget about the troubles of the other members of the family and have some "me time" – to do things that Diana herself would enjoy doing.

3.32 In the real world, Diana's case is **a fairly common one**[16] and most people would also agree with the psychiatrist's advice (do you?). However, if psychological egoism were true, then that advice would make no sense. Diana would have always pursued her own well-being. In other words, psychological egoism conflicts with our everyday way of looking at things.

The evolutionary objection

3.33 Evolutionary biology provides a different type of evidence against psychological egoism (**Sober, 1999, ch. 7, sect. 8**).[17] **Elliot Sober**[18] begins from the observation that human beings tend to take care of their children and that they do so for a longer period of time than other animal species. Most human parents take care of their children because they naturally desire to help them.

3.34 According to evolutionary biology, there must be **an evolutionary explanation**[19] for human parents' desire to take care of their children. What evolutionary advantage would caring for offspring for long periods of time give to humans? An evolutionary biologist would be quick to point out that human populations that cared for their offspring would be likely to outcompete human populations that did not. Caring populations would raise more offspring to maturity and therefore grow their societies.

3.35 Psychological egoism and psychological altruism offer competing explanations for the parents' desire to help their children. They are alternative pictures of the mechanism that leads human parents to take care of their children. According to the psychological egoists, human parents want to care for their children when doing so will increase their own well-being. In contrast, according to the psychological altruists, parents are motivated to care for their children when doing so will increase their children's well-being.

3.36 Even an egoistic desire for well-being would guide parents to take care of their children. When a parent believes that **their child is in pain**,[20] they too experience anxiety and discomfort. In this situation, by taking care of your child's pain you can benefit yourself. For this reason, the psychological mechanism which egoists ascribe to parents would usually make the parents do the same acts as the altruistic mechanism.

We can, however, compare these psychological mechanisms to determine which would be more advantageous in evolutionary terms. Would either the altruistic or the egoistic motive make human beings more likely to survive as a species in difficult circumstances? The answer to that question would provide a scientific argument in favor of one of these positions. 3.37

One important difference between the motives is that the altruistic mechanism is more direct. If a parent believes that their child is in discomfort, she would want to help the child directly. In contrast, according to the egoistic picture, a parent would not be motivated to help her child merely because of the child's discomfort. She would need to feel anxious herself and she would have to believe that her own distress would be alleviated if she took care of her child. The egoistic motive provides a more complicated, two-step answer to the question of why a parent cares for a child. 3.38

Evolutionary forces tend to create the most effective and reliable ways to increase fitness in a population. The egoistic explanation has more parts that can go wrong. There would be cases in which parents would not experience anxiety when the child felt pain, or they would fail to form the required beliefs about the means to alleviate their anxiety. So the egoistic parents would be less likely to take care of their children. It follows that a population of such parents would be less likely to survive. For this reason, evolution is more likely to produce populations with altruistic motives. Admittedly, it is true that this argument against psychological egoism is very speculative. You might think that the slight evolutionary advantage offered by altruistic motivations just could not be decisive enough for determining what kind of psychological makeup evolution has given us. 3.39

To summarize, the best arguments for ethical egoism rely on psychological egoism as their first premise. These arguments also make use of other general philosophical principles. Even if we accepted those principles, we still have strong reasons to doubt the truth of psychological egoism. Because of this it is unlikely that there are sound arguments for ethical egoism. 3.40

Moore's Argument against Ethical Egoism*

3.41 This section will explore a famous flawed argument against ethical egoism. It was first presented by **G.E. Moore** in his book *Principia Ethica* (**1903, ch. 3, sect. 59**; see also Hutchinson, 2001, sect. 6).[21] Moore's argument attempts to show that ethical egoism is not even a coherent position.

3.42 For Moore's argument, we must first reformulate ethical egoism using slightly different terminology. We saw that ethical egoism is the view that each person is morally required to pursue only their own well-being. It would perhaps be simpler to say that ethical egoism is the theory that each person is morally required to pursue what is good for them. This would contrast ethical egoism with ethical altruism, according to which we ought to promote what is good for others.

3.43 Moore claimed that ethical egoism formulated in this way is self-contradictory. He first believed that the notion of "what is good for me" is unclear. He was puzzled by what people mean when they say that eating vegetables is good *for you*. Moore knew what we mean when we talk about things being good in a more abstract sense: it's good that we can treat diseases with antibiotics, it's good that we have clean water to drink, and so on. These claims make perfect sense.

3.44 So we can talk about what's good in general. Can we use this general notion to understand what the phrase "what is good for you" means? Moore proposed a way to do this: to say that something is good for you is to say that it would be good generally if you had it. If you claim that vegetables are good for you, you mean that it would be good if you ate vegetables. This is a general claim: it would be good if you ate vegetables in exactly the same way as it would be good if a cure for cancer were discovered.

3.45 Moore's next step was to state that, if something is good generally, it can't be the case that only you have reasons to pursue it. If it really is good that the number of people living in poverty is shrinking, then we all have reasons to pursue this goal in different ways. So, if a state of affairs would be generally good, then everyone has reasons for bringing about that outcome.

3.46 This means that if it were good for you to eat vegetables – that is, if it were good generally that you ate them – then everyone else too would have reasons to help you to eat them. Likewise, if ethical egoism means that it would be good for you to be happy, then it also means that we all should help you to be happy. However, this directly conflicts with the definition of ethical egoism, which was supposed to be the view that you are required only to pursue your own well-being. Now others too have reasons to help you pursue it. In this way, according to Moore, ethical egoism itself leads to the conclusion that ethical egoism can't be correct.

Here is a summary of Moore's argument: 3.47

1. According to ethical egoism, you are required to pursue only what is good for you.
2. Let us assume that only your own happiness is good for you.
3. According to ethical egoism, you are therefore required to pursue only your own happiness.
4. To say that something is good for Sally is to say that it is good generally that Sally has that thing. To say that happiness is good for Sally is thus to say that it would be generally good if Sally were happy.
5. If some state of affairs is good generally, then all of us – *including you* – have reasons to bring it about. If Sally's happiness is good generally, then you have reasons to help her to be happy.
6. Given statements 4 and 5, you have reasons to promote what is good for Sally. If her happiness is good for her, then you have reasons to promote her happiness.
7. So, if ethical egoism is true, you are required to pursue only your own happiness and you also have reasons to promote Sally's happiness. This is inconsistent.

What should you make of this intriguing argument? Does it show that ethical egoism is self-contradictory? Few people believe that the argument works. It is more difficult to say where exactly it goes wrong. 3.48

Problems of Moore's argument*

There is some agreement about what the main problem is. The argument shows that ethical egoism is self-contradictory *only* if the ethical egoist is committed to all the steps of the argument. If there is any premise in the argument which an ethical egoist can reject, then her position is at least consistent. 3.49

Are there any elements in Moore's argument which the egoist need not accept? **C.D. Broad** argued that egoists can reject the fifth premise of the argument (Broad, 1942).[22] They could always deny that whenever some state of affairs is good generally then everyone has reasons to bring about 3.50

that state of affairs. In other words, even if world peace would be good, you might not have reasons to help bring it about. Saying this would make ethical egoism consistent.

3.51 There is one even less plausible step in Moore's argument: the claim that the only possible way to understand the phrase "good for you" is to understand it to mean "good generally for you to have." Moore himself understood all forms of goodness in this universal way. But why should the egoist agree with him in this? Why can't the egoist claim that, in addition to being good generally, things can be good relative to individuals? On this view, your happiness is good for you because it is good relative to you that you are happy. In this way, your happiness could also be both good for you and bad for me because it would be good relative to you and bad relative to me.

3.52 This still leaves the egoist with a challenge: to explain what it means for things to be good relative to persons. Is this similar to a situation in which something is expensive for you but not to someone with more money? However, there might also be a way for the egoist to avoid even this challenge. Ethical egoism was formulated above by using the notion of well-being: it is the view that you are morally required to pursue your own well-being. This view does not make any claims about what is good and therefore Moore's objection can't be used against it. If an argument has no connection to taxation at all, you cannot object to it by saying that it is based on a wrong view of taxation.

3.53 There are no easy ways to refute ethical egoism. If you want to do so, you must be able to argue that ethical egoism leads to implausible moral verdicts about individual cases. For example, you could argue that ethical egoism would lead to the position that it is morally right to kill people when this is in your interests, which contradicts many of our dearly held beliefs. However, we will see next that arguing against egoism in this way turns out to be difficult: often the best means to increase your own well-being is to conform to these dearly held beliefs.

Gauthier's Contractarianism

3.54 This section focuses on an ethical theory that attempts to eliminate the conflict between the demands of prudence and the demands of morality. According to this theory, the best way to make your life better is follow the ethical rules that we all intuitively accept. The name of this theory is **contractarianism**,[23] because it understands right and wrong in terms of a contract that rational egoists would make. This theory has been best described by **David Gauthier**[24] in his book *Morals by Agreement* (Gauthier, 1986). To understand this theory, let us first consider why cooperation is paradoxical for egoists and then how Gauthier's view emerges as a solution to these paradoxes.

The paradox of social cooperation

In order to survive and to live well **you need to cooperate with other** 3.55
people.[25] If you lived on your own in the wild, life would be **a struggle**.[26] If people lived solitary lives, we would not have invented farming, technology, science, art, restaurants, libraries, cars, and so on. Therefore, it is in the selfish interests of each individual to live together with others in a society.

Despite this, from the perspective of egoists, social cooperation is a 3.56
problem. If we all pursue our own interests selfishly when living together with other people, we all end up being worse off than we would be if we all acted less selfishly. To see this, consider the following typical example of social cooperation (Smith, 2001, pp. 230–231).

Imagine that you and I are neighbors. We are the only people living on 3.57
our street, which has no streetlights. Our street is very narrow, and it has tricky tight corners. Because of this and the fact there are no streetlights on our street, it is likely that we will each have two accidents per year. I will have one accident on my own part of the street and one on yours. Similarly, you will have one accident yearly on your own part of the street and one on mine. The cost of each of these accidents would be $1000 for the driver.

If we both erected a streetlight on our properties, no accidents would 3.58
occur. It would cost $1200 to put up and maintain one streetlight for a year. Unfortunately, this means that, if I only consider my own well-being, it would not be worthwhile for me to put up a streetlight even if the two accidents cost me $2000 while the light costs $1200. To see why, let us first illustrate the situation with a simple table (see Table 3.1).

From your perspective (where it says *You* in the table), there are two 3.59
possible future scenarios depending on what I will do. In one situation, I erect my streetlight, whereas in the other scenario I decide not to do so. In the first alternative, if I erect my streetlight and you do so too, this will cost you $1200, which is the price of one streetlight. In contrast, if I erect my streetlight and you will not do so, you will only have to pay for one accident on your own dark part of the street, which will cost you $1000. So, if I erect

Table 3.1 A decision table

		Me	
		Erect a streetlight	Do not erect a streetlight
You	Erect a streetlight	Cost to you: $1200 [one streetlight, no accidents] Cost to me: $1200 [one streetlight, no accidents]	Cost to you: $2200 [one streetlight, one accident] Cost to me: $1000 [one accident, no streetlight]
	Do not erect a streetlight	Cost to you: $1000 [one accident, no streetlight] Cost to me: $2200 [one streetlight, one accident]	Cost to you: $2000 [two accidents, no streetlight] Cost to me: $2000 [two accidents, no streetlight]

a streetlight, you are $200 better off not putting up a streetlight on your property.

3.60 In the second alternative, I decide not to erect a streetlight. In this case, if you erect a streetlight, this will cost you $1200 plus the one accident that you will have on my dark property ($1000). So, the overall cost for you in this situation would be $2200. In contrast, if you do not erect a streetlight in this situation, this will cost you two accidents – the total of $2000. In this case as well, you are better off if you don't erect a streetlight.

3.61 This means that, no matter what I do, you are better off not erecting a streetlight on your property. I will come to the same conclusion on the basis of similar egoistic reasoning. This case is paradoxical because, although we try to be selfish, we end up being worse off. We both will have two accidents and end up being $2000 out of pocket. If we had acted less selfishly and erected our streetlights, this would have cost each of us only $1200. So, by pursuing our selfish interests strategically, we end up losing $800.

3.62 Cases like this are called **prisoner's dilemmas**.[27] By definition, **in these cases**[28] the best outcomes for everyone cannot be reached by a group of egoists who maximize the satisfaction of their selfish interests. These cases are called prisoner's dilemmas because they are often illustrated with an example of two prisoners who are considering whether to confess their crimes or not. It is then self-interestedly rational for both prisoners to confess even if this leads both parties to be worse off than they would have been if they both had remained silent.

Prisoner's dilemmas are common in everyday life. It is in your selfish interests not to pay the bus fare and at the same time use a public transport system that is funded by other people paying their fair share. If we all think in this way, then no one pays for their tickets and the whole system of public transportation collapses. As a result, we all end up worse off. Likewise, it is in the interests of petrol stations to cut their prices when others keep them constant. However, when everyone does this, all stations end up being worse off. 3.63

Contractarianism as a solution

If you can't reach the best outcome for yourself acting egotistically, how can you then reach that outcome? One answer to this question would be a set of principles that told us also to consider the well-being of others. If each of us adopted a principle that required us to build streetlights to prevent accidents, then we would erect our streetlights and be better off as a result. 3.64

According to David Gauthier's contractarianism, the principles that help us in situations like these have the following two essential features (Gauthier, 1986, p. 6): 3.65

1. Such principles must be impartial enough and they must constrain our egoism enough in order to count as proper moral principles. A principle like "Kill other people when it helps you!" does not count as a proper moral principle. However, principles that require us to consider the interests of others in cooperation cases are not like this and this is why they are proper moral principles.
2. Accepting and following such principles makes sense even for egoists. Doing so gives them more of what matters to them – their own well-being.

What would these principles look like? Gauthier's answer to this question is that these mutually beneficial moral principles would result from negotiating and bargaining (Gauthier, 1986, ch. 5). If you want to live together with others, you know that aiming only at your own well-being is not the way to go. Therefore we must agree on some general principles of behavior that benefit us all. Which principles should we then accept? 3.66

3.67 Gauthier has a simple solution to this problem. You should accept the principles that distribute the benefits of social cooperation according to how much each individual contributes. In the streetlight case above, if we both contribute equally by paying $1200 for the streetlight to be erected on our property, then it is only right that we benefit equally. In contrast, if I contributed $1800 and you paid only $600, then I would deserve more benefits than you. This much is intuitive. If you own 75% of our shared venture, then you should also get 75% of the benefits.

3.68 What does all of this have to do with morality? Consider a familiar moral principle such as "keep your promises," "tell the truth," "do no harm," and "do not kill." These principles are attempts to solve the problem that purely selfish behavior causes. If we all constrain our behavior by following these principles, then we can reap the benefits of cooperation: we can live together in a society. Thus each of us contributes to the social functioning of society by giving up certain forms of behavior. By doing so, we are entitled to a share of the benefits gained from social cooperation.

The compliance problem

3.69 The fundamental problem with this view is this: why should you stick to the bargain? It makes more sense for you to pursue your own well-being. As we have seen, you will be better off if you stick to the rules and cooperate with others. However, the best possible outcome for you would be to get others to cooperate and yet not have to contribute to the cooperation yourself. You pursue your own well-being most effectively by being a **freeloader**[29] – by letting others do the hard work and then enjoying the benefits yourself.

3.70 Furthermore, if you are not a freeloader, you will end up being a stooge. You will do the hard work and follow the rules while others take advantage of you. This means that you seem to have no reason to follow the moral agreement. And because everyone else will reason in the same way, we end up back in the unfortunate situation in which everyone fails to cooperate.

3.71 **A classic solution** to this **compliance problem** was famously endorsed by **Thomas Hobbes** (**Hobbes, 1660, ch. 17**).[30] He thought that in order to produce the right kind of conditions for mutually beneficial cooperation we must create an all-powerful institution that can punish everyone who fails to comply. If failing to keep your agreements means imprisonment, then clearly it is in your selfish interest to keep them.

David Gauthier's contribution to this debate was his demonstration that external coercion is not required (Gauthier, 1986, ch. 6). According to Gauthier, even without external punishments it can be rational for selfish agents to comply with moral principles that actually serve their interests. Consider a situation in which you are deciding whether you should constrain your egoistic behavior to comply with the mutually beneficial moral principles. Gauthier offers you two reasons to do so. 3.72

Reason one: Risk of exclusion If you fail to comply with the moral principle, you will be excluded from future social cooperation. **Even if you get away with breaking the rules once or twice, eventually you will be excluded from the social compact**[31] and unable to cooperate with others. 3.73

Reason two: Risk of revealing your true motives Even if others can't read you like an open book, they will still be able to recognize your selfish motives. If they see that you are not disposed to keep your part of the deal, they will be unlikely to enter agreements with you. You will therefore have more opportunities to do things with others if you are naturally inclined to play by the rules. And, according to Gauthier, once you have acquired this disposition to keep your end of the bargain, then it will also be rational for you to do so. 3.74

Summary

To summarize the contractarian position, if you fail to cooperate with others, your life will be lonely and poor. Therefore, social cooperation is in your selfish interests. Because mutually beneficial cooperation requires some basic rules, the basic rules of morality that form the basis for society result from self-interested bargaining. Gauthier's theory also explains why it is in your best interests to comply with the moral principles agreed to: 3.75

- Without such moral dispositions others would not trust you.
- If others thought you would not follow the rules, they would not cooperate with you.

In many ways, Gauthier's ethical theory is appealing. It does not rely on mysterious, self-evident moral truths. Rather, it shows that the correct moral principles result from ordinary self-interested bargaining between people who want to live and work together. This view can also explain why 3.76

you should do what morality requires. It tells you that only by being moral will you be able to enjoy the benefits of social cooperation. In Gauthier's theory, being a good person pays off.

Problems with Gauthier's Theory

3.77 Despite the attractions of Gauthier's theory, few moral philosophers currently accept it. There are three main problems.

Objection 1: Scope of moral concern

3.78 Even if this view can justify many intuitive moral principles, it can't justify all of them. Gauthier's theory tells you how to treat those people whose cooperation is beneficial to you. With them, you need to agree on the principles of cooperation. Gauthier's theory is thus an attempt to explain the content of these rules and why you should comply with them.

3.79 This view of morality leaves too many individuals outside the social contract (Hooker, 2000, p. 7). Consider those who do not contribute to society, such as small babies, frail elderly people, severely disabled and ill people, animals, very poor people, and people who are nasty, evil, or psychopaths. Arguably, if you consider your purely selfish interests, your life will go just as well if you do not cooperate with any of these people. You have no selfish reasons to cooperate with the members of these groups.

3.80 Therefore, Gauthier's theory fails to give you any reason to treat these groups morally, so you should be able to do to these groups whatever is in your selfish interests. This is surely wrong. We don't think that you can mistreat people who are too young or too old to contribute to society, torture animals, or fail to help the poor. So, Gauthier's view does not support all the moral principles we intuitively accept.

Objection 2: Deception

3.81 Gauthier's argument is based on the claim that you cannot hide your motives from others. But is this true (Sayre-McCord, 2001)? It is in your interests to deceive others about your selfish motives whenever you can get away with it. Freeloaders do not always get caught in the real world, let alone **in films.**[32] Even if you do get caught occasionally, there will always be plenty of other people to deceive. Gauthier's theory does not explain why we should not deceive others when we can.

Objection 3: Acting for right reasons

The last problem is perhaps the most general one. It is also the most controversial. Many people believe that acting morally is not merely a matter of doing the right thing, but also doing it for the right reasons (Prichard, 1912). Consider a friend who helps you only because by doing so she can hang out with your other friends. In this situation, it is true that she does what is right. After all, she is helping you. However, if she helps you only for selfish motives, then she fails to act in the morally appropriate way. 3.82

Gauthier's view is like the friend who helps for the wrong reasons: it seems to suggest that you could act morally for the wrong reasons. Ultimately, the theory suggests that the reason you should keep your promises or refrain from killing other people is to enjoy the benefits of cooperation. According to this view, the reason not to attack another person is not that it is wrong to hurt them, but rather that not doing so will benefit you in the long run. This reasoning fails to fit our intuitions about what morally appropriate agency requires. You should treat other people well because they deserve it. 3.83

Summary and Questions

The fundamental question in normative ethics is: "Which actions are right and which actions are wrong?" Ethical theories are systematic attempts to answer this question. This chapter focused on two theories: ethical egoism and ethical altruism. Ethical egoism claims that it is morally right to pursue your own well-being, whereas according to moral altruism, acting rightly requires promoting the well-being of others. 3.84

The chapter presented two strong arguments in favor of ethical egoism. Both of these arguments begin from psychological egoism. According to it, we can be moved to act only by the prospect of our own well-being. The first argument concludes from this that because you cannot do anything else than pursue your own well-being, nothing else can be morally required of you. The second argument, in contrast, was based on a specific view about practical reasons. According to this argument, you must always have sufficient reasons to do what is right. The argument asserts that you can 3.85

only have reasons to do what helps you achieve your goals. This means that only those actions that serve your goals can be morally right. If your goal is to pursue your own well-being, as psychological egoism claims, it must be morally right for you to do so.

3.86 The chapter then considered how plausible psychological egoism is as a premise of these arguments. It argued that psychological egoism fails to fit our understanding of many ordinary situations and it also conflicts with evolutionary psychology.

3.87 The next topic was Moore's attempt to show that ethical egoism is self-contradictory. Moore analyzed what is good for you in terms of you having something that is good generally. This led him to believe that egoists are committed to the idea that you also have reasons to help others to pursue their own well-being. Moore's argument fails because egoists do not need to accept his claims about what is good for you.

3.88 The last sections discussed David Gauthier's contractarianism. This theory argues that even egoists have reasons to accept a set of basic moral principles. Without such principles egoists would be worse off because they could not cooperate with other people effectively. The chapter concluded by considering the reasons why Gauthier's theory has not been universally accepted.

3.89 What should we, then, conclude about the relationship between morality and self-interests on the basis of this discussion? Can the two be reconciled after all? The views discussed in this chapter attempted to do this by bringing morality closer to what is in our selfish interests. This will always remain an uphill struggle. There will always be cases in which the morally right course of action just seems to come apart from what is in our selfish interests.

3.90 Other views such as virtue ethics (which will be discussed in Chapter 5 below), in contrast, try to reconcile morality and selfish interests by bringing selfish interests closer to morality. These views will tell you that acting morally itself makes your life go better. It seems rather implausible that this would be always true. Many bad people have lived at least reasonably good lives.

3.91 Because of this, perhaps we should just accept that there are two distinct sources of requirements. Prudence and what is good for us as individuals requires us to do certain things. Morality often requires us to do those very same things, but there will always be some cases in which morality requires us to do what is not very good for us as individuals. Sometimes, in order to do the right thing we must make sacrifices.

What should we then say about the strength of these requirements? In many cases, moral requirements are undoubtedly stronger than your own interests. There will be only a few cases in which you should overall do what is, morally speaking, the wrong thing to do. But perhaps there are some cases in which what is in your own interests matters more than morality. There might, for example, be cases in which you should put your survival first, even if, morally speaking, you should save the lives of many other people. 3.92

Based on the philosophical resources introduced in this chapter, consider the following questions: 3.93

1. What is the difference between psychological egoism and ethical egoism?
2. On pages 57–59 I explained two arguments for ethical egoism. How could you best summarize these arguments in a premise/conclusion form (see my summary of Moore's argument on p. 63)?
3. What objections to ethical egoism can you think of?
4. What could a defender of psychological egoism say in response to my two objections to the thesis?
5. What other prisoner's dilemma type of situations can you think of? Draw a choice table for one of these situations.
6. How serious are the problems of contractarianism?

Annotated Bibliography

Broad, C.D. (1942) "Certain Features of Moore's Ethical Doctrines," in *The Philosophy of G.E. Moore*, ed. Paul Schlipp (New York: Tudor), pp. 41–67. This article is famous for its criticism of Moore's objection to egoism.

Darwin, Charles (1971) *Descent of Man*, full text available at http://www.infidels.org/library/historical/charles_darwin/descent_of_man/, accessed February 21, 2014. Darwin's second book on evolutionary theory, in which he focused on how human beings evolved.

Feldman, Fred (1978) *Introductory Ethics* (Englewood Cliffs, NJ: Prentice Hall). This textbook clearly explains the traditional ethical theories. It is especially good on consequentialism and egoism.

Gauthier, David (1986) *Morals by Agreement* (Oxford: Clarendon Press). Gauthier's brave and sophisticated attempt to show that conforming to ordinary moral standards is rational because it is in our selfish interests.

Gibbard, Allan (1990) *Wise Choices, Apt Feelings: A Theory of Normative Judgement* (Oxford: Oxford University Press). An expressivist theory of normative judgments (see Chapter 8 below) in which Gibbard tries to understand judgments of right and wrong in terms of accepting norms of rationality that govern our emotion of blame.

Hampton, Jean (1993) "Selflessness and the Loss of Self," *Social Philosophy and Policy*, *10*(1), 135–165, full text available at http://philosophyfaculty.ucsd.edu/faculty/rarneson/Courses/HAMPTONselflessness.pdf, accessed February 21, 2014. An interesting article trying to argue that, on some occasions, selflessness can be bad and selfishness good.

Hobbes, Thomas (1660) *The Leviathan*, full text available at http://oregonstate.edu/instruct/phl302/texts/hobbes/leviathan-contents.html, accessed February 21, 2014. A hugely influential early formulation of social contract theory in which Hobbes describes the state of nature and the sovereign as a solution to the paradox of social cooperation.

Hooker, Brad (2000) *Ideal Code, Real World* (Oxford: Oxford University Press). The best contemporary formulation and defense of rule-consequentialism, which also includes insightful critical discussions of many alternative views in normative ethics.

Hutchinson, Brian (2001) *Moore's Ethical Theory* (Cambridge: Cambridge University Press). A thorough commentary on G.E. Moore's moral philosophy. The chapter on Moore's objection to egoism is especially helpful.

Joyce, Richard (2001) *The Myth of Morality* (Cambridge: Cambridge University Press). A recent book defending fictionalism in metaethics in which Joyce grounds his view on a strong connection between right and wrong, and reasons.

Moore, G.E. (1903) *The Principia Ethica*, full text available at http://fair-use.org/g-e-moore/principia-ethica, accessed February 21, 2014. A classic defense of non-naturalist realism in metaethics in which Moore also made his famous argument against egoism.

Prichard, H.A. (1912) "Does Moral Philosophy Rest on a Mistake?" *Mind*, *21*, 3–37, full text available at http://mind.oxfordjournals.org/content/XXI/81/21.full.pdf, accessed February 21, 2014. A complicated yet rewarding article on why many moral theories fail because they cannot account for the reasons we have for doing the right thing.

Rachels, James (2003) *The Elements of Moral Philosophy*, 4th ed. (New York: McGraw-Hill). A popular introduction to ethics which has a reasonably good chapter on egoism.

Sayre-McCord, Geoffrey (2001) "Deceptions and Reasons for Being Moral," in *Contractarianism and Rational Choice*, ed. Peter Vallentyne (Cambridge: Cambridge University Press), pp. 181–195. Sayre-McCord argues that Gauthier's view ignores some people's ability to deceive others and the benefits of doing so.

Scanlon, T.M. (1998) *What We Owe to Each Other* (Cambridge, MA: Harvard University Press). In this classic book, Scanlon attempts to make sense of right and wrong in terms of principles that no one could reasonably reject. He also nicely clarifies what we are talking about when we talk about right and wrong in the first place.

Shafer-Landau, Russ (2010) *The Fundamentals of Ethics* (Oxford: Oxford University Press). See the bibliography of Chapter 1 above.

Shaver, Robert (2010) "Egoism," in *The Stanford Encyclopedia of Philosophy* (Winter 2010 edition), ed. Edward N. Zalta, full text available at http://plato.stanford.edu/entries/egoism/, accessed on February 21, 2014. In this overview article, Shaver distinguishes between psychological, ethical, and rational egoism and discusses the merits of these views.

Sidgwick, Henry (1907) *The Methods of Ethics*, 7th ed. See the bibliography of Chapter 1 above.

Smith, Holly (2001) "Deriving Morality from Rationality," in *Contractarianism and Rational Choice*, ed. Peter Vallentyne (Cambridge: Cambridge University Press), pp. 229–253. A rich critical discussion of Gauthier's thesis according to which it is rational, in a self-interested sense, to be a constrained maximizer.

Smith, Michael (1994) *The Moral Problem* (Oxford: Blackwell). This book formulates the basic challenge in metaethics (see Part Three in this book) in an illuminating way. A part of his positive view is moral rationalism – the idea that right and wrong are tied to reasons.

Sober, Elliot (1999) "Psychological Egoism," in *The Blackwell Guide to Ethical Theory*, ed. Hugh Lafollette (Oxford: Blackwell), pp. 129–148, full text available at http://www.joelvelasco.net/teaching/tawp/Sober%2000%20-%20psych%20egoism.pdf, accessed February 21, 2014. Sober first clarifies what psychological egoism is and then discusses the main objections to it in an illuminating way.

Stern, Robert (2004) "Does 'Ought' Imply 'Can'? And Did Kant Think It Does?" *Utilitas*, *16*(1), 42–61, full text available at http://eprints.whiterose.ac.uk/298/1/sternr1.pdf, accessed February 21, 2014. A surprisingly accessible article on the "ought implies can" principle. It considers the main motivations for the principle and its different formulations.

Online Resources

1 Chris Heathwood's clear explanation of what normative ethics is: http://spot.colorado.edu/~heathwoo/phil1100/lec3_neb.pdf.
2 Key ethical theories for dummies: http://www.dummies.com/how-to/content/a-snapshot-of-key-ethical-theories.html.

3 Internet Encyclopedia of Philosophy on psychological egoism: http://www.iep.utm.edu/psychego/.
4 See section 2b for ethical egoism: http://www.iep.utm.edu/egoism/.
5 Feldman's homepage: http://people.umass.edu/ffeldman/ and a real-life case: http://mg.co.za/article/2011-11-26-former-unionist-richard-kawie-faces-arrest.
6 Henry Sidgwick's formulation of the so-called dualism of practical reason: http://archive.org/stream/methodsofethics00sidguoft#page/496/mode/2up.
7 Top ten evil dictators: http://popten.net/2010/05/top-ten-most-evil-dictators-of-all-time-in-order-of-kill-count/.
8 Information about Mao Zedong and the Great Leap Forward: http://en.wikipedia.org/wiki/Mao_Zedong and http://en.wikipedia.org/wiki/Great_Leap_Forward.
9 Rachels' chapter and Shaver's overview article on egoism: http://plato.stanford.edu/entries/egoism/ and http://www.faculty.umb.edu/lawrence_blum/courses/306_09/readings/rachels_ethical.pdf.
10 This is called overgeneralization: http://voices.yahoo.com/understanding-avoiding-distorted-thinking-overgeneralization-8826523.html.
11 Raoul Wallenberg saved the lives of thousands of Jews in Nazi-occupied Hungary during World War II: http://www.jewishvirtuallibrary.org/jsource/biography/wallenberg.html.
12 Wikipedia on ought implies can: http://en.wikipedia.org/wiki/Ought_implies_can and Robert Stern's explanation and evaluation of the principle: http://eprints.whiterose.ac.uk/298/1/sternr1.pdf.
13 Superman turning back time: http://www.youtube.com/watch?v=TjgsnWtBQm0.
14 Wikipedia on evolutionary biology: http://en.wikipedia.org/wiki/Evolutionary_biology.
15 Jean Hampton's article "Selflessness and the Loss of Self": http://philosophyfaculty.ucsd.edu/faculty/rarneson/Courses/HAMPTONselflessness.pdf.
16 At least advertisers seem to think so: http://www.over40females.com/blog/health/self-sacrificing-mothers-%E2%80%93-give-yourself-gift-2012-begins.
17 Elliot Sober's article "Psychological Egoism": http://www.joelvelasco.net/teaching/tawp/Sober%2000%20-%20psych%20egoism.pdf.
18 Sober's homepage: http://sober.philosophy.wisc.edu/.
19 Natural selection explained clearly: http://www.youtube.com/watch?v=0SCjhI86grU.
20 A baby crying: http://www.youtube.com/watch?v=qS7nqwGt4-I.
21 G.E. Moore: http://plato.stanford.edu/entries/moore/ and *Principia Ethica*: http://fair-use.org/g-e-moore/principia-ethica/chapter-iii.
22 The life and works of C.D. Broad: http://plato.stanford.edu/entries/broad/.

23 An overview of contractarianism and its main problems: http://plato.stanford.edu/entries/contractarianism/.

24 The life and works of David Gauthier: http://en.wikipedia.org/wiki/David_Gauthier.

25 Charles Darwin describes this nicely in Chapter 4 of *Descent of Man*: http://www.infidels.org/library/historical/charles_darwin/descent_of_man/chapter_04.html.

26 In Thomas Hobbes's words, life would be "solitary, poor, nasty, brutish, and short": http://oregonstate.edu/instruct/phl302/texts/hobbes/leviathan-c.html.

27 Wikipedia on prisoner's dilemmas: https://en.wikipedia.org/wiki/Prisoner's_dilemma.

28 An illustration of a prisoner's dilemma from a British game show: http://www.youtube.com/watch?v=zpahL4fu5R8.

29 A clear discussion of the so-called free-rider problem: http://plato.stanford.edu/entries/free-rider/.

30 Steven B. Smith's lecture on sovereignty as a solution to the state of nature problem: http://www.youtube.com/watch?v=lyZJ1lDULNw; Hobbes's life and works: http://plato.stanford.edu/entries/hobbes/; and Chapter 17 of Leviathan: http://oregonstate.edu/instruct/phl302/texts/hobbes/leviathan-c.html#CHAPTERXVII.

31 President George W. Bush having difficulties with this idea: http://www.youtube.com/watch?v=eKgPY1adc0A.

32 A scene from *Dirty Rotten Scoundrels*: http://www.youtube.com/watch?v=axAA2egWeaY.

4

CONSEQUENTIALISM AND KANTIAN ETHICS

This chapter will discuss two influential traditions of ethical thought. The 4.1
first one of these is consequentialism. The most famous version of consequentialism is **utilitarianism**,[1] which was famously defended by Jeremy Bentham and John Stuart Mill. Bentham summarized this view by claiming that "it is the greatest happiness of the greatest number that is the measure of right and wrong (**Bentham, 1777**)."[2] This **greatest happiness principle** is not helpful because it doesn't tell whether (i) you should go for the *greatest amount of happiness* or (ii) attempt to make *as many people happy as possible*. There are situations in which you just can't do both.

It is better to begin from what is special about all **consequentialist** 4.2
ethical theories (Mulgan, 2007; Bykvist, 2010; Driver, 2012).[3] Consequentialism is best understood as a family of ethical views that share the same structure. The next section will explain what this structure is and the different versions of consequentialism that share it. The second section will then discuss John Stuart Mill's famous argument in favor of utilitarianism. This argument is important because it clearly reveals the important moral ideals that continue to motivate utilitarians.

After consequentialism we will look at **Immanuel Kant**'s ethical theory, 4.3
which is based on the **Categorical Imperative**.[4] This principle requires that you should "never…act otherwise than so that [you] could also will that [your] maxim should become a universal law (**Kant, 1785, 4:402**)."[5] We will find out the best way to understand this principle and look at Kant's arguments to the conclusion that this is the fundamental principle of morality.

This Is Ethics: An Introduction, First Edition. Jussi Suikkanen.

4.4 Philosophers have recently come to see the debates about ethical theories in a new light (see Parfit, 2011). Philosophers used to see consequentialism and **Kantian ethics** as competing theories about what is right and wrong. As a result the defenders of these theories looked for cases in which their opponents' view seems to get things wrong about what you should do. The end of this chapter will go through some of these cases.

4.5 However, nowadays philosophers don't really care about these sorts of cases. This is because both consequentialism and Kantian ethics are very flexible. When there is an alleged counterexample to these views their defenders can always reformulate their view so as to avoid the problem. This is possible because the central parts of these theories can be understood in so many different ways. As a result the defenders of these views seem to be able to agree on what is right and wrong. The last section of this chapter will explain all of this in more detail.

Consequentialism

4.6 In order to understand consequentialism you need to know first that there are two distinct families of moral qualities. First of all, there are **evaluative qualities**. You talk about them when you use words such as "value," "good," "bad," "desirable," "worthwhile," and "utility." You can, for example, say that it is good that so many people help the poor.

4.7 In addition to these evaluative qualities, there are also **deontic qualities**. You talk about them when you use words such as "ought," "must," "should," "right," "permissible," "wrong," "reasons," "duty," and "obligation." You can use these words to describe how people are to act. If you say that Ben ought to keep his promise, you are telling him what to do.

4.8 The fundamental idea of **consequentialism** is that you can only make sense of the deontic qualities in terms of the evaluative ones. Therefore, according to the core idea of consequentialism, what is good is always prior to and more important than what you ought to do and what is right or wrong. This is to say that consequentialists think that truths about good and bad explain all the truths about right and wrong.

4.9 Consequentialist theories therefore always have two separate elements. Let us call the first one of these **the evaluative element**, which is a **theory of value**.[6] Such a theory attempts to capture which things are good. Theories of this type play a crucial role in all forms of consequentialism.

Imagine that you are in a situation in which you have the following options: 4.10

A. Call a friend.
B. Watch television.
C. Travel to France.

Suppose that, for some reason, these are your only options. The value theory element of a consequentialist view allows you to rank these options in terms of how good their consequences are.

We can use a very silly theory of value to illustrate how this works. This silly (and blatantly false) theory of value says that nothing except how many rubber ducks there are in the world has value. Rubber ducks and only rubber ducks are good. Let us also imagine that whether you do A, B, or C affects the number of rubber ducks there will be. Traveling to France makes some people want to produce more rubber ducks whereas calling a friend makes them want to destroy few. As a result this theory of value means that traveling to France is your best option and calling a friend your worst one. 4.11

In order to be able to always rank your options like this in terms of how good their consequences are, all consequentialist theories must thus give an account of what is good. They have to describe what makes outcomes better – like the rubber ducks did in the previous example. Instead of silly rubber duck views, real consequentialists obviously want to offer you more plausible and realistic theories of value which can tell us what kind of outcomes are genuinely good. Note that when you compare how good your options are it does not matter how far in the future the relevant goods are created or who gets them. All consequences matter equally just as long as they are better consequences than the consequences of your other alternatives. 4.12

The second element of all forms of consequentialism is the so-called **deontic**[7] element. It uses the evaluative ranking of the options to specify which options it is right and wrong to choose. One deontic element could say that it is always wrong to do the act that is ranked the lowest. This deontic element would mean in the previous case that it is wrong for you to call a friend. All forms of consequentialism therefore tell us what is right and wrong by relying on the evaluative rankings of the options. This explains why, according to these views, what is good is always prior to what 4.13

is right (Rawls, 1971, p. 24). As we'll see, consequentialists also disagree about which sort of deontic element to use in their theory.

Utilitarianism

4.14 **Utilitarianism**[8] illustrates nicely the basic structure of consequentialism. According to this theory, happiness, and only happiness, has value. Utilitarians therefore rank your options by how much happiness they bring about. Again, it does not matter who experiences this happiness and when. Utilitarians then add that an action is right if and only if it has the best consequences – that is, when the action brings about more general happiness than the other actions which you could do in your situation.

4.15 In many cases this view has intuitive consequences. Why is it, for example, wrong to rape someone? Utilitarians have a plausible answer to this question. It is true that the rapist will get some fleeting happiness from the act of rape. However, the rape will also make its victim deeply unhappy. It will also affect the happiness of the victim's friends and family, and more generally will create a negative atmosphere. On balance then, rape has horrible consequences, which makes it the wrong thing to do according to utilitarians.

4.16 Utilitarianism also has more controversial consequences. Consider **William Godwin**'s famous example: you can save either a skillful surgeon or your mother (**Godwin, 1793, vol. I, book II, ch. 2**).[9] In this case, you will produce more general happiness if you save the surgeon. If you don't save your mother, you and your family will be unhappy and your mother will no longer experience any happiness. However, if you don't save the surgeon then a whole lot more people will be just as unhappy and unable to experience happiness – all the other people whom the surgeon's skills could help. For this reason the utilitarians rank the option of saving the surgeon above saving your mother. This means that according to utilitarianism, it is right for you to save the surgeon (the option with the best consequence) and wrong for you to save your mother.

4.17 Utilitarianism is not the only version of consequentialism. All forms of consequentialism have an evaluative element and a deontic element. When consequentialists formulate their views, they can pick and mix different combinations of evaluative and deontic elements from the following alternatives. The following sections will introduce some of the most important versions of consequentialism. These versions will be motivated by the problems of the standard form of utilitarianism.

Deliberation procedure vs. criterion of rightness

Some consequentialists put their theory forward as a **deliberation procedure** and others as a **criterion of rightness** (**Bales, 1971**).[10] A deliberation procedure, funnily enough, is what you use to decide what to do. If a consequentialist says her theory is the correct deliberation procedure, then this means that you have to think about, and rank, the consequences of your available options when you're deciding what to do. 4.18

The trouble is that understanding consequentialism like this undermines the whole point of the theory. Deliberating in this consequentialist way requires too much time – you will usually have lots of options open to you, and remember you have to think about the long-term consequences of what you do. If you went about things in this way, you'd never get anything done. In this way consequentialism is self-undermining: if you use it to decide what to do, the consequences are bad. 4.19

The alternative is to think that consequentialism is a criterion of what is right. It only says that it is always right to do what has the best consequences. This leaves it open how you should go about deciding what to do. It could be that you can get better consequences by following simple, tried-and-tested moral rules of thumb than by working out the details of every decision you have to make. 4.20

Direct vs. indirect forms of consequentialism

Act-consequentialism is the best example of **a direct consequentialist theory**. Consider the previous case in which you can either lie or tell the truth. Act-consequentialism says that what is right for you to do in this situation depends only on how good the consequences of these actions will be. If lying has good consequences, then is right for you to lie. The rightness and wrongness of your acts is thus *directly* a result of how good the consequences they have are. Many people think that this view makes bad actions such as lying to other people too easily permissible. 4.21

Indirect forms of consequentialism that attempt to avoid this problem are slightly more complicated (Adams, 1976; Hooker, 2000). On these views we first evaluate the consequences of something other than acts. Whether an act is right or wrong then depends on those other things. **Rule-consequentialism**[11] is a good example of indirect consequentialism. According to this theory, you need to first consider the consequences different rules would have if they were adopted by everyone. Whether an 4.22

act is right then depends on whether it is permitted by the rules that have the best consequences.

4.23 So, in the previous case, a rule that allows you to lie would probably have catastrophic consequences. If everyone lied, you couldn't trust anyone! This is why the best rules forbid you to lie. This means that rule-consequentialism tells you to tell the truth even if this would have bad consequences in the given situation. Some people think that for this reason rule-consequentialism better matches what we intuitively think is right and wrong.

Utilitarianism vs. richer conceptions of value

4.24 As explained above, utilitarians think that only happiness is good and they understand happiness in terms of the balance of our pleasurable and painful experiences (**Mill, 1861, ch. 2, para. 2**).[12] So, according to their view, right actions always maximize the amount of pleasure and minimize the amount of pain. In many cases, this theory of value seems to have embarrassing consequences. Imagine living in a society in which the vast majority experiences pleasure from the misfortunes of a small minority. According to basic utilitarianism, in this situation it would be right for the majority to discriminate against the minority. This would, after all, make the society a happier place overall.

4.25 This hedonistic theory of value is not the only option for consequentialists. Firstly, if you like the idea of utilitarianism but you don't like hedonism, you could think that only well-being is good and then understand well-being in terms of desire satisfaction. Your view would then say that it is always right to maximize the general amount of desire satisfaction. You could also accept a **perfectionist**[13] form of consequentialism according to which it is always right to maximize the realization of human capabilities (Hurka, 1993).

4.26 Even more value pluralist forms of consequentialism could claim that:

1. Some basic acts like breaking of promises, killing, and lying are bad in themselves.
2. Some things like human interaction, knowledge, virtue, and aesthetic pleasures are good in themselves.

These views would then go on to argue that it is always right for you to act in ways that minimize the number of bad acts done, and maximize the amount of intrinsically good things. This consequentialist theory would not care about how happy people are.

All these different theories of value will create very different evaluative rankings of options. As a result, they will lead to very different conclusions about what is right and wrong. This is important because many objections to consequentialism assume very simplistic theories of value, which are only optional for the consequentialist. The more sophisticated theories of value can help consequentialists to avoid these objections. For example, in the case of the previous case where the majority enjoys discrimination, a form of consequentialism that says that discrimination is bad in itself will tell you not to discriminate, which is exactly what you want to hear. 4.27

Actual vs. expected value

Some consequentialist views rank options in terms of **the value of their actual consequences** and the rest in terms of the **expected value** of their consequences.[14] Consider a case in which you offer a friend of yours a glass of **water**.[15] Sadly, your friend dies as a result of this because someone had, unbeknownst to you, poisoned the water. Did you do anything wrong? 4.28

The actual consequences of your friendly act were horribly bad. The consequences of not offering your friend a drink would not have been equally bad. Therefore, if the actual consequences of your acts matter, then you did something wrong in this case. Most people think that this is an absurd view – you didn't know that the water was poisoned. To avoid this problem, many consequentialists point out that your act had very good expected consequences. You didn't expect your friend to die. They then say that according to more plausible versions of consequentialism, it is always right to do what has the best expected consequences. 4.29

The expected value of an act is determined by: 4.30

i. what potential outcomes the act has;
ii. how likely these different outcomes are; and
iii. how much value they contain.

The better the potential outcomes of a given act are and the more likely these good outcomes are, the more expected value the act has (for how the expected value of an option is calculated more precisely, see paragraphs 10.82–10.85 below). The likely outcome of offering someone water is that they will enjoy drinking it. It is highly unlikely that they will die. Because of this, even if the actual outcome of your act – that your friend died – was bad, your act of offering her water still had a lot of expected value. The expected value form of consequentialism therefore fits the intuition that you don't do anything wrong if you harm people by accident.

Maximizing vs. satisficing

4.31 Consequentialists can also accept different deontic elements. So far we have only discussed **maximizing** versions of consequentialism. They claim that it is always right to do whatever has the best consequences, and that it is wrong to do anything else. Maximizing forms of consequentialism thus claim that you should always maximize the good.

4.32 In contrast, **satisficing** versions of consequentialism claim that you should always do what has *good enough* consequences (**Slote, 1984**).[16] Imagine a situation in which your options are ranked in terms of how good their consequences are. In this case a satisficing theory does not require you to pick the best option but rather only an option that has at least a certain level of good consequences. If going to Amsterdam has almost as good consequences as going to Paris (which would be best), then this view allows you to choose either option. Some people think that satisficing versions of consequentialism are more plausible because they leave us more freedom to choose between many morally permissible options.

Mill's Argument for Utilitarianism

4.33 Now you know what the core idea of consequentialism is and you are familiar with the main versions of consequentialism. Why should you be a consequentialist in the first place? This section explains **John Stuart Mill**'s famous answer to this question.[17] Many people think that his argument in favor of utilitarianism is a complete disaster. However, there is more to Mill's argument than first meets the eye. Mill's argument is important because it reveals the fundamental moral ideals on which consequentialist thinking is based.

4.34 Mill's argument can be quoted here almost in full:

> The only proof capable of being given that an object is visible, is that people see it…In the like manner…the sole evidence it is possible to produce that anything is desirable, is that people do actually desire it…No reason

> can be given why the general happiness is desirable, except that each person, so far as he believes it to be attainable desires his own happiness. This, however, being a fact, we have not only all the proof which the case admits of, but all which it is possible to require, that happiness is a good; that each person's happiness is a good to that person, and the general happiness, therefore, a good to the aggregate of all persons. **(Mill, 1861, ch. 4, para. 3)**[18]

As you saw above, all consequentialist theories have two elements. Mill only addresses the first one in his argument. He assumes without an argument that it is always right to do what has the best consequences. His argument's main aim is to show that only happiness can make the consequences of an act good: that "happiness is desirable, and the only thing desirable, as an end" (Mill, 1861, ch. 4, para. 2). He also wants to show that everyone's happiness is equally desirable. 4.35

The first stage of Mill's argument to this conclusion compares the visibility of objects to the desirability of outcomes. Mill appears to think that, because an object is visible when it is seen, an outcome is similarly desirable when it is desired. Given that you probably desire your own happiness, this enables Mill to conclude that your own happiness must be desirable for you. 4.36

In the second stage of the argument Mill directly states, on the basis of the previous claim, that everyone's general happiness must also be desirable as an end. As you can see, Mill suggests in the quote above that *because* your happiness is good for you therefore general happiness must be a desirable end for all of us. 4.37

The final part of the argument attempts to argue that only general happiness is a desirable end (Mill, 1861, ch. 4, paras 4–7). This part of the argument is a response to an objection and it takes place just after the quoted passage. You could object that people in fact desire many other things than happiness. You can desire food and conversation, for example. Doesn't it follow from Mill's own argument that these things too must therefore be desirable? 4.38

Mill's response to this objection is that you always first desire food and conversation as a means to happiness. However, once you eat food and take part in conversation, you will come to realize how pleasant these experiences are in themselves. As a consequence, these goods become an element of your happiness. In desiring food and conversation, you are then in the end desiring the pleasant experiences that constitute your happiness. 4.39

Because of this, you do not really desire anything else except happiness, and thus only happiness is desirable.

The problems with Mill's argument

4.40 We can now list Mill's mistakes. Firstly, Mill merely assumes without any argument half of what he is supposed to prove. The assumption that it is always right to do what has the best consequences is not supported by any part of the argument whatsoever. However, unless you show all parts of a theory to be true, you do not successfully prove that the theory is correct.

4.41 The second step of Mill's argument relies on a problematic analogy between visibility and desirability (**Moore, 1903, ch. 3, sects 39–40**).[19] It is true that the things you see are visible. This is because to be visible is to be something that is capable of being seen. However, it is not true that to be desirable is to be something that people can desire. You can desire to count blades of grass but this does not make doing so desirable. Instead, to be desirable is to be something that is *worth* desiring. As the previous example illustrates, there are many things we desire that are not worth desiring and thus are not desirable. The second step of Mill's argument is thus equally flawed.

4.42 The third step of his argument is even worse (**Sidgwick, 1907, p. 388**).[20] Mill just bluntly asserts that because your happiness is good for you, the general happiness of everyone must therefore be a desirable goal for each of us. However, this is just what Mill's opponents want to deny. Egoists who do not care about others, for example, claim that only their own happiness is a desirable goal for them. Mill gives no reason for the egoists to change their mind. If you read the quote above carefully from the egoist's perspective, nothing it in addresses your views.

4.43 The last step of Mill's argument is not any better either (**Moore, 1903, ch. 3, sect. 43**).[21] Perhaps it is true that we can only desire experiences that are pleasant and that these experiences are also desirable. Even in this case, you could still desire these experiences for other reasons than the pleasures they provide you. Consider **Picasso's Guernica**.[22] Even if you get pleasure from looking at this magnificent painting, many of us want to spend time looking at it for other reasons too. It is desirable to look at this painting because it illustrates the horrors of the Spanish Civil War in an acute way.

Saving Mill's argument

At this point, you might think that Mill's argument is hopelessly flawed. 4.44
Despite this, Geoffrey Sayre-McCord convincingly argues that Mill's argument still contains some of the most important ethical ideas that support consequentialism (**Sayre-McCord, 2001**).[23]

It is true that Mill doesn't argue for the other half of utilitarianism. This is 4.45
not because he was a bad philosopher. Mill did not argue for the claim that right actions have the best consequences because this was believed to be self-evidently true when he was writing (**Moore, 1903, ch. 1, sect. 17**).[24] Imagine that you have two options: one that is very good and another that is not good at all. Isn't it obvious in this case that you should choose the better option? What possible reason could there be for making things worse?

The second step of Mill's argument is not too bad either. If you read the 4.46
long quote above carefully, you notice that Mill never claims that to be desirable is to be what people desire. All he says is that what people desire is *good evidence* for what is desirable. This has to be correct. Consider all the things that you desire. Most of those things have to be good, right? One plausible explanation for this is that we desire things just because we take them to be good in some way.

The third step of the argument is the most important one. This is the 4.47
step where Mill moves from the idea that your happiness is good for you to the conclusion that everyone's happiness is a desirable goal for all of us.

If you want to be charitable to Mill, you should read this quick step in 4.48
the following way. Your happiness is desirable for you – it is a worthwhile goal for you. We can then compare your happiness to my happiness. If you do this, you must recognize that they seem to be exactly alike. In fact, the only thing that distinguishes your happiness from mine is that your happiness belongs to you and mine to me. But, if your happiness is otherwise just like mine and your happiness is something worth pursuing, then shouldn't my happiness too be worth pursuing even if it is not yours?

This reasoning captures the important moral insight behind Mill's argu- 4.49
ment. **When you consider two things and you can't find any relevant differences between them, you must consider them to be equally good.**[25] If there are no significant differences between your and my happiness, and your happiness is desirable, then mine must be too. In fact, given that there are no important differences between your happiness and other people's happiness, then everyone's happiness must be equally desirable – just as Mill argued.

4.50 We can therefore understand the main crux of Mill's argument as a challenge. If you don't want to be a utilitarian, you must either deny that your own happiness is desirable or you must explain what makes your happiness different from other people's happiness. This difference cannot be that your happiness belongs to you whereas mine belongs to me given that your car is not better than mine merely because it is yours. Unless you can respond to this challenge, Mill's reasoning requires you to accept utilitarianism.

4.51 This important insight also reveals the fundamental ethical ideals behind consequentialism. The argument Mill is making here is that my happiness can't be any more important than anyone else's happiness. Everyone's happiness must therefore count equally. In this way, Mill is grounding his utilitarianism on an appealing idea of the basic moral equality of everyone. This idea that we should be impartial is in many ways appealing. It supports the idea that you should not treat people differently on the basis of their gender, ethnicity, wealth and social class, sexual orientation, and so on. When Mill was writing, this idea was very radical, and even today many people continue to resist the idea that we all matter equally, morally speaking.

Kantian Ethics

4.52 Even if Mill's argument makes utilitarianism appealing, there are also good alternatives. You already know what these alternatives must be like. Non-consequentialist ethical theories have to specify what is right and wrong without relying on what is good. The opponents of consequentialism thus need an alternative starting point. This section introduces one of the main alternatives to consequentialism: Kantian ethics. The beginning of the section explains how Kant thought that you could use the so-called **universalization test** to determine what principles it is right and wrong to act on. The second part of the section will then investigate the main arguments for Kant's view. These are at the same time arguments for why we should follow the principles that pass Kant's test.

The good will

4.53 **Immanuel Kant** thought that we could start from our own wills (**Kant, 1785**; for **an overview of Kant's ethics**, see **Johnson, 2008**; see also O'Neill, 1975; Hill Jr., 1992; Herman, 1993; Korsgaard, 1996; Timmermann,

2007).[26] He argued that you can work out what is right and wrong by first thinking about when we admire other people for their actions. When do their actions have "moral worth," as Kant put it? Assuming that we admire people for their right actions and blame them for their wrong actions, answering this question would reveal to us what is right and wrong. Kant's insight was that the way we praise and blame others seems to have little to do with the consequences of their actions. Instead, what seems to matter is what people are intending to do. This is why he thought that whether you act rightly depends on the quality of your will rather than on how good the consequences of your actions are.

Kant observed that whether you admire others for what they do depends 4.54
on what motivates them to act. Consider the act of **saving someone's life**.[27] You can save others for different reasons: because you need a hostage, or because you love the person in need, or because you just think that this is your duty. Even if the act is the same in all these cases, saving a person for the first reason has no moral worth whereas saving them for the last reason would be admirable. What motives do you then need to have for your acts to be morally admirable?

According to Kant, in order to answer this question you must look at 4.55
the principles on which people act. Kant called our subjective principles that lead us to act **maxims**.[28] They have the following form (O'Neill, 1975, p. 37):

In my circumstances C, I do act A in order to achieve an outcome O.

Whenever you act, you must therefore have in your mind a principle that specifies the circumstances you are in (C), what you aim to achieve in them (O), and what you intend to do in order to bring about that outcome (A).

Kant believed that no subjective principle of action can ever make your 4.56
action morally admirable. Within the principle on which you act, the relevant outcome you want to achieve appears as an incentive for you. One maxim you often act on is "When I am in a supermarket, I buy sugar in order to have coffee later." Within this maxim, the prospect of being able to drink coffee offers you an incentive to buy sugar. It offers such an incentive to you because you want to have sugar in your coffee.

Because of this connection to desires, Kant thought that our maxims are 4.57
too unstable and superficial to make our actions morally admirable. Certain outcomes offer you incentives to act in the way you do because of what you want to achieve. If you happened to want something else, then you would

not act on these maxims. If you didn't happen to like coffee, you would not act on your sugar-buying maxim. Because we have limited control over what we want, Kant thought that we could not be praised for acting in the way we do on the basis of our desires. Imagine that Amanda takes care of her mother merely because she desires to see her mother happy. According to Kant, you should not praise Amanda in this situation, because she could have just as well wanted to pursue her own career instead. Because it is just luck that Amanda helps her mother, she doesn't deserve to be admired for doing so.

4.58 Kant thought that this shows that your acts are morally admirable only if you first test whether your maxim can be **universalized** (Kant, 1785, pp. 4:400–4:402). All universalized versions of maxims, which Kant calls **universal laws**, have the following form (O'Neill, 1975, p. 61):

> Whenever anyone is in the circumstances C, they will do act A in order to achieve an outcome O.

As you can notice, here the "I" in the maxim has been replaced with "anyone" and "they." Kant then claims the fundamental principle of morality is the following:

> **Categorical Imperative**: "never…act except in such a way that [you] could also will that [your] maxim should become a universal law." (Kant, 1785, p. 4:402)

So, according to Kant, we should praise your acts only if you are acting on a maxim which you have tested for whether you can will that maxim also to be a universal law.

The universalization test

4.59 **There are two ways in which you could fail to will a maxim to be universal law.**[29] Sometimes when you attempt to will your maxim to be a universal law, you fail the **contradiction in conception** test. Other times when you try to do so, you fail the **contradiction in will** test. In both cases, your maxim cannot be consistently willed to be a universal law and the Categorical Imperative forbids you to act on that maxim.

4.60 Kant used the following examples to illustrate these two tests (Kant, 1785, pp.4:422–4:423). Consider first the maxim:

> Whenever I am in need, I make a false promise in order to get some cash.

We can then formulate this maxim into the following universal law:

> Whenever anyone is in need, they will make a false promise in order to get some cash.

The problem here is that it is impossible to imagine circumstances in which this is a universal law. If the false promises maxim were accepted by everyone, the whole practice of making promises would collapse. In those circumstances you would not be able to get money by making a false promise. No one would believe you. So you can't actually imagine a scenario where everyone makes false promises to get what they want. For this reason, the false promises maxim can't be consistently willed to be a universal law – it fails the contradiction in conception test. This is why the Categorical Imperative rules out acting in this way. 4.61

There is also another way in which a maxim can fail to be universalizable. Consider the maxim: 4.62

> Whenever I see someone in urgent need of help, I will not help them in order to avoid sacrificing my own happiness.

If we universalize this maxim into a universal law, we get:

> Whenever anyone sees another person in urgent need of help, they will not help the needy in order to avoid sacrificing their own happiness.

In this case, you can imagine what the world would be like if this were a universal law everyone followed. It would be a pretty nasty world, but not impossible. For this reason, willing this maxim to be a universal law does not fail the contradiction in conception test.

Kant thought that you still couldn't consistently will this maxim to be a universal law. In the world in which no one helps others, you would still have some goals. As a rational person you must want to take the steps required to secure those goals. And some of those goals will require the help of others. If everyone is acting selfishly constantly, then you won't be able to achieve these aims. This means that, because you want things that will require other people's help to secure, you can't consistently will the 4.63

selfish maxim to be a universal law. This is why this maxim fails the contradiction in will test and why the Categorical Imperative does not allow you to ignore the suffering of others.

Duties, right and wrong

4.64 Kant thought that these two tests can be used to illuminate **different kinds of duties**.[30] Before you act, you should will your maxim to be a universal law. If you can't even imagine a situation in which your maxim is a universal law, like in the case of the false promise, then you have **a perfect duty** not to act on that maxim. This means that you must never act in that way.

4.65 If you can consistently imagine the situation but cannot consistently will that state of affairs to obtain, like in the case of the selfish maxim, then you only have **an imperfect duty**. When you have an imperfect duty to help others this means that you must adopt the general aim of helping others but you only need to do so on some occasions – you have some level of discretion.

4.66 If before you act you check and find out that your maxim can be consistently willed to be a universal law, then you will act in a morally admirable way. In this situation, it is not a coincidence that you do the right thing. You do not act merely because you happen to want something, but rather in this case your will has the general form of a law. Kant said that a person whose will has this form acts from respect for the law as such. She will not be making lying promises and she will be helping others because this is her duty. She would do this even if she happened to want to do something else. Because people like this reliably do what is right, Kant thought that we should admire them.

4.67 Kant also uses this view to capture what is right and wrong. An action is merely permissible if and only if at least in principle you could will the relevant maxims for that action to be universal laws. This means that you can act in a morally permissible way even if what you do is not morally admirable. This happens when you act on a maxim which (i) you haven't tested with the universalization test, but which (ii) would pass the test in any case. Consider the act of helping your parents because it makes them happy. Let's assume that you have not universalized your maxim and therefore you are not doing anything admirable according to Kant. However, what you do is still permissible because at least you could have consistently willed your maxim to be a universal law if you had tested it.

Wrong acts are then, according to Kant, ones the maxims of which you couldn't consistently will to be universal laws. Take the act of killing another person in ordinary circumstances. It is very difficult to find a maxim for this action such that you could consistently will it to be a universal law. It is also easy then to see why Kant isn't a consequentialist. When he describes what is right and wrong he doesn't make any claims about which outcomes are good. He only considers which maxims can be consistently willed to be universal laws. 4.68

Why do the right thing?

You now have some idea of what Kant said about right and wrong. But why should you believe him? What are the arguments for thinking that the universalization test can tell us what is right and wrong? 4.69

One thing we know is that there are good reasons to do right actions and also good reasons to avoid acting wrongly. We have reasons to help other people and reasons not to kill them. This simple thought helps us to see what the best arguments for Kant's theory and the universalization test are. If Kant can explain to you why you should act only on the maxims that pass this test and avoid acting on maxims that don't pass it, then he makes a strong case for his view. He could in this situation argue that only the acts that pass his test are right as those are the only acts that we have good reasons to do. 4.70

Does Kant then say anything really useful about why you should do the right thing? There was already one answer to this question above. According to Kant, when you act in a morally admirable way you act from respect for the law. Kant claimed that we are awed by the fact that we can give our maxims the general, universal form of laws. We respect the fact that we are willing our maxim to apply to everyone regardless of their personalities. You probably agree that this answer to the previous question seems too abstract. It is unlikely to convince everyone of the fact that it is important to act on maxims that pass the universalization test. Let us see if there are any better arguments for Kant's theory. 4.71

Reason 1: Exceptions A better and more concrete way to answer the previous question is to think about how repulsive it is if someone thinks that they have special moral privileges. Consider a person who thinks that it is all right to jump queues and at the same time does not allow others to do the same. This person wants to make an exception of herself, which makes 4.72

us all angry. There is something fundamentally wrong about not granting the same moral status to everyone.

4.73 If you agree with this, then you should not try to make an exception of yourself either. You should grant everyone else the same moral entitlements that you demand for yourself. One good way to understand the Categorical Imperative is to think of it as a test for when you are not demanding to be treated in a special way. If you can will your maxims to be universal laws, you are saying to others that they too can act in the same way. The reason for following the Categorical Imperative is that, on this suggestion, doing so respects other people's equal moral status as rational agents. The first important positive argument for the Universalization test is then based on the moral ideal of equality.

4.74 *Reason 2: Freedom* Kant's second reason for why you should not do what is wrong is more complicated (Kant, 1785, part 3; Korsgaard, 1996, pp. 160–167). It is based on the idea that it is extremely important to be free. We can appreciate this argument if we consider a heroin addict. An addict is a paradigm example of someone who is not free. This is because the addict simply can't resist the strong urge to get heroin. No matter what she wants personally, she is a slave of her addiction – the strongest desire she has.

4.75 Kant believed that if your desires are in control of your behavior then you aren't any freer than the addict. In this case your different desires battle for supremacy and, each time, the one that wins is responsible for what you do. Yet there is no difference between acting from the same irresistible desire every time and acting from whichever desire happens to be strongest in each case. Here too you are a slave of your passions.

4.76 As a result, Kant recognized that acting freely requires being able to stand back from your desires and use your reason to decide which desire to act on. Only this makes you free by enabling you to avoid being at the mercy of your desires. How can you then use your reason to decide which desire you are to act on?

4.77 Kant offers you two alternatives. One is that when your reason considers your desires, it just arbitrarily jumps behind one of them for no further reason. So, in one case your reason jumps behind your desire to raise a family, in another behind your desire to run a marathon, and so on. In this situation, you would be free from your natural inclinations, but this type of freedom as arbitrary behavior would not help you to be in positive control of your actions.

The other alternative your reason has is to use *a special principle* to decide which desire you are to satisfy. This principle must be able to guarantee that what you happen to want can't influence what you do. Kant believed that a principle of practical reason is like this only if it has the form of a universal law as described by the Categorical Imperative. You can help your mother independently of what you want only if your will is committed to the principle "Whenever anyone's mother is ill, they will help their mother in order to make them feel better." This is why in order to be free you must follow the Categorical Imperative, which requires you to do the right thing. 4.78

So, to summarize, Kant believed that being free is incredibly important for all of us. He then argued that freedom requires not letting your desires decide what you do, and that this is only possible if your will follows the Categorical Imperative. Roughly put, according to Kant, acting morally is the only way to be free and there is nothing more important than that. This means that the second important argument for the universalization test is based on the importance of freedom and the idea that using this test is the only way in which we can be truly free from the forces of nature. 4.79

Counterexamples and Convergence

We then have the following candidates for the ultimate principle of morality: 4.80

Utilitarianism: An act is right if and only if it brings about more general happiness than the other options which you have at the time of action.

Categorical Imperative: An act is right if and only if you could consistently will your maxim for the act to be a universal law.

If you want to challenge these principles, you should come up with counterexamples to them. These examples should show that Utilitarianism and the Categorical Imperative do not match with what you intuitively think is right and wrong.

This concluding section of the chapter describes famous counterexamples to the previous principles and also offers some responses to them. It aims to show just how flexible consequentialism and Kantian ethics 4.81

are as ethical theories. As a result, these views can agree about what is right and wrong.

Counterexamples to utilitarianism

4.82 Consider first the following counterexamples to Utilitarianism:

> *Riots*. Suppose that a police officer shoots a young man and then claims that he appeared to be reaching for a gun. However, you saw that the victim was not carrying a gun or acting in any threatening way whatsoever. The relations between the police and the local community are already tense. If the true nature of the events were revealed, this would lead to rioting and a lot of innocent people would suffer. You are asked to testify that the young man was really reaching for a gun. If you say so, the riots will be avoided. (McCloskey, 1965)

> ***Transplant***.[31] You are a doctor who has five dying patients. Each of these patients has a different central organ failing. A healthy, lonely, orphan comes to see you. You could kill him and distribute his organs to your five patients. By doing so you would lose one life but save five equally good lives.

> ***Promise***.[32] You have promised to take your child to the park. Your neighbor has three children. If you break your promise and take them to the park instead, your child will be sad but your neighbor's children will be happy.

> ***Poverty***.[33] You have $50 in your wallet and quite a bit more in your bank account. You could use your $50 for a nice meal or you could give it to charity. If you donate the money to charity, you save a number of people from extreme poverty. In fact, you could either use the money in your bank account for your own projects or for saving the lives of a large number of people.

4.83 Utilitarianism has implausible consequences in all these cases. In *Riots*, you should make the false statement because this helps you to stop the riots and the suffering they cause. In *Transplant*, utilitarianism requires you to cut up the orphan because doing so will make more people happy. In *Promise*, utilitarianism says that you should break your promise and take the neighbor's children to the park instead of your own. Finally, in P*overty* utilitarianism requires you to give almost all your wealth to charity because by doing so you would create more happiness than by keeping the wealth yourself. These are not the right things to say about these cases.

Counterexamples to the Categorical Imperative

The Categorical Imperative seems to have equally objectionable consequences in the following cases: 4.84

> ***Murderer***.[34] A man rings your doorbell. He wants to know where your sister is. You know that the man is a murderer who has come to kill your sister. The only way to save her is to lie about her whereabouts.
>
> *Dinner*. Your neighbors invite you to dinner on a Friday night. Should you go? (Herman, 1993, p. 138)
>
> *Theft*. Imagine that the author of this book is short of money. In this case, would it be permissible for the only Finnish philosopher working at the University of Birmingham to steal from others? (Parfit, 2011, p. 289)
>
> ***Charity***.[35] As a conscientious person, you want to give $250 to a charity because this is more than what the average person donates.
>
> ***Judge***.[36] You are the judge at a murder case. The evidence shows beyond doubt that the suspect committed the murder. Are you permitted to punish him?

When you apply the Categorical Imperative to these cases, you must test whether you could will your maxim to be a universal law. In *Murderer*, your maxim of action would be something like "Whenever a murder asks, I will lie to them in order to save my sister." You should then consider whether you could will this maxim to be a universal law. If everyone accepted this maxim and this were common knowledge, you could not deceive the murderer by lying to him in those circumstances. For this reason, you can't consistently will your maxim to be a universal law in *Murderer* and thus the Categorical Imperative says you should not lie. 4.85

4.86 Likewise in *Dinner*, when you try to universalize your maxim of visiting your neighbors on Friday nights, you can't imagine a situation in which we all go to our neighbors' party at the same time. Our neighbors too would be away in that scenario. As a result, the Categorical Imperative seems to rule out dinner parties.

4.87 In *Charity*, it is similarly impossible to imagine a situation in which everyone successfully gives more money to charity than the average. It is impossible for everyone to do so. Therefore, the Categorical Imperative says that it is wrong to give more money to charity than the average. In contrast, in *Theft*, given that the author of this book is the only Finnish philosopher working at the University of Birmingham, you can easily imagine a situation in which all Finnish philosophers working at the University of Birmingham steal from other people. If you happened to be me, you could easily will everyone to act on this maxim. The Categorical Imperative thus allows me to steal from others.

4.88 In *Judge*, it is less clear whether the judge can will his seemingly good maxim to be a universal law. Perhaps the judge is acting on the following maxim: "Whenever I am a judge in a murder case and there is overwhelming evidence of the crime, I will follow the law and punish the murderer." When the judge tests whether he can will this maxim to be a universal law, he must consider a situation in which he stands accused of a murder in a situation in which the judge in his case has adopted this maxim. In this situation, the judge will have goals which he can't pursue if he goes to prison and for this reason he can't consistently will his maxim to be a universal law. The Categorical Imperative therefore seems to say that judges should not punish criminals.

Utilitarian and consequentialist responses to the counterexamples*

4.89 The first three counterexamples to utilitarianism are easy to deal with. If you are a consequentialist, you can accept that these cases show Utilitarianism to fail. They nicely illustrate that the amount of happiness can't be the only thing that makes outcomes good. If you accept a richer theory of value, then consequentialism can easily give right answers in these cases.

4.90 In *Riots*, you can think that lying, punishing innocents, and letting real criminals go unpunished are bad things in themselves. This would mean that you can make the world a better place in *Riots* by not giving the false testimony. As a result, consequentialism would claim that it would be wrong for you to do so.

Likewise, in *Transplant*, you could accept that an outcome in which killings take place is much worse than one in which some people are merely allowed to die. This would again mean that the world will be a better place if you do not kill the orphan even if this entails five deaths from natural causes. Finally, in *Promise*, you could argue that keeping promises and protecting parental relationships are good in themselves. This would mean that here too you can make the world a better place by taking your own child to the park. 4.91

Therefore, in all these cases, if you don't focus only on how people's happiness will be affected, the world can be made a better place by the intuitively right actions. The relevant outcomes are better because the guilty are punished, people are not killed, promises are kept, and children can rely on their parents. If the intuitively right choices make things go best in this richer way, then consequentialism leads to the correct conclusions about these cases. 4.92

Poverty is the biggest challenge for consequentialists. Intuitively you are not required to give all your wealth away in order to help the poor. Most people believe that you are only required to give a small percentage of your income to charity and only on the condition that the charities effectively help the poor. 4.93

It is harder for the consequentialist to argue that the world would not be a better place if extreme poverty were eradicated. For this reason, it is more difficult for the consequentialists to explain why you are not required to do more to help others. Doing so, after all, seems to make things go better according to reasonable theories of value. 4.94

In response, consequentialists could try to argue that the extreme poverty of others is not very bad "relative to you" when you don't suffer from it. They could claim that the consequences of your actions are best relative to you when you successfully carry out your ordinary personal projects, whatever they happen to be. If consequentialism then only required you to make the world best relative to you and not impartially best, the *Poverty* case would not be a problem. 4.95

This response has several drawbacks. First of all, the move to what is good relative to you seems to be motivated only by the fact that it allows the consequentialist to escape the problems caused by *Poverty*. It also requires you to reject the fundamental insight of Mill's argument in favor 4.96

of utilitarianism. Why would the world be a better place relative to you if you were happy instead of someone else even when your happiness is just like theirs? If there is no good answer to this question, then consequentialism requires us to help other people a lot more than we intuitively think is right. Given the amount of extreme poverty in the world and the suffering it causes, perhaps consequentialists should endorse this consequence of their view.

Kantian responses to the counterexamples*

4.97 Let us then consider the counterexamples to the Categorical Imperative. A Kantian response to these cases would need to show that the relevant maxims that correctly guide us to

- lie to the murderer,
- go to our neighbor's dinner party on a Friday,
- give more money to charity than the average, and
- punish the guilty murderers

can be willed to be universal laws. Kantians also need to be able to explain why the author of this book should not steal as the only Finnish philosopher working at the University of Birmingham. If you are a Kantian, there are two things you can say in response to these objections. You can claim that either we have not considered the right maxims or that we have misunderstood how the relevant universalization tests work.

4.98 For example, in *Murderer* the murderer is likely to hide the fact that he is a murderer from you and for this reason he will not normally expect that you know that he has come to kill your sister (Korsgaard, 1996, p. 136). If he told you that he has come to kill your sister, he would be less likely to succeed. Because of this, the murderer will not know that you know that he is a murderer, and therefore he is likely to believe what you say about your sister's whereabouts. Consider then the maxim "Whenever there is a murderer at the door, I will lie about my sister's whereabouts." If murderers do not expect people to lie to them and they don't know that the people on the door know that they are murderers, everyone could act on this maxim even if it were a universal law. Because of this, the Categorical Imperative does not forbid you to lie in *Murderer*.

4.99 Consider *Dinner* next. Kantians believe that this case reveals a mistaken way to apply the universalization test. It is impossible for everyone to go to their neighbors' dinner parties on Fridays. However, you should instead consider whether you could will everyone to feel free to visit their neighbors on Fridays – *if they so wanted to*. Because everyone will not want to visit their neighbors, this is easy enough to imagine and will to be the case. Because of this the Categorical Imperative does not forbid us to enjoy dinner parties.

The problem in *Theft* is that the maxim of action is so specific that you can easily will it to be a universal law. No contradiction follows if everyone would steal if they were a Finnish philosopher working at the University of Birmingham. The problem with this objection is that it assumes that you can choose your maxim of action. It assumes that you could adopt more or less specific principles to act on. This seems too optimistic. 4.100

It is more natural to think that maxims are action-guiding intentions which you have in your mind in some implicit form. As such natural intentions, they will be less specific than the fine-grained Finnish philosopher maxim assumed by this objection. Consider then the less specific and more natural maxim "Whenever I need money, I just take it from others to satisfy my needs." If you imagine circumstances where everyone acts on this maxim, you will quickly notice that this leads to a collapse of the whole system of private property. Thus, given that no one can universalize a more natural general maxim for stealing, the author of this book is not permitted to steal even if he is the only Finnish philosopher working at the University of Birmingham. 4.101

What about *Charity*? In this case, you need to distinguish between morally admirable and morally permissible actions. The Categorical Imperative clearly says that it is permissible for you to give more money to charity than the average. After all, there are many other universalizable maxims that enable you to give $250 to charity. For example, it is easy to universalize the maxim "Whenever I have enough money, I will give $250 to charity in order to help the poor." This is why it is admirable to act on this maxim if you have first universalized it. 4.102

It is true, though, that the maxim which explicitly guides you to give more money to charity than the average cannot be universalized. This means that acting on this maxim wouldn't be morally admirable, according to Kant. This must be the right thing to say. A person who acts on this maxim does not care about the poor people but rather only about how much she gives more than others. This doesn't sound like a very good thing. 4.103

Finally, the Kantian response to *Judge* is perhaps the most intriguing one. Many Kantians believe that the judge's maxim can in fact be 4.104

universalized. According to them, the judge can will his maxim to be a universal law even when he considers cases in which he is the murderer. They claim that, if you are not convicted for your crimes, then you are not considered to be morally responsible for your actions. Sometimes we do not punish children for their misbehavior because we think that they just couldn't help it. If someone says this to you, it is likely that you will find it demeaning and offensive. They are comparing you to a misbehaving child who just cannot help it. Therefore, if you are rational, you want to be convicted because this recognizes that you are a rational adult who is responsible for their actions. This is why the judge can will to be punished in situations in which he is the murderer and why therefore he can consistently will to universalize his maxim when he is punishing the murderer.

Convergence*

4.105 Both consequentialists and Kantians can therefore deal with the main counterexamples to their fundamental ethical principles. If this is true, then both consequentialist and Kantian ethical theories can fit our pre-theoretical intuitions about what is right and wrong. This means that these theories can also agree about right and wrong.

4.106 Why do Kantians and consequentialists then disagree despite this? Perhaps the best way to understand why they still disagree is to think that they have different views about what makes the intuitively right acts right. Consequentialists claim that the acts which we all believe to be right are right because they bring about the best outcomes. In contrast, Kantians claim that these acts are right because the relevant maxims for them can be willed to be universal laws. Consequentialists and Kantians give competing explanations for why certain acts are right even if they can agree on which acts are right.

4.107 You should also be aware that the consequentialists and Kantians must pay a high price for dealing with the counterexamples in the previous ways. Consequentialists tend to either change their theory of value or the deontic elements of their views in order to avoid the counterexamples. In the same way, Kantians usually reformulate the relevant maxims or the universalization test for the same reason. If these changes to their views are not motivated by anything more than the desire to avoid the counterexamples, then consequentialist and Kantian views threaten to become less and less intuitively appealing. This is true especially if these theories include a vast number of fixes that are needed to deal with all the individual cases. Such theories are no longer supported by simple ethical ideals such as the moral equality of everyone that motivated us to accept these views in the first place.

Summary and Questions

This chapter began by introducing the structure of all consequentialist ethical theories. These views first rank all options in terms of how good their consequences are, and then they explain what is right and wrong in terms of the resulting rankings. We then considered the main differences between different forms of consequentialism and John Stuart Mill's famous argument in favor of consequentialism. Even if this argument has many problematic steps, it is important because it captures some of the most fundamental ethical ideas there are. 4.108

The second half of this chapter explained the basic ideas behind Immanuel Kant's theory of ethics. This theory is based on the Categorical Imperative principle which requires you to see whether you can universalize the principles on which you act. If you can do this, your actions will have moral worth. Kant also explained what is right and wrong in terms of the principles that can be willed to be universal laws. He also argued that you should do the right thing because this gives everyone an equal moral status and it also makes you free. 4.109

The final part of the chapter introduced famous counterexamples to Kantian and consequentialist theories. It also argued that these theories are flexible enough to deal with these cases and because of this they can agree about what is right and wrong. 4.110

Based on the philosophical resources introduced in this chapter, consider the following questions: 4.111

1. What is the structure of all consequentialist ethical theories?
2. Is consequentialism better understood as a deliberation procedure or as a criterion of rightness?
3. Think of cases in which the following theories disagree about which actions are right and wrong:
   i. direct vs. indirect consequentialism;
   ii. utilitarianism vs. forms of consequentialism with richer theories of value;

   iii. actual value vs. expected value consequentialism; and
   iv. maximizing vs. satisficing forms of consequentialism.

   In each case, consider which theory is more plausible.
4. Consider whether you can will the following maxims to be universal laws when you act on them:
   i. I will plagiarize my essay in order to get a good grade.
   ii. I will tell white lies to my friends about how they look in order to keep them happy.
   iii. I will only buy ready-made meals so as to avoid the hassle.
5. Can you think of new counterexamples to utilitarianism and the Categorical Imperative which weren't covered in this chapter? What would consequentialists and Kantians say in response to these cases?

Annotated Bibliography

Adams, Robert Merrihew (1976) "Motive Utilitarianism," *Journal of Philosophy*, *73*, 467–481. A formulation of an indirect version of utilitarianism according to which we should first consider what good consequences different motivations have and then evaluate actions on the basis of their motives.

Bales, Eugene R. (1971) "Act-Utilitarianism: Account of Right-Making Characteristics or Decision-Making Procedure," *American Philosophical Quarterly*, *8*(3), 257–265, full text available at http://people.umass.edu/philo160/Bales%20AU.pdf, accessed February 26, 2014. An article in which Bales emphasizes the distinction between decision-making procedures and standards of rightness.

Bentham, Jeremy (1776) *Fragment on Government*, full text available at http://www.efm.bris.ac.uk/het/bentham/government.htm, accessed February 26, 2014. Bentham's early work in which he argued that utilitarianism could be used to make politics more rational and scientific.

Bykvist, Krister (2010) *Utilitarianism: A Guide for the Perplexed* (London: Continuum). In this clear and accessible textbook Bykvist examines utilitarian responses to the standard objections.

Driver, Julia (2012) *Consequentialism* (New York: Routledge). An up-to-date textbook on consequentialism which emphasizes how many different forms of consequentialism there are and how these views can be used to address objections to consequentialism.

Foot, Philippa (1967) "The Problem of Abortion and the Doctrine of Double Effect," *Oxford Review*, *5*, 5–15, full text available at http://www2.econ.iastate.edu/classes/econ362/hallam/readings/footdoubleeffect.pdf, accessed February 26, 2014. A classic article in which Foot introduced the famous trolley and transplant cases.

Godwin, William (1793) *An Enquiry Concerning Political Justice, and Its Influence on General Virtue and Happiness*, full text available at http://www.efm.bris.ac.uk/het/godwin/pj.htm, accessed February 26, 2014. This book is known for the famous illustration of the impartiality of consequentialism. However, in addition to good consequences, Godwin also emphasizes the perfection of human virtue.

Herman, Barbara (1993) *The Practice of Moral Judgment* (Cambridge, MA: Harvard University Press). In this book Herman investigates what Kantians should say about moral judgments and persons. She argues that Kant had a richer and less formal view on these issues than is often assumed.

Hill, Jr., Thomas (1992) *Dignity and Practical Reason in Kant's Moral Theory* (Ithaca: Cornell University Press). An admirably balanced examination of Kant's ethics. Hills also applies Kant's views to contemporary moral issues such as terrorism.

Hooker, Brad (2000) *Ideal Code, Real World* (Oxford: Oxford University Press). See the bibliography of Chapter 3 above.

Hurka, Thomas (1993) *Perfectionism* (Oxford: Oxford University Press). See the bibliography of Chapter 2 above.

Johnson, Robert (2008) "Kant's Moral Philosophy," in *The Stanford Encyclopedia of Philosophy* (Spring 2008 Edition), ed. Edward N. Zalta, full text available at http://plato.stanford.edu/entries/kant-moral/, accessed March 10, 2014. A detailed and comprehensive overview of Immanuel Kant's moral philosophy, which presents Kant's views in a both accessible and positive light.

Kant, Immanuel (1785) *Groundwork of the Metaphysics of Morals*, full text available at http://www.gutenberg.org/ebooks/5682, accessed on February 26, 2014. In this rich, rewarding, and complicated short book, Kant lays down the foundations of his ethics, which include three formulations of the Categorical Imperative, and the connection between morality and free will.

Kant, Immanuel (1797) "On a Supposed Right to Lie from Altruistic Motives," full text available at http://bgillette.com/wp-content/uploads/2011/01/KANT supposedRightToLie.pdf, accessed June 4, 2013. Kant's defense of the idea that you must always tell the truth.

Korsgaard, Christine (1996) *Creating the Kingdom of Ends* (Cambridge: Cambridge University Press). A collection of groundbreaking articles on Kant's ethics.

McCloskey, H.J. (1965) "A Non-Utilitarian Approach to Punishment," *Inquiry*, 8, 249–263. A famous article criticizing utilitarianism on the grounds that it will lead to unjust punishments.

Mill, John Stuart (1861) *Utilitarianism*, full text available at http://www.gutenberg.org/files/11224/11224-h/11224-h.htm, accessed February 26, 2014. See the bibliography of Chapter 1 above.

Moore, G.E. (1903) *Principia Ethica*. See the bibliography of Chapter 3 above.

Mulgan, Tim (2007) *Understanding Utilitarianism* (Durham: Acumen). In this highly readable textbook Mulgan covers the history of utilitarianism, the main arguments for the view, the nature of well-being, and the main objections to utilitarianism.

O'Neill, Onora (1975) *Acting on Principle* (New York: Columbia University Press). A clear and careful reconstruction of Kant's ethics. Especially good on how we should understand maxims and universalization.

Parfit, Derek (2011) *On What Matters*, Vols. 1 and 2 (Oxford: Oxford University Press). In these two volumes, Parfit attempts to show that if we understand different ethical theories correctly, these theories can agree about what is right and wrong.

Rawls, John (1971) *A Theory of Justice* (Cambridge, MA: Harvard University Press). See the bibliography of Chapter 2 above.

Ross, W.D. (1930) *The Right and the Good*. First three chapters available at http://www.ditext.com/ross/right.html, accessed February 26, 2014. An important formulation of intuitionism in both normative ethics and metaethics, which also contains influential objections to consequentialism.

Sayre-McCord, Geoffrey (2001) "Mill's 'Proof' of the Principle of Utility: A More than Half-Hearted Defense," *Social Philosophy & Policy*, *18*(2), 330–360, full text available at http://www.unc.edu/~gsmunc/Mill/Mill_Proof.pdf, accessed February 26, 2014. A wonderful, charitable reinterpretation of Mill's often misunderstood argument.

Sidgwick, Henry (1907) *The Methods of Ethics*, 7th edition. See the bibliography of Chapter 1 above.

Singer, Peter (1972) "Famine, Affluence, and Morality," *Philosophy and Public Affairs*, *1*, 229–243. A famous article which provides a strong consequentialist argument to the conclusion that we should do more to help poor people around the world.

Slote, Michael (1984) "Satisficing Consequentialism," *Proceedings of the Aristotelian Society, Supplement 58*, 139–163, full text available at http://www.princeton.edu/~ppettit/papers/1984/Satisficing%20Consequentialism.pdf, accessed February 26, 2014. An attempt to avoid many of the problems of consequentialism by formulating a view that requires you to do what has good enough consequences.

Timmermann, Jens (2000) "Kant's Puzzling Ethics of Maxims," *Harvard Review of Philosophy*, *8*, 39–52, full text available at http://www.harvardphilosophy.com/issues/2000/Timmermann.pdf, accessed February 26, 2014. A clear explanation of maxims and their role in Kant's ethics. The article also deals with many of the so-called puzzle maxims.

Timmermann, Jens (2007) *Kant's Groundwork for the Metaphysics of Morals: A Commentary* (Cambridge: Cambridge University Press). A detailed, page-by-page commentary of Kant's *Groundwork* which defends Kant's view from many objections and misconceptions.

Online Resources

1 A detailed historical overview of utilitarianism: http://plato.stanford.edu/entries/utilitarianism-history/.
2 Bentham's *Fragment on Government*: http://www.efm.bris.ac.uk/het/bentham/government.htm.
3 An overview of different forms of consequentialism and their advantages: http://plato.stanford.edu/entries/consequentialism/.
4 The life and works of Kant: http://plato.stanford.edu/entries/kant/ and a video that explains the Categorical Imperative: http://www.youtube.com/watch?v=FBNX6pp5efA.
5 The first section of *Groundwork*: http://ebooks.adelaide.edu.au/k/kant/immanuel/k16prm/chapter1.html.
6 Overview of value theory: http://plato.stanford.edu/entries/value-theory/.
7 See the brief description in the beginning: http://plato.stanford.edu/entries/logic-deontic/.
8 Roger Crisp explains clearly what utilitarianism is in a podcast: http://philosophybites.libsyn.com/roger_crisp_on_utilitarianism.
9 The life and works of Godwin: http://plato.stanford.edu/entries/godwin/, and the relevant chapter from his *Enquiry Concerning Political Justice*: http://www.efm.bris.ac.uk/het/godwin/pj2.htm.
10 R. Eugene Bales' article "Act-Utilitarianism: Account of Right-Making Characteristics or Decision-Making Procedure": http://people.umass.edu/philo160/Bales%20AU.pdf.
11 Overview of rule-consequentialism: http://plato.stanford.edu/entries/consequentialism-rule/.
12 Mill's famous definition of happiness: http://www.gutenberg.org/files/11224/11224-h/11224-h.htm#CHAPTER_II.
13 Overview of perfectionism in ethics: http://plato.stanford.edu/entries/perfectionism-moral/.
14 Overview of this distinction: http://plato.stanford.edu/entries/consequentialism/#WhiConActVsExpCon and a video of how to calculate expected consequences: http://www.youtube.com/watch?v=DAjVAEDil_Q.
15 A real-life version of the case: http://www.dailymail.co.uk/news/article-2174877/Its-poison-help-Holiday-mothers-final-words-drinking-water-bottle-filled-cleaning-fluid.html.

16 Explanation of the word: http://en.wikipedia.org/wiki/Satisficing and Slote's article "Satisficing Consequentialism": http://www.princeton.edu/~ppettit/papers/1984/Satisficing%20Consequentialism.pdf.

17 Mill's life and works: http://plato.stanford.edu/entries/mill/.

18 Chapter 4 of Mill's *Utilitarianism*: http://www.gutenberg.org/files/11224/11224-h/11224-h.htm#CHAPTER_IV.

19 Chapter 3 of *Principia Ethica*: http://fair-use.org/g-e-moore/principia-ethica/chapter-iii.

20 Sidgwick's objection to Mill: http://archive.org/stream/methodsofethics00sidguoft#page/388/mode/2up.

21 Moore's further objection to Mill: http://fair-use.org/g-e-moore/principia-ethica/s.43.

22 Picture of Guernica: http://www.pablopicasso.org/images/paintings/guernica.jpg.

23 Sayre-McCord's article "Mill's 'Proof' of the Principle of Utility: A More than Half-Hearted Defence": http://www.unc.edu/~gsmunc/Mill/Mill_Proof.pdf.

24 Moore on the connection between right and good: http://fair-use.org/g-e-moore/principia-ethica/s.17.

25 Overview of this so-called "supervenience" thesis: http://plato.stanford.edu/entries/supervenience/.

26 Anthony Grayling on why Kant was one of the greatest philosophers of all time: http://www.bbc.co.uk/radio4/history/inourtime/greatest_philosopher_immanuel_kant.shtml, Marianne Talbot's introductory lecture on Kant's ethics from Oxford: http://www.youtube.com/watch?v=Vz5ZslW6Bzw, the full text of the *Groundwork*: http://www.gutenberg.org/ebooks/5682, and Johnson's overview article on "Kant's Moral Philosophy": http://plato.stanford.edu/entries/kant-moral/.

27 Life-saving stories: http://carnegiehero.org/.

28 Jens Timmermann's article "Kant's Puzzling Ethics of Maxims": http://www.harvardphilosophy.com/issues/2000/Timmermann.pdf.

29 Brad Hooker's clear explanation of these tests: http://www.richmond-philosophy.net/rjp/back_issues/rjp1_hooker.pdf.

30 Paul Guyer's explanation of perfect and imperfect duties: http://www.rep.routledge.com/article/DB047SECT10.

31 Philippa Foot's article "The Problem of Abortion and the Doctrine of Double Effect": http://www2.econ.iastate.edu/classes/econ362/hallam/readings/footdoubleeffect.pdf.

32 Chapter 2, "What Makes Right Acts Right," from W.D. Ross's *The Right and the Good*: http://www.ditext.com/ross/right2.html.

33 Peter Singer's article "Famine, Affluence, and Morality": http://www.utilitarian.net/singer/by/1972----.htm.

34 Kant's article "On a Supposed Right to Lie from Altruistic Motives": http://bgillette.com/wp-content/uploads/2011/01/KANTsupposedRightToLie.pdf.

35 This example comes from Derek Parfit as reported by Brad Hooker: http://www.richmond-philosophy.net/rjp/back_issues/rjp1_hooker.pdf.

36 An objection also made by Brad Hooker: http://www.richmond-philosophy.net/rjp/back_issues/rjp1_hooker.pdf.

5

INTUITIONISM, PARTICULARISM, AND VIRTUE ETHICS

The end of the previous chapter explained why consequentialists and Kantians can agree about what is right and wrong. Despite this, these views offer us competing views about what ultimately *makes* acts right and wrong. When we talk about what makes acts right and wrong, we are looking for what explains why some acts are right and others wrong. *In virtue of what* do acts have these fundamental moral qualities? 5.1

Consequentialists and Kantians offer direct answers to these questions. According to consequentialists, right acts are right because they have the best consequences of the options available to you. According to Kantians, the rightness of these same acts is best explained by the fact that you can consistently will a maxim to do these acts to be universal laws. These traditional theories of what makes acts right face a serious problem, which was first presented by **W.D. Ross** in his wonderful 1930 book ***The Right and the Good*** (Ross, 1930).[1] 5.2

Ross's Objection to Consequentialism and Kantian Ethics

Both consequentialist and Kantian theories assume that there is just *one* general principle which explains what makes right acts right. Acts can't be right for any other reason than that they either have best consequences or they can be done with universalizable maxims. For these reasons, these theories are **monist** ethical theories.[2] 5.3

This Is Ethics: An Introduction, First Edition. Jussi Suikkanen.

5.4 W.D. Ross was one of the first to challenge the basic assumption shared by all monist theories (**Ross, 1930, ch. 2**; Dancy, 1991).[3] He observed that there are many very different kinds of right and wrong acts. Consider the following wrong acts: failing to keep a promise, rape, destroying a unique piece of art, not giving money to charity, failing to develop your talents, not respecting your parents, making fun of other people's deeply held religious beliefs, polluting the environment, and fraud.

5.5 Why are these acts wrong? Explaining why any one of these acts is wrong is easy. It is wrong to rape another person because this both hurts them and undermines their sexual autonomy; it is wrong not to respect your parents because you owe your existence to them; it is wrong to destroy a unique piece of art because this denies other people important aesthetic experiences, and so on.

5.6 When you explain why different acts are wrong in this simple way you give different reasons for why different acts are wrong. Whichever wrong act you take, there is always a concrete ordinary explanation for why that act is wrong. However, in each case the explanation is different. We do not therefore intuitively assume that there is just one thing which makes all wrong acts wrong and right acts right.

5.7 This simple observation is a serious problem for the traditional ethical theories. The ordinary explanations for why different acts are right and wrong seem to be sufficient. If you can fully explain **why Joe should not rape Jill** by talking about the importance of her own sexual choices, then it seems that the traditional ethical theories become redundant.[4] You no longer need to talk about which acts have the best consequences or which maxims could be universalized. Already, before this, we can understand why the act which we are considering is wrong.

5.8 This simple case also reveals another flaw in the traditional ethical theories, which is distinct from the previous idea that different things make different acts right. You want to think that something about Jill as a person explains why it would be wrong for Joe to rape her. You want to think that she matters as an individual and, because she matters, there are things that Joe should not do to her. In contrast, Kantians claim that something about Joe's willing makes it wrong for him to rape Jill, and similarly consequentialists claim that something about the consequences of this act for everyone explains why Joe should not rape Jill. These theories thus deny that other people as individuals are the source of our moral reasons.

If you like the previous two lines of reasoning, then you will be drawn 5.9
to accept **a pluralist theory in normative ethics**.[5] These views take seriously the idea that different things explain why different acts are right and wrong. This chapter will explain the basic elements of these views. The next section begins from W.D. Ross's own theory, which is known as **intuitionism** in normative ethics. After this, we will consider an even more radical pluralist view called **particularism**.[6] The last section of the chapter will consider **virtue ethics**, which combines elements from both traditional ethical theories and pluralism.

Intuitionism in Normative Ethics

Ross concluded from the previous considerations that many different 5.10
things matter for their own sake (Ross, 1930, ch. 2). He furthermore thought that it is a basic fact that these things matter for their own sake. You can't use a single, more fundamental ethical principle to explain why they matter. This means that, ultimately, different right acts are right for different reasons and different wrong acts are similarly wrong for different reasons.

Prima facie duties

Ross used confusing terminology to formulate his own positive view. He 5.11
based his theory on the notion of **prima facie**[7] duties. Ross gave the following list of these duties (**Ross, 1930, ch. 2, para. 9**):[8]

1. *Duties of fidelity.* These duties are based on our past actions such as **promises.**[9] The duty of fidelity means that if you have promised to do something then you have a prima facie duty to keep your promise.
2. *Duties of reparation.* These duties are based on our past wrong actions. For example, if you steal money from someone else, you have a prima facie duty to pay that money back.
3. *Duties of gratitude.* These duties are based on previous actions of other people. For example, if someone helps you, you have a prima facie duty to thank them.
4. *Duties of justice.* These duties are based on the idea that goods must be distributed according to merit. If someone contributes more in a

team, there is a prima facie duty to give them a bigger share of the rewards.

5. *Duties of beneficence.* These duties rest on the fact that there are other people whose condition we can improve. Given that there are millions of people living in extreme poverty, we have a prima facie duty to help them.
6. *Duties of self-improvement.* These duties are based on the fact that we can become better people. If you have an opportunity to make yourself kinder, then you have a prima facie duty to take that opportunity.
7. *Duty of non-maleficence.* We have a prima facie duty to not harm other people.

5.12 What is it to be a **prima facie duty**? Very simply put, you should understand Ross's list to offer you a list of general qualities of acts that make them right *to some degree*. For example, some acts have the quality of being what you have promised to do. By saying that there is a prima facie duty of fidelity, Ross really meant to say that the fact that you have promised to do an act makes doing that act right to some degree. You can also understand Ross to be claiming that this quality of an act – that you have promised to do it – gives you some **reason** to do the act (Dancy, 1991; Stratton-Lake, 2002, pp. xxxiii–xxxvii).[10] That you have promised to do something counts in favor of keeping the promise, to a degree.

5.13 For what it's worth, there is also a more complicated understanding of Ross's prima facie duties. This is because the Latin phrase "prima facie" doesn't really mean "to some degree," but rather "provisionally" or "at first sight." In Latin, the appropriate phrase for qualities of acts that make them right to some degree is "pro tanto," which also is often used in literature. In any case, according to this more complicated understanding of Ross's view, prima facie duties are right-makers not because they have some weight, but rather because of the presence or absence of other right- and wrong-making considerations. Here prima facie duties make the act right provisionally, barring other intervening considerations. For the sake of simplicity, the rest of this chapter will focus on the simpler understanding of Ross's view, but it's worth knowing that there is also an alternative and more complicated reading of his theory.

5.14 Ross thus offers you a list of things that can make acts right to some degree. The moral significance of these things can conflict. Take the act of saving a drowning child. According to Ross, you have a prima facie duty to do this act because you are under the duty of beneficence. The fact that you could help the child therefore makes the act of saving her right to some degree. You can also at the same time have a prima facie duty to not save the child. This is the case if you have promised to meet your friend in town. Given the prima facie duty of fidelity, the fact that you have promised makes not saving the child also right to some degree.

There are, then, cases where you have a prima facie duty both to save a child and to not save her. This just means that there are reasons for and against doing many acts. So far, Ross has only described what these reasons are by giving you a list of prima facie duties. Despite this, his theory already has an important advantage over the traditional ethical theories. It can accommodate the basic intuition that different acts are right and wrong for different reasons. 5.15

How do you know?

Why are *these* the qualities that are relevant to what we should do? In response to this challenge, Ross argued that experience helps us all to learn what makes different acts right (**Ross, 1930, ch. 2, para. 32**).[11] He hoped that if you consider your experiences carefully enough, you will agree with his list. 5.16

According to Ross, you first recognize in a particular situation which features of that situation are morally relevant. In the previous case, you first notice that there is a reason to help the child because this saves her life, and a reason not to do so because doing so requires breaking a promise. You feel that in this case the child's situation counts in favor of saving her whereas your promise counts against doing so. 5.17

Ross claimed that from this experience of a particular case you will naturally draw more general conclusions about what makes acts right and wrong. You will realize that the desperate circumstances of others count in favor of helping them in all other cases too. Likewise, you will recognize that breaking a promise is always wrong to a degree. In this way, by generalizing from concrete situations you have been in, you come to know what makes acts right and wrong in other situations too. 5.18

You probably first learned mathematics in the same way. A small child learns that $2 + 2 = 4$ by first counting two apples, then another two apples and finally the four apples she then has. At some point the child will realize from this that whenever she counts two objects and another two objects she will end up with four things. By making this generalization from her experience, the child learns a self-evident universal truth that $2 + 2 = 4$. 5.19

According to Ross, that it is always right to a degree to keep your promises is, in the same way, a universal and self-evident principle.

5.20 This story explains why Ross's list of the prima facie duties contains the items it does. Ross believed that these principles cannot be derived from any single, deeper, ethical source. He only learned these principles through first experiencing which qualities of actions are morally significant in particular cases. He then generalized from these situations to the general self-evident principles on his list. He is not saying that his list is the final word on the matter. Perhaps there are individual situations in which we will discover new prima facie duties that Ross missed.

Prima facie duties and actual duties

5.21 The previous story leaves one important question unaddressed. So far, Ross has only explained what makes acts right to a degree, which isn't enough. What you really want to know is what your **actual duties** are. What should you do *all things considered*? To answer this question, Ross needs to tell you how you can get from knowing that a certain act is both right to a degree and wrong to a degree to whether you should do it overall. He needs to tell you how to get to what you ought to do from all the prima facie duties that are morally relevant in your situation.

5.22 You might think that there is an easy answer to this question. Consider the previous life-saving case. That the child is drowning is a very strong reason to save her, whereas the fact that you have made a promise to your friend is only a weak reason against saving the child. Perhaps we should also make general judgments about the weights of the prima facie duties on the basis of these types of individual cases.

5.23 If prima facie duties had constant weights, you could solve the problem in this way. On the basis of individual cases, you could create a table that numerically represented the weights of the prima facie duties. Perhaps a part of the table could look like that shown in Table 5.1.

Table 5.1 Prima facie duties with weights

Prima facie duty	**Weight**
Beneficence	9
Fidelity	4
Gratitude	2
…	…

Whenever you needed to make a decision about what you should do overall, you could just consult this table. You would first consider which prima facie duties apply in your situation and you could then make an overall judgment about what you ought to do by looking up how strong these duties are from the table. Problem solved!

Ross thought that you could not solve the problem in this way (**Ross, 1930, ch. 2, para. 29**).[12] He denied that the prima facie duties have the same weights in all situations. According to him, that an act has a certain quality can be a strong reason to do the act in one situation but only a weak reason to do it in another. 5.24

Consider shoplifting. The fact that you would be stealing makes it always wrong to a degree to shoplift. Intuitively this fact does not always give everyone an equally strong reason not to steal. **If your children are starving and you have no other means to save them,**[13] then that you would be stealing is only a weak reason for you not to shoplift. Yet the same consideration – that you would be stealing – can be a strong reason not to steal if you only want to steal **because you are bored.**[14] 5.25

If the weights of the prima facie duties vary like this, then you can't make an overall judgment about what you ought to do merely by consulting a table. Instead, you need to know how strong these duties happen to be in your concrete situation. In some cases, this will be easy. When you need to choose between saving someone's life and keeping a trivial promise, you'll know what to do. Yet many situations we face are far more complicated. Ross thought that in many such cases you won't be able to fully know what you ought to do, all things considered, in concrete situations. In the complex cases, you can only rely on your best judgment. 5.26

When you grew up, your upbringing gave you a moral sensibility. If it works correctly, it enables you to see what the right thing to do is in the situations you face. By thinking about the relevant features of the situation, you can come to understand how strong the different prima facie duties are in the particular situation. These judgments are not always obvious or self-evident. Your sensibility can always be clouded by bias, emotions, tiredness, or ignorance. This is why you can't always be fully confident about your overall judgments. 5.27

Ross thus failed to give a neat theoretical answer to the question of what you ought to do overall in particular situations. He understood that the moral reality we face is messy. There are always many different morally significant factors present and how important these factors are varies. All you can do is to rely on your best judgments. This requires sensitivity rather 5.28

than calculation in the same way as seeing how beautiful **the Sistine Chapel**[15] is requires sensitivity rather than theorizing.

Particularism

5.29 Intuitionism makes the requirements of morality more complicated than Kantian ethics or utilitarianism. However, **Jonathan Dancy** has **recently argued that even Ross failed to go far enough in this respect** (Dancy, 1991, 1993, 2004).[16] According to Dancy, Ross didn't see just how messy morality is.

Prima facie duties and holism

5.30 Dancy has argued that there are counterexamples to Ross's prima facie duties even if they only attempt to capture what makes acts right to a degree (Dancy, 1991, p. 228). Ross's basic assumption was that different morally significant qualities have a **constant valence**. To understand what this means, let us consider an example.

5.31 You have a reason to send your aunt a Christmas card. She has helped you throughout the year and sending a card helps you to thank her for this. Here the fact that your aunt has helped you makes it right to a degree to express your gratitude by sending the card.

5.32 Your dentist too has helped you throughout the year by fixing your teeth. It follows from Ross's assumption that here too it is right to a degree to tell your dentist how thankful you are. In fact, *whenever* someone has helped you, you have at least some reason to express your gratitude. According to Ross, this consideration – that someone has helped you – could never fail to be a reason to thank them or make it wrong to do so. This is what it means for this consideration to have a constant valence.

5.33 Ross thought that the same goes for all prima facie duties. They all capture general qualities of acts that always count in favor of doing the acts. You always have some reason to keep your promises, to help others, and so on. Thus, a reason for an act can never switch sides and become a reason against acts. Another way to put this is that something that makes an act right in one case can never make another act wrong in another context.

5.34 Dancy thinks that this assumption is wrong. We often do have reasons to do the acts that are on Ross's list of prima facie duties. However, contrary to what Ross assumed, a quality of an act that makes the act right to a degree in one situation can make the same act wrong elsewhere. Whatever is a reason for doing an act in one case can be a reason against doing the same act in other contexts. This would mean that no quality of acts can be morally significant in all situations in the same way.

This powerful objection to prima facie duties can easily be illustrated 5.35
with examples. For instance, Ross assumed that the fact that you have promised is always a reason to keep your promise. That you have promised to do an act always makes the act in question right to a degree. Is this really the case?

Consider the following example (Dancy, 1993, p. 60). Imagine that you 5.36
have borrowed a book from Mark. You have also promised to return the book to him as soon as you have read it. Suppose that you then find out that Mark has stolen that book from the library. In normal cases, you should return the book to Mark because you have promised to do so. Yet in this situation you have no reason at all to return the book to Mark. In this case, that you have promised to do so does not make the act of returning the book to Mark right.

Similarly, the duty of beneficence says that you always have some reason 5.37
to make a large number of people happy. Yet consider a case in which you can do this by hanging an innocent person publicly (Dancy, 1991, p. 228). Even if the hanging would make a lot of people happy, in this case that consideration is no reason at all to hang the victim.

Dancy accepts that many qualities of acts tend to make acts right to a 5.38
degree. He only insists that even these considerations can be morally neutral or even wrong-making in some cases. This thesis is called **practical reasons holism**. Holism says that:

> Any quality of acts that usually counts in favor of doing them can, in other situations, count against doing acts that have that quality.

This is to say that whatever makes some acts right can in other circumstances make other acts wrong.

Holism and particularism*

Dancy used to argue that a view called **particularism** follows from 5.39
holism.[17] Those who think that particularism is false are called **generalists**. **Unfortunately, what particularists and generalists disagree about is controversial.**[18]

5.40 Very broadly, there are two things at issue in this debate. One of them is about whether you could capture what is right and wrong with a set of easily learnable principles. Generalists claim that this is possible whereas particularists deny this. The second question is about whether you must use moral principles in everyday moral thinking. Particularists claim that morally admirable people can get by without relying on any principles whereas generalists deny this.

5.41 Which one of these views is right? Let us assume that holism is true. Thus whatever makes some acts right can in other contexts make other acts wrong. Does particularism follow from this thesis? That is, does holism itself entail that what is right and wrong cannot be captured with a fairly simple set of basic moral principles?

5.42 Here you will need new philosophical terminology. Take a quality that tends to make acts right, to a degree, like doing what you have promised to do. We saw above that even this quality fails to make acts right in some contexts (recall the example of the stolen book). In these cases, there is always a special explanation for why this happens. That you had promised does not have its normal significance in the previous case because the book was stolen. Likewise, that an innocent person would be hanged explains why in the second case you have no reason to make others happy.

5.43 These explanations refer to so-called **disabling conditions**. That the book was stolen is a disabling condition because it prevents your promise from making it right for you to return the book. In this terminology, holism is the view that there are disabling conditions that explain why considerations that are usually good moral reasons fail to be such reasons in other contexts. Does the existence of disabling conditions then mean that what is right and wrong cannot be captured with a finite set of moral principles?

5.44 This does not seem to follow (Ridge and McKeever, 2006, ch. 2). What is right and wrong can be described with a simple set of principles if the disabling conditions can be built into the simple moral principles. You could add explicit exceptions to Ross's prima facie duties. Perhaps the first principle should say:

> Keeping promises is right to a degree *except when* you have promised to return stolen property.

Likewise the fifth principle should perhaps say:

> You should try to improve the situation of others except when this requires hanging an innocent person.

Of course, these two additions will not be able to deal with all cases. You could hope, however, that even if the principles contained all the needed exceptions they would still be simple enough to learn. In this situation generalists too could accept holism.

In order to argue against this suggestion, the particularists need to show that there are so many exceptions to the prima facie duties that they could not be described by a set of principles you could learn. This would show that the situations we face in ordinary life are too complex for any useful moral principles. 5.45

Knowing what is right*

This leads us to the second disagreement between particularists and generalists. Let us accept for a moment that what is right and wrong cannot be captured with simple principles, because there are just too many exceptions to learn. You could think that even in this case people could act in a morally admirable way. This would mean that you can act morally even if you are not following any moral principles when you decide what to do. 5.46

How could you then know what is right and what is wrong if you can't rely on principles? This question is even more difficult for the particularists than it was to Ross. Ross thought that whether an act is right in a particular situation depends only on how strong the relevant prima facie duties are in that situation. If you can figure out the weights of these duties in the particular case, you will know what you should do. 5.47

The situation is much worse for the particularists. According to them, there are always many morally relevant considerations present in the situations you are in. Whether these considerations make acts right or wrong and to what degree depends on the particular features of the situation. How on Earth could you then know what you ought to do? 5.48

The particularists give the same answer to this question as Ross. They rely on the idea that, because of your moral upbringing, you have a moral sensibility that enables you to see what is right and wrong in the situations you face (McDowell, 1981; McNaughton, 1988, pp. 55–62; Dancy, 2004, pp. 143–148). By using these sensibilities carefully, you can also come to understand what reasons you have in particular cases. This answer leads to three questions: 5.49

i. What are moral sensibilities?
ii. How do you get one?
iii. How does a moral sensibility help you to see what is right?

5.50 Neither Ross nor particularism itself helps you to answer these difficult questions. Many intuitionists and particularists have therefore concluded that you need to rely on virtue ethics to solve these problems. For this reason, the rest of this chapter will explain the basic idea of virtue ethics and how virtue ethics can supplement Rossian pluralism and particularism.

Virtue Ethics

5.51 We've so far seen ethical theories that attempt to address the following two questions:

- Which actions are right?
- What makes these actions right?

Virtue ethicists believe that these are the wrong questions to start with (**Anscombe, 1958**).[19] They claim that we should first consider the following questions:

- How should you live?
- **What kind of a person should you be?**[20]

Only once you have addressed these more fundamental questions should you begin to think about what is right and wrong.

5.52 You can therefore understand the disagreement between virtue ethics and other ethical theories as a disagreement about the order of explanation in moral philosophy. The traditional theories begin from right and wrong. They then use these notions to explain how you should live (you should do what is right) and what kind of person you should be (one who does the right thing).

5.53 In contrast, virtue ethicists begin from the good life and the character traits that are needed for it. They then attempt to explain what is right and wrong in terms of these character traits. Where other views go from right and wrong to virtuous people, virtue ethics goes from virtuous people to right and wrong.

There are many different forms of **virtue ethics**[21] (for a textbook, see 5.54
Athanassoulis, 2013; for more advanced books, see Slote, 2001, Hursthouse, 1999, Foot, 2001, and Annas, 2011; and for collections of articles, see Crisp and Slote, 1997, and Darwall, 2003). What follows will be a combination of the most traditional and popular forms of virtue ethics.

Flourishing

Let's begin again from plants. Consider **an elm tree.**[22] There are obvious 5.55
standards that you can use to evaluate whether an elm tree is doing well. An elm is flourishing if it has a tall and strong trunk, deep roots, lots of green leaves, and it produces plenty of seeds. Likewise, an elm tree is struggling if it is diseased, if it has lost leaves and its leaves are dry, and if its branches have cracked.

You can use similar natural criteria for evaluating the lives of animals. 5.56
Consider **wolves.**[23] A flourishing wolf will have sharp teeth, shiny fur, and strong muscles. However, when you evaluate how well a wolf is doing, you do not only evaluate its physical condition. You also need to take into account what the wolf is doing. It is natural to think that in order to live well a wolf must take part in activities that are natural for wolves. These might include living in wilderness, belonging to a pack, having offspring, hunting with other wolves, and being able to howl.

Virtue ethicists think that you can use similar, species-specific standards 5.57
for evaluating the lives of people. Like in the case of plants, you can first evaluate the health of human beings by using natural standards. Like in the case of animals, you can also assess the flourishing of people by considering whether they can successfully take part in the activities that are natural for human beings.

As mentioned in Chapter 2, Aristotle claimed that two activities are 5.58
fundamental for human beings (**Aristotle, circa 350 BC, book X, sects 7–8**).[24] Firstly, he thought that you can only live well as a human being if you live with other people. We are social animals and therefore we naturally interact with other people. We are born to form families, friendships, businesses, and political communities. Your life is going well if you can successfully take part in these forms of socializing.

5.59 The second essential human activity is using reason. This means both using your theoretical reason to investigate the world and also using your practical reason to navigate your way around it. The latter requires both making choices in individual cases and also forming long-term plans with other people.

5.60 The activities that are natural for a species can in this way be used to understand when a member of that species flourishes. You can use this account of good lives to understand virtues and vices (**Aristotle, circa 350 BC, book II, sect. 6**).[25] Both **virtues** and vices are stable character traits. Virtues are excellences which you need for the activities that constitute living well. In contrast, vices are stable character traits that prevent you from living a good human life. As character traits, virtues consist of three different components: an intellectual component (which allows you to form the beliefs that you need for acting successfully), an emotional/affective component, and a motivational component.

5.61 Here are a few examples to illustrate this picture. Consider honesty, which is a stable disposition to tell the truth and to keep your word. In order to have this disposition you will need:

i. certain beliefs about how much truth it is appropriate to reveal in different cases;
ii. certain emotions like feeling guilty if you have been dishonest and feeling good about telling the truth; and
iii. a desire to tell the truth and a desire not to lie.

5.62 It is easy to see how this disposition can help you to live well. If you are a reliable person, it will be easier for you to form personal relationships with other people. It will also be easier for you to live with other people in society. People who lie to one another will struggle to live together because they can't rely on what others say.

5.63 Courage can similarly be understood as a disposition to take appropriate risks for worthwhile causes. Having this disposition also requires both correct beliefs and appropriate emotional reactions and motivations. Consider a person who is either a coward or a reckless person. If you are a coward, then you are too shy to enter relationships with other people because doing so would require putting yourself on the line. Likewise, a reckless person will fail to live a good life, because at some point her luck will run out.

5.64 This should give you a sense of the character traits that enable you to live a good life. This leads to the following three questions about virtues:

1. How can virtuous character traits be acquired?
2. In addition to being virtuous, what more is required for acting virtuously?
3. Could the notion of virtuous actions also be used to account for what is right and wrong?

The rest of this section will focus on these questions in this order.

Virtue acquisition

According to Aristotle, you are not born virtuous (Aristotle, circa 350 BC, 5.65
book I, sect. 9 and **book II, sect. 1**)[26]. **Instead, he believed that you can acquire virtues only through practice**.[27] This is inevitably a social process. Our society rewards you for acting in certain ways and it disapproves of other ways of acting. People are thankful if you help them, they pay for skills and knowledge, and they trust you with their secrets if you can keep your word. Because of this, there are many ulterior motives for doing what is considered to be right.

In this situation, you can acquire virtues by first imitating those who are 5.66
successful in our society (**Aristotle, circa 350 BC, book II, sects 1 and 4**).[28] When you first practice following their lead, you are often motivated by selfish desires. You want to get the same rewards (fame and money, usually) as your idols.

When you take part in different activities for these selfish reasons, you 5.67
will at some point acquire new cares and concerns. You come to see the internal rewards of the things you are doing and so you begin to enjoy these activities for their own sake. It becomes a part of your second nature to regard it as worthwhile to spend time with friends, to explore nature around you, and to pursue excellence in sports, arts, and sciences. When these new cares and concerns have become a part of who you are, you have acquired new virtues – dispositions that help you to live well.

Note that this view about virtues exposes you to **moral luck**[29] 5.68
(Athanassoulis, 2005, ch. 3). You can acquire the traits that count as excellences only if the activities that are constitutive of living a good life are rewarded in your community. If your society fails to appreciate telling the truth, then there will be fewer opportunities to practice honesty for ulterior motives. In this situation, it would be very difficult to become an honest person. You would not be able to learn why telling the truth matters for its own sake.

Acting virtuously

5.69 The next important element of virtue ethics is the distinction between merely doing what a virtuous agent would do and acting virtuously yourself. There are many cases in which you can do what a virtuous agent would do without acting virtuously. Perhaps the reason why Keith does not shoplift is that he is too afraid of getting caught. In this case Keith does what a virtuous agent would do without acting virtuously.

5.70 Aristotle claimed that you act virtuously only if you satisfy three further conditions (**Aristotle, circa 350 BC, book II, sect. 4**).[30] First of all, in order to act virtuously you must know what you are doing. If you keep your promise virtuously, you must know that you are keeping a promise. Return again to the case in which you have borrowed a book from Mark and promised to return it. Imagine that you then forget all about this. If you, in this case, give the book back to Mark as a birthday gift, you fail to act virtuously even if you do the same thing as what a virtuous agent would do.

5.71 Secondly, in order to do an act virtuously, you must aim to do the act for "what it is" (for Aristotle's view on choice and voluntary action, see **Aristotle, circa 350 BC, book III**).[31] This condition says that acting virtuously requires acting for the right reasons. When you act virtuously in the previous case your reason for returning the book to Mark must be that by doing so you will keep a promise. Therefore, when a virtuous agent acts virtuously, she finds the activities that constitute human flourishing desirable for their own sake. Keeping a promise is a part of living successfully with other people, and therefore an honest person finds keeping promises rewarding as such.

5.72 Finally, acting virtuously also requires that a stable character trait leads you to do the act in question. If you keep your promise virtuously, then you could not have been tempted to do anything else. In this situation, you are also prepared to defend your choice of keeping the promise. That your character leads you to do the virtuous act guarantees that you do this reliably. It is not merely a matter of luck that you end up doing the right thing.

5.73 To summarize, according to Aristotle, acting virtuously requires:

i. acting knowingly;
ii. aiming to do the act for the right reasons – for the act it is; and
iii. acting on the basis of stable character traits.

If you do not satisfy these conditions, then you are merely doing what a virtuous agent would do but you are not acting virtuously. This account of acting virtuously will finally help us to formulate a virtue theory of right and wrong.

Right and wrong acts

If you are virtuous, you will have all the knowledge, emotional dispositions, 5.74
and motives that are required for the activities that constitute living well. Because of this you will have **practical wisdom**.[32] If you have practical wisdom, then you will always know what options you have and your emotions and motives help you to see which one of them is the most worthwhile. This means that whatever situation you take, there is something that a flourishing virtuous agent would do in that situation.

You can use this idea to give a theory of what is right and wrong 5.75
(**Hursthouse, 1991;** 1999, ch, 1).[33] According to the resulting view:

> An act is right if and only if it is what a virtuous person would do in the relevant situation (i) knowingly, (ii) for the act it is, and (iii) from a stable character trait.

This view says that how a virtuous agent reacts to different situations determines what is right and wrong. You might think that this leads to a problem. Assuming that you are not a fully virtuous person yourself, how could you ever apply this theory? How could you ever know what a virtuous agent would do?

Here's a brief sketch of how you could apply the view. You begin from 5.76
the idea of a flourishing human being. This leads you to consider what activities you need to do in order to live well. You then consider what character traits would be needed for pursuing these activities successfully. What kind of beliefs, emotions, and motivations do you need, for example, in order to live with other people and in order to use both theoretical and practical reason effectively in deliberation? Presumably virtues such as courage, being just, kindness, loyalty, honesty, curiosity, and generosity would be required for these activities.

You can then use these virtue terms to formulate simple ethical princi- 5.77
ples. These include principles such as "Do what is just!" "Be kind!" "Be courageous!" "Avoid cruelty!" and so on. By trying to apply these rules the

best you can, you can come to approximate what a fully virtuous agent would do in the concrete situations you face. The only really hard cases will be ones in which these rules seem to conflict. Sometimes doing what is honest seems to require being cruel. It is only in these cases that you have to rely on the judgments of fully virtuous agents themselves.

Two Objections to Virtue Ethics

5.78 Should you accept virtue ethics as an ethical theory of right and wrong? This final section will consider two main problems with the theory. One of these is the idea that virtue ethics is circular as a theory of right and wrong, and the second is that it doesn't give the right advice to people who are not fully virtuous themselves.

Circularity

5.79 Here is, once again, the way in which virtue ethics is supposed to work. You begin from a flourishing human life and the activities that constitute it. You then use these notions to describe which character traits are required for taking part in the relevant activities successfully. After this, you finally use these virtues to explain what is right and wrong.

5.80 This explanatory chain fails if you need to rely on right and wrong at the earlier stages of the explanation. Imagine that you couldn't explain which character traits count as virtues merely by talking about what is required for human flourishing. In this case, you would need to rely on what is right and wrong to determine which character traits count as virtues. If you had to do this, then virtues could not be used to give an account of right and wrong without objectionable **circular thinking**[34] (Das, 2003).

5.81 Consider, for example, the virtue of honesty. If you have this character trait, you will tell the appropriate truths on the appropriate occasions. This description of honesty relies on appropriate truths and appropriate occasions. To be honest is not to tell all the truths you know in every situation. You only have to tell the truths that are relevant on the appropriate occasions.

5.82 How can you know which truths it is appropriate to tell in which situations? What does honesty really require? A virtue ethicist must be able to answer these questions by relying only on the activities that constitute flourishing for human beings. However, it seems as though successful social interaction and theoretical and practical reasoning are far too indeterminate as ideas to tell us which truths you must tell and when.

At this point, there is a temptation to say that honesty requires you to 5.83
tell the truth *when it is right to do so*. However, saying this means reversing the order of explanation. It requires assuming that there are antecedent facts about which acts are right and wrong. If you must help yourself to such facts about right and wrong to explain what virtues are, then you are no longer using human flourishing and character traits that count as excellences to explain what is right and wrong. In effect, you have given up virtue ethics.

Improving yourself

The second problem with virtue ethics is that we are not all virtuous agents 5.84
ourselves (**Johnson, 2003**).[35] This leads virtue ethics to implausible conclusions about what is right and wrong. Imagine that John is an alcoholic, whose drinking is making him and other people suffer. John is then offered an excellent opportunity to give up drinking. He is offered a place at an efficient **rehab**[36] center free of charge. Should he take this opportunity?

According to virtue ethics, whether John should go to rehab depends on 5.85
what a fully virtuous agent would do in his circumstances. The problem is that a fully virtuous person would not be an alcoholic in the first place, because alcoholism is not compatible with having the character traits that count as human excellences. But if a fully virtuous person would not go to rehab, then according to virtue ethics it would also be wrong for John to go there. This must be mistaken. Virtue ethics thus fails to capture what is right and wrong.

Virtue ethics and moral sensibility

Despite these problems, virtue ethics still plays an extremely useful role. 5.86
The previous sections suggested that both Ross and particularists fail to explain how you can know what you should do overall. Whenever you are making a decision, you always have many moral reasons for and against all the alternatives you have. According to Ross and the particularists, there are no general principles that could tell you how strong these reasons are in the particular situation you are in.

5.87 All Ross and the particularists can say is that you must rely on your moral sensibility in order to see what you ought to do in the situation you face. Your sensibilities enable you to see what the morally relevant considerations are in your situation and in what way they matter. This helps you to make accurate judgments about what you ought to do.

5.88 Virtue ethics is important because it helps us to understand what a moral sensibility is and also how it reacts to the reasons we have. According to virtue ethicists, a moral sensibility is a set of stable character traits that consist of beliefs, emotions, and motivational dispositions. You acquire these character traits through a moral upbringing when you are a child.

5.89 When you are a child, you play and interact with other people. As a child, you want to imitate others and you are also rewarded when you do this successfully. During this process you acquire new cares and concerns. You learn to enjoy reading, sports, chatting to other people, and so on for their own sake. You also come to appreciate keeping promises, helping others, telling the truth, and taking risks.

5.90 When you grow up, these new cares and concerns are fine-tuned by the people around you. Through the examples, praise, and criticism they give you, your concerns come to be highly sensitive to the features of the situations you are in. You come to care more about telling the truth in some cases (like **in court**) than in others (like **when playing poker**).[37] This is how you come to have a highly complex set of finely tuned and sensitive moral concerns.

5.91 This story explains how you can know what you should do all things considered, even when you live in a morally complex world. When you see some action to be the right thing to do overall, this observation is based on the balance of how strongly your different cares and concerns react to the features of your situation. This is how you can know what you ought to do without relying on any explicit general moral principles.

5.92 For example, when you became honest you started to care about telling the truth. However, you were not brought up to be sensitive to truth telling always in the same way. Your concern for truth was shaped so that in some cases you feel strongly that you must tell the truth. In this case, you see the fact that you would be telling the truth as a strong reason to do so. In other circumstances, such as when you are playing poker, you feel less inclined to tell the truth. In this way, your cares and concerns that constitute your virtues enable you to see what reasons you have in particular situations.

Of course the previous sketch still needs many details filled in about how your virtuous dispositions can react to the morally relevant considerations in the situations you are in. One good, positive quality of this story is that it is available for Rossians, particularists, and virtue ethicists alike. All these views, which attempt to be faithful to the idea that moral decisions are often difficult, can use this story to attempt to understand how you can still often make sound moral judgments. 5.93

Summary and Questions

This chapter started from W.D. Ross's powerful objection to traditional ethical theories. Consequentialists and Kantians assume that just one quality of all right acts explains why these acts are right. Consequentialists say that certain acts are right because they maximize the good whereas Kantians say that these acts are right because you can consistently universalize their maxims. According to Ross, these views fail because different features of acts make different acts right and wrong. 5.94

The middle part of the chapter outlined Ross's own intuitionist view in normative ethics. According to this view, there is a list of considerations which can make acts right to a degree. These so-called prima facie duties cannot be derived from any more fundamental ethical principles, and how strong these duties are varies in different contexts. Particularists think that there are no prima facie duties. They think that whatever makes some acts right in certain contexts can make other acts wrong elsewhere. That an act makes a lot of people happy is usually a good reason to do it, but not when it requires hanging someone. 5.95

The last sections of the chapter introduced virtue ethics. Virtue ethics focuses on how you should live and what kind of a person you should be. It tries to answer these questions by considering activities that are typical for human beings and that therefore constitute human flourishing. Virtues are character traits that enable you to take part in these activities successfully. 5.96

Virtue ethicists argue that right actions are what a fully virtuous agent would characteristically do in the given situation. The chapter concluded by explaining why virtue ethics is problematic as an account of what is right and wrong and why it is still important because it can help us to understand how you can know what you should do, all things considered. 5.97

5.98 Based on the philosophical resources introduced in this chapter, consider the following questions:

1. Say what makes the following acts wrong:
   i. cheating on your taxes;
   ii. telling a white lie to your friend about what they are wearing;
   iii. plagiarizing an essay.
2. What obligations were on Ross's list of prima facie duties? What is it for these duties to be prima facie duties? Should we add anything to the list or remove anything from it?
3. What do Ross and the particularists disagree about?
4. Describe how virtue ethicists define:
   i. happiness;
   ii. virtue;
   iii. virtuous action;
   iv. right and wrong.
5. How could virtue ethicists try to answer the two objections?

Annotated Bibliography

Annas, Julia (2011) *Intelligent Virtue* (Oxford: Oxford University Press). According to Annas's neo-Aristotelian view, virtues are dispositions to act in ways that constitute human happiness. Annas also explains how virtues require practical reasoning, which can be learned through practice in the same way as other skills.

Anscombe, G.E.M. (1958) "Modern Moral Philosophy," *Philosophy*, *33*(124), 1–19, full text available at http://www.pitt.edu/~mthompso/readings/mmp.pdf, accessed February 26, 2014. An interesting but difficult article which continues to have a huge influence on moral philosophy. It single-handedly revived Aristotelian virtue ethics as a live option.

Aristotle (circa 350 BC) *Nicomachean Ethics*. See the bibliography of Chapter 1 above.

Athanassoulis, Nafsika (2005) *Morality, Moral Luck and Responsibility: Fortune's Web* (Basingstoke: Palgrave Macmillan). An interesting discussion of moral luck in the contexts of Aristotelian virtue ethics and Kant's ethics.

Athanassoulis, Nafsika (2013) *Virtue Ethics* (London: Bloomsbury). An up-to-date textbook on virtue ethics which goes through both Aristotle's theory and the most recent developments in contemporary virtue ethics.

Crisp, Roger and Michael Slote (eds.) (1997) *Virtue Ethics* (Oxford: Oxford University Press). This collection of articles contains all the essential articles on virtue ethics including articles both clarifying the view and making objections to it.

Dancy, Jonathan (1991) "An Ethic of Prima Facie Duties," in *A Companion to Ethics*, ed. Peter Singer (Oxford: Blackwell), pp. 219–229. A wonderfully clear explanation of Ross's intuitionism.

Dancy, Jonathan (1993) *Moral Reasons* (Oxford: Blackwell). An original defense of particularism about practical reasons on the basis of an argument which rests on internalist views of moral motivation (see Chapter 8 below).

Dancy, Jonathan (2004) *Ethics without Principles* (Oxford: Oxford University Press). In this more recent defense of particularism, Dancy begins from holism in the theory of practical reasons and argues from it to particularism and realism in metaethics.

Darwall, Stephen (ed.) (2003) *Virtue Ethics* (Oxford: Blackwell). This anthology contains both classic readings by Aristotle, Hutcheson, and Hume and the most famous contemporary articles on virtue ethics.

Das, Ramon (2003) "Virtue Ethics and Right Action," *Australasian Journal of Philosophy*, *81*(3), 324–339. This article describes the most recent accounts of right and wrong in virtue ethics and argues convincingly that these views are circular in a vicious way.

Foot, Philippa (2001) *Natural Goodness* (Oxford: Oxford University Press). In this book, Foot argues that there are natural norms for evaluating the life of human beings just in the same way as there are natural norms for evaluating the life of plants and animals. She then uses this account to explore practical rationality, happiness, and morality.

Hursthouse, Rosalind (1991) "Virtue Theory and Abortion," *Philosophy and Public Affairs*, *20*(3), 223–246, full text available at http://www.debatechamber.com/wp-content/uploads/2010/07/hursthouse-on-abortion.pdf, accessed February 26, 2014. A famous article in which Hursthouse specifies a virtue ethical theory of right and wrong and responds to the objection that virtue ethics is not sufficiently action-guiding. She shows how the view can be applied to the debates about abortion.

Hursthouse, Rosalind (1999) *On Virtue Ethics* (Oxford: Oxford University Press). A book which focuses on virtue ethics as a theory of right and wrong actions. It also contains an interesting discussion of moral motivation and a long investigation of whether virtues are objective and natural qualities.

Johnson, Robert (2003) "Virtue and Right," *Ethics*, *113*, 810–834, full text available at http://www.tc.umn.edu/~ston0235/3311/johnson.pdf, accessed February 26, 2014. This article argues forcefully that virtue ethics cannot account for the fact that we are often required to improve our characters.

McDowell, John (1981) "Non-Cognitivism and Rule-Following," in *Wittgenstein: To Follow a Rule*, ed. Steven Holtzman and Christopher Leich (London: Routledge and Kegan Paul), pp. 141–162. John McDowell has defended realist views in metaethics by using the resources of virtue ethics. This influential early article discusses moral perception in the framework of Wittgenstein's rule-following considerations.

McNaughton, David (1988) *Moral Vision: An Introduction to Ethics* (Oxford: Blackwell). A wonderfully opinionated metaethics textbook. One of the best things about this book is how it makes John McDowell's views in ethics more accessible.

Ridge, Michael and Sean McKeever (2006) *Principled Ethics – Generalism as a Regulative Ideal* (Oxford: Oxford University Press). In this book, Ridge and McKeever argue that Dancy was wrong to claim that particularism follows from holism about practical reasons. They also defend the idea that we should at least attempt to find general moral principles in our moral thinking.

Ross, W.D. (1930) *The Right and the Good*. See bibliography of Chapter 4 above.

Slote, Michael (2001) *Morals from Motives* (Oxford: Oxford University Press). Slote's virtue ethics draws from the sentimentalist tradition of David Hume and Francis Hutcheson. According to this view, we should try to understand right and wrong in terms of actions that are based on virtuous motives such as benevolence and caring.

Stratton-Lake, Philip (2002) "Introduction," in W.D. Ross, *The Right and the Good*, ed. Philip Stratton-Lake (Oxford: Oxford University Press), pp. ix–lviii. An admirably clear overview of the main points of *The Right and the Good*, which also contains an excellent bibliography of secondary literature on Ross.

Väyrynen, Pekka (2011) "Moral Particularism," in *Continuum Companion to Ethics*, ed. Christian Miller (London: Continuum), full text available at http://www.personal.leeds.ac.uk/~phlpv/papers/moralparticularism.pdf, accessed February 26, 2014. A very careful and thorough discussion of what the disagreement between particularists and generalists is about.

Online Resources

1 The life and works of W.D Ross: http://plato.stanford.edu/entries/william-david-ross/ and the first three chapters of his *The Right and the Good*: http://www.ditext.com/ross/right.html.
2 Monism as compared to pluralism: http://plato.stanford.edu/entries/value-pluralism/.
3 Chapter 2 of *The Right and the Good*: http://www.ditext.com/ross/right2.html.
4 An interesting and illuminating online discussion on the wrongness of rape: http://answers.yahoo.com/question/index?qid=20090606193308AAOhOHi.

5 A clear explanation of the so-called "value pluralism": http://plato.stanford.edu/entries/value-pluralism/.
6 Overview of particularism: http://plato.stanford.edu/entries/moral-particularism/.
7 Chris Heathwood's clear lecture slides on the topic: http://spot.colorado.edu/~heathwoo/phil1100/lec14_ross.pdf.
8 Chapter 2 of *The Right and the Good*: http://www.ditext.com/ross/right2.html.
9 An overview of different philosophical views on promises: http://plato.stanford.edu/entries/promises/.
10 An overview of philosophical work on practical reasons: http://plato.stanford.edu/entries/reasons-just-vs-expl/.
11 See the paragraph beginning with "The general principles of duty are obviously not self-evident…": http://www.ditext.com/ross/right2.html.
12 See the paragraph beginning with "Our judgements about our actual duty in concrete situations…": http://www.ditext.com/ross/right2.html.
13 An interesting discussion of the rights and wrongs of stealing if you are starving: http://www.debate.org/opinions/is-it-moral-to-steal-food-for-the-benefit-of-a-starving-person-if-that-is-the-only-means-by-which-the-food-may-be-obtained.
14 Top 10 celebrity shoplifters: http://xfinity.comcast.net/slideshow/entertainment-celebshoplifters/.
15 A picture of the frescoes in the Sistine Chapel: http://www.wga.hu/art/m/michelan/3sistina/3ceil_ho.jpg.
16 Jonathan Dancy's homepage: https://webspace.utexas.edu/jpd346/www/Site/Welcome.html and Dancy talking about particularism on philosophybites: http://philosophybites.com/2012/06/jonathan-dancy-on-moral-particularism.html.
17 Dancy explaining particularism on the Craig Ferguson Late Late show: http://www.youtube.com/watch?v=_V4vQhpRwi4 and overview of debates about particularism: http://plato.stanford.edu/entries/moral-particularism/.
18 Pekka Väyrynen's wonderful overview of the particularism vs generalism debates: http://www.personal.leeds.ac.uk/~phlpv/papers/moralparticularism.pdf.
19 A useful encyclopedia entry on virtue ethics: http://www.iep.utm.edu/virtue/ and G.E.M. Anscombe's famous article "Modern Moral Philosophy": http://www.pitt.edu/~mthompso/readings/mmp.pdf.
20 Roger Crisp interviewed on Plato, Aristotle, and virtues at the web site Philosophy Bites: http://philosophybites.com/2008/10/roger-crisp-on.html.
21 A clear overview of virtue ethics: http://plato.stanford.edu/entries/ethics-virtue/.
22 Information on elm trees: http://en.wikipedia.org/wiki/Elm.
23 Information on wolves: http://en.wikipedia.org/wiki/Wolf.

24 Book X of Aristotle's *Nicomachean Ethics*: http://classics.mit.edu/Aristotle/nicomachaen.10.x.html.
25 Book II of the *Nicomachean Ethics*: http://classics.mit.edu/Aristotle/nicomachaen.2.ii.html.
26 Books I and II from the *Nicomachean Ethics*: http://classics.mit.edu/Aristotle/nicomachaen.1.i.html and http://classics.mit.edu/Aristotle/nicomachaen.2.ii.html.
27 Tamar Gendler from Yale explaining acquisition of virtues: http://www.youtube.com/watch?v=reZA81S0zfI.
28 Book II of the *Nicomachean Ethics*: http://classics.mit.edu/Aristotle/nicomachaen.2.ii.html.
29 Overview article on moral luck: http://plato.stanford.edu/entries/moral-luck/.
30 Book II of the *Nicomachean Ethics*: http://classics.mit.edu/Aristotle/nicomachaen.2.ii.html.
31 Book III of the *Nicomachean Ethics*: http://classics.mit.edu/Aristotle/nicomachaen.3.iii.html.
32 A computer animation summary of Aristotle on practical wisdom: http://www.youtube.com/watch?v=CmtcjyZNej8.
33 Hursthouse's famous article "Virtue Theory and Abortion": http://www.debatechamber.com/wp-content/uploads/2010/07/hursthouse-on-abortion.pdf.
34 Examples of circular reasoning: http://ksuweb.kennesaw.edu/~shagin/logfal-pbc-circular.htm.
35 Robert Johnson's article "Virtue and Right": http://www.tc.umn.edu/~ston0235/3311/johnson.pdf.
36 Amy Winehouse on rehab: http://www.youtube.com/watch?v=MbyUEe2Junk.
37 Getting caught in court: http://www.youtube.com/watch?v=g8pvAJ587-c and poker players discussing lying: http://www.youtube.com/watch?v=_yRmJzzgmJQ.

Part Three

METAETHICS

6

SUBJECTIVISM, RELATIVISM, AND DIVINE COMMANDS

The previous three chapters explored normative ethics. The main questions in these chapters were: 6.1

- Which acts are right and which acts wrong?
- What makes acts right and wrong?
- How should you live? What kind of a person should you be?

The discussion of these questions assumed that there are truths about right and wrong. We've understood ethical theories as attempts to capture these truths.

Many people find the whole idea of moral truths mysterious. At this 6.2
point you move from normative ethics to **metaethics**.[1] In normative ethics you are still taking part in ordinary moral debates. Outside the philosophy seminars we usually think about more specific moral questions. We wonder about whether it would be wrong to lie to a friend or fail to keep a particular promise. We also often disagree about whether cheating on taxes is wrong or whether it should be permissible to have an abortion. In normative ethics you just think about these questions more systematically.

When you move to **metaethics**,[2] you move from ordinary moral debates 6.3
to a more theoretical level (for metaethics textbooks, see Fischer, 2011; Kirchin, 2012; Miller, A., 2013). From the theoretical standpoint, you then start to think about what is going on in the ordinary moral debates. You can ask questions such as:

This Is Ethics: An Introduction, First Edition. Jussi Suikkanen.

- What do moral words mean?
- **Can moral statements be objectively true?**[3]
- Are there moral properties and what are they like?
- What constitutes making a moral judgment, psychologically speaking?

Metaethics therefore doesn't investigate what is right and wrong; rather it is interested in the nature of moral language and thinking, and whether there are moral properties or objective moral truths. These metaethical questions will be the topic of the next three chapters.

6.4 Many people are **deeply skeptical**[4] when they first consider these metaethical questions. They find the idea that there could be objective moral truths suspicious. As a result they naturally attempt to find more down-to-earth ways of making sense of moral language and thought.

6.5 Here is one way to make this move. It is natural to use the model of law to understand morality (**Anscombe, 1951**).[5] After all, for an act to be wrong is a bit like for it to be against the law. Both law and morality are important standards for evaluating what we do. This is true even if some legal acts are morally wrong and some illegal actions are morally right. For example, even if it is legal to cheat on your partner, doing so can still be morally wrong.

6.6 In the case of law, someone has to make the law for there to be a law. There has to first be a sound legislative process, which usually takes place in a parliament. The outcome of such a process is a law, which requires you to do some things and forbids you to do others. Therefore, things do not just happen to be legal or illegal, but rather someone has to make it the case that things are permitted and forbidden by the law (see Hart, 1961).

6.7 If you use the analogy of law to understand morality, then you will also think that things don't just happen to be right or wrong, but rather some acts are wrong because someone first made it the case that they are wrong. If you follow this line of thought, then moral standards too must be created by voluntary acts of an agent or a group of agents. This view of morality is called **voluntarism**.

6.8 This chapter discusses three metaethical views which all take this intuitive voluntarist line of reasoning seriously (see also Shafer-Landau, 2004). The first view is called **subjectivism**.[6] On this view what is right and wrong depends on what you approve and disapprove of as an individual. The second theory is called **relativism**.[7] This is the view that what is right and wrong is determined by what your society accepts and forbids. The last theory is called the **divine command theory**.[8] According to it, moral standards are based on the commands of God.

Subjectivism

One knee-jerk reaction to metaethical questions is to insist that "It's all just a matter of opinion!" If you have this reaction too, then you will love subjectivism. It is an attempt to develop the idea that morality is just a matter of opinion into a proper metaethical theory that answers the basic questions in metaethics. However, you will need to be careful because subjectivism is difficult to make consistent. 6.9

Subjectivism is best understood as a theory of what moral words mean. There are very few genuine defenders of this view in metaethics today (but see **Dreier, 1990**).[9] **Thomas Hobbes** seemed to endorse subjectivism when he wrote: 6.10

> But whatsoever is the object of any man's appetite or desire, that is it which he for his part calleth good; and the object of his hate and aversion, evil; and of his contempt, vile and inconsiderable. For these words of good, evil, and contemptible are ever used with relation to the person that useth them: there being nothing simply and absolutely so; nor any common rule of good and evil to be taken from the nature of the objects themselves (**Hobbes, 1660, ch. 6**).[10]

Here Hobbes makes an interesting claim about what you mean when you say that something is good.

You personally approve of certain actions and disapprove of others. According to subjectivism, when you say that an act is good or right all you mean is that you approve of the act. Likewise, when you say that an act is wrong all you mean is that you disapprove of the act. Subjectivists therefore think that making claims about what is right and wrong **reports** what you approve or disapprove of. When you discuss moral questions, in the end you are just talking about your own attitudes. You are describing whether or not you like different acts. 6.11

This view is easy to illustrate with an analogy. Consider claims about what is yucky and yummy. It is natural to think that when you say that **rhubarb is yucky**[11] and raspberries yummy, all you are really saying is 6.12

that you like raspberries but not rhubarb. In this way, the words "yucky" and "yummy" are devices for telling other people about what you like and don't like. According to subjectivists, the meaning of moral words can be explained exactly in the same way.

Advantages of subjectivism

6.13 Subjectivism has many appealing features. Firstly, it means that morality is just a matter of opinion, which many people believe anyway. This is because, according to subjectivism, all there is to being right or wrong is that you approve or disapprove of the act.

6.14 Another nice thing about this view is that it doesn't make moral qualities mysterious. If saying that an act is right just means that you approve of it, then you will easily know which acts are right. All you need to do is to find out what you approve of, which you can usually tell yourself. Sciences like evolutionary psychology can, moreover, shed light on why you approve of different acts. If subjectivism is the correct theory of what moral words mean, then this also tells you what is right and wrong.

6.15 Subjectivism can, in addition, explain two important features of our moral discourse. Firstly, it can explain how some moral utterances are true and others false by providing the conditions under which your moral utterances are true. If you say "**waterboarding**[12] is wrong," then, according to subjectivism, this utterance is true if and only if you are against waterboarding and false otherwise.

6.16 Secondly, subjectivism can also explain the practical nature of moral judgments (see Chapter 8 below). **There is a match between what people say is right and wrong and what they are motivated to do.**[13] People who claim that eating meat is wrong tend not to want to eat meat, for example.

6.17 Subjectivism makes sense of this observation. When you say that an act is right you are reporting your positive attitudes toward the act. Given that you have that attitude it is not a surprise that you will want to do what you think is right. Take Sam, who says that it is wrong to eat meat. When he says this he means that he disapproves of eating meat, which explains why he doesn't want to eat meat.

Objections to subjectivism

6.18 Despite these advantages of subjectivism very few people who work in metaethics accept the view. This is mainly because:

- subjectivism doesn't fit our moral experience;
- subjectivism makes you morally infallible; and
- subjectivism can't explain moral disagreements.

Objection 1: Experience Consider your own moral experiences: fairly 6.19
often you first come to think that some act is wrong and only then you begin to disapprove of the act. Many people like fur coats before it is explained to them how much **the minks suffer in their tiny cages.**[14] This leads many people to conclude that wearing fur is morally problematic and because of this they will have negative attitudes toward fur coats.

The problem is that this simple story would be ruled out by subjectivism. According to subjectivism, you always first disapprove of certain actions. Once you do this you can then call these actions wrong. This would make it impossible for you to begin to disapprove of an act because you first think that it is wrong.

Objection 2: Infallibility Secondly, even if you can often know what is right 6.20
and wrong, it is hard to accept that you are infallible about it. Most of us are humble enough to admit that we can be wrong about what is right and wrong. **Sometimes we even realize that we have been morally blind.**[15] Furthermore, there are situations in which it is really hard to tell whether some act is wrong. Consider **cloning animals.**[16] Is this right or wrong? This case raises so many different ethical issues that it is hard to be certain.

Subjectivism is unable to account for these facts (**Rachels, 2003, ch. 3**[17]; 6.21
Shafer-Landau, 2004, ch. 3). According to it, when you say that an act is right you mean that you disapprove of the act. If you know what you disapprove of, you will always know what is wrong. Knowing what is right and wrong would not be any harder than knowing what you like, which is something you usually know with ease. For subjectivism, moral knowledge is therefore so easy to come by that you couldn't be mistaken or struggle to find an answer. This isn't what it's like.

Objection 3: Disagreement Finally, subjectivists can't explain how you 6.22
could have moral disagreements with other people (**Moore, 1922, sect. 26**).[18] Let's imagine that you and Ben are talking about whether terrorist suspects should be subjected to waterboarding. You say that it would be wrong to do so whereas Ben claims that it wouldn't. Intuitively in this case you disagree with Ben. There is something that you are convinced of that Ben just doesn't accept.

6.23 Subjectivists can't make sense of this disagreement. According to them, when you say that waterboarding is wrong you mean that you disapprove of it. Likewise, when Ben says that waterboarding is right he only reports that he is for it. In this case, Ben can agree with what you say and you can accept what he says. Ben can happily agree that you do not like waterboarding and you can equally well accept that he is for it.

6.24 This means that, according to subjectivism, there is no disagreement between you and Ben. In fact, in all cases where it looks as if people disagree about moral questions, people would just be talking about their own attitudes and therefore talking past one another. This consequence of subjectivism is difficult to accept. You really want to hold on to the idea that we can have genuine moral disagreements.

Relativism

6.25 Many people try to avoid these problems with subjectivism by accepting a view called **moral relativism** instead (**Harman, 1975**; **Lafollette, 1991**).[19] According to relativism, when you talk about right and wrong, you are not talking about your own personal preferences, but rather about what the moral code in your society permits and forbids.

6.26 A moral code is a set of prescriptions. One moral code could, for example, contain the following prescriptions:

- Do not lie!
- Do not steal!
- Tell the truth!
- Do not kill except when this is the only way to save your life!

Actual moral codes are like this (only a bit more complicated!). A society's moral code is the set of prescriptions which most people in the society accept. These prescriptions therefore influence what people do and what they are praised and criticized for.

6.27 Relativism is also a theory of what you mean when you say that an act is right or wrong. There are two different versions of relativism. The first version is called **appraisal relativism**. According to it, when you say that it is wrong to lie, this utterance means that your own society forbids stealing. Appraisal relativism makes the truth of moral utterances relative to the moral code which is accepted in the speaker's society.

The second version of relativism is called **agent relativism**. According to it, when you say that it is wrong for Natasha to commit fraud, you mean that the moral code in Natasha's own society forbids committing fraud. On this view, the relevant moral standards are not the ones in your society but rather the ones accepted in the society of the agent whose actions you are evaluating. For the sake of simplicity, the rest of this section will focus on appraisal relativism even if I will occasionally refer to agent relativism too. 6.28

Perhaps the best way to understand appraisal relativism is to think that, according to it, simple moral sentences like "lying is wrong" are **incomplete expressions (Boghossian, 2006).**[20] When you use this sentence the context you are in completes your utterance. Whenever anyone says that "lying is wrong," they always therefore really mean that: 6.29

Lying is wrong relative to F.

"Relative to F" is here a hidden parameter which is not explicitly mentioned in the sentence you utter. As you recall, according to relativism, a moral claim is always about what the moral code of your society accepts. The placeholder "F" stands for this code. This way of understanding relativism is motivated by the idea that otherwise relativism quickly leads to contradictions. Without the additional parameter, it could be true both that *lying is wrong* and *lying is not wrong* as long as there is one society which accepts lying and one which forbids it.

The context in which you say "lying is wrong" determines which moral code you are referring to. This explains how when Bill, as an American, says that "lying is wrong," in his context he means that: 6.30

Lying is wrong relative to the American moral code.

Similarly, when Hans as a German says that "lying is wrong," in his context he means that:

Lying is wrong relative to the German moral code.

This is how the context in which the speaker is completes what the speaker means. This also explains why relativism does not lead to contradictions. It can be true both that lying is wrong relative to code A and not wrong relative to code B.

Advantages of relativism

6.31 Relativism too has many theoretical advantages. Like subjectivism, it makes right and wrong scientifically investigable. You can **empirically investigate**[21] which moral norms are accepted in your society, and evolutionary psychology can help you to understand why these norms were accepted instead of others.

6.32 Relativism can also explain under what conditions moral utterances are true. If you say that it is wrong to steal, this claim is true when the moral standards of your society forbid stealing. Given that you probably accept the moral standards of your own society yourself, this view can furthermore explain why you are motivated to do what you think is right. If you correctly report that your society's standards forbid stealing and you accept those standards, then you will not want to steal.

6.33 Even more importantly, relativism can avoid many problems of subjectivism. It fits the idea that you can come to disapprove of an act because you discover that it is wrong. Because of peer pressure we often come to share other people's attitudes. Thus it isn't a surprise that you can disapprove of eating meat when everyone else is against it too.

6.34 Relativism furthermore explains how you can be mistaken about moral questions and how some moral truths can be difficult to discover. It is not always easy to know which acts are permitted in your society. Consider sleeping with many people at the same time. Is this wrong? According to relativism, this question is whether the moral standards of your society forbid adultery. **This is something that you can easily be mistaken about and also something that isn't easy to find out.**[22] Relativism can therefore explain how you can make moral mistakes and why moral knowledge isn't always easy to get.

6.35 Finally, relativism enables you to disagree with Ben about whether waterboarding is wrong. When you and Ben disagree about whether waterboarding is wrong you really disagree about what your society's stance toward waterboarding is. You are saying that most people in your society are against waterboarding whereas he is saying that most people in your society are not against it.

6.36 Relativism has one more important advantage. Many people are impressed by a scientific truth called **descriptive cultural relativism.**[23] This is the observation that different societies have different moral codes (Benedict, 1946). **In some societies people give tips whereas in other societies this is considered to be demeaning.**[24] This leads many people to think that we should adopt the attitude of tolerance toward other cultures. Even if you think that we should tip generously, you don't want to force other societies to adopt this practice. You want to accept that tipping can be right in your society but wrong in Sweden. Many people continue to believe that accepting relativism in metaethics is the best way to tolerate other cultures and their moral norms.

There are, therefore, many good reasons to accept relativism in metaethics. **Despite this, surprisingly few philosophers working in metaethics are relativists in this sense.**[25] The next section will look at some of the main reasons for this. 6.37

Problems of relativism

Problem 1: Disagreement It is not clear whether the relativists can really avoid the problems with subjectivism. Consider moral disagreements again. Relativism can easily explain how the members of the same society can disagree. In disagreements like the one between you and Ben, you are making conflicting claims about what your society accepts. 6.38

However, consider people who are not members of same society (Shafer-Landau, 2004, p. 41). For example, take the following exchange between Irish Róisín and Swedish Anna who are talking about whether it is wrong to have an abortion: 6.39

RÓISÍN: It would be wrong to have an abortion.
ANNA: No, there wouldn't be anything wrong with it.

In this situation, Róisín and Anna definitely disagree. However, according to relativism, they could not do so because they would be talking about different topics. Relativists would claim that Róisín is talking about what is accepted in Ireland whereas Anna is talking about what people accept in Sweden. In this situation the disagreement between them goes away. Anna can accept that people in Ireland are against abortions and Róisín can admit that the Swedes have nothing against them.

Relativism thus makes moral disagreements between members of different societies impossible. However, this is not plausible – you can disagree with people from other cultures even about moral questions. Many of us, for example, strongly disagree with the practice of **female genital mutilation**[26] that is widely practiced in many societies. 6.40

6.41 *Problem 2: Moral fallibility* Relativists also face problems when they attempt to explain moral fallibility and moral knowledge. The relativist says that moral claims are about what most people in your society think. Admittedly, this is something that you can be wrong about and also something that you might struggle to find out. However, things are not so straightforward.

6.42 Consider this question: Should you give money to charity? What evidence should you take into account when you answer this question? According to relativism, the only way to answer this question is to find out what other people in your society think. This is counterintuitive. What most people think does not seem all that important when you consider whether you should give money to charity. It would be far more important to know how desperately people need help, how effective different charities are, and how much you could afford to help. One implausible consequence of relativism, therefore, is that information about what other people think would always be best evidence for what is right and wrong.

6.43 *Problem 3: Tolerance* The third problem is related to what motivates many to be moral relativists in the first place (**Pojman, 2000**[27]; Shafer-Landau, 2004, pp. 30–33). Does it really follow from relativism that you should tolerate what the members of other societies do?

6.44 The claim that "it is wrong to force the members of other cultures to live in the same way as you" is a moral claim. In this respect, it is just like the claim that "lying is wrong." Relativism is a general theory of what claims like this mean. So, if you claim that lying is wrong, you mean that most people in your society are against lying. Then, according to relativism, when you say that it is wrong to coerce other societies to live in the same way, you mean that most people in your society are against this.

6.45 The problem is that this claim need not be true – **some societies are not tolerant**.[28] The members of these societies believe that you can force other people to follow your way of life. In the relativist framework, if you are a member of this type of intolerant society then you would be mistaken if you said that it is wrong to force other societies to live like you. The upshot is that relativism is not the best way to defend tolerance. Notice that this objection also applies to agent relativism. Imagine that you come across a foreign society whose members just can't tolerate other cultures. Are they doing anything wrong by being intolerant? If agent relativism is true, they are not, because on that view everyone's actions should be measured by the moral standards of the society they belong to.

Problem 4: Multiculturalism The last problem with relativism is my personal favorite (Shafer-Landau, 2004, ch. 10). Many of us belong to many different societies. I belong both to Finnish and English societies. I spent the first 28 years of my life in Finland and since then I have lived in England for 10 years. Imagine that I tell you that "you should always go to the **sauna**[29] naked." 6.46

According to appraisal relativism, my utterance is true if most people in my society are in favor of going to the sauna naked. This is hopeless. **All Finns go to the sauna naked.**[30] In contrast, **English people never go to the sauna naked.**[31] They are horrified by this Finnish tradition. So is my utterance true or not? If I am a member of the Finnish society it is true, and if I am a member of the English society it isn't. If I belong to both societies then my utterance is both true and false – which would be a blatant contradiction. To avoid this, the relativist would need to explain which society I really belong to. There doesn't seem to be a non-arbitrary way of deciding this. 6.47

Divine Command Theory

So far, this chapter has explained why moral standards cannot be set by individuals or societies. If moral standards must be set by someone despite this, then you must look for alternative sources of morality. Many people draw from this the conclusion that moral standards must have a supernatural source. According to this view, which has been popular throughout the history, acts are right and wrong because **God**[32] as a divine being made them so. This view is called **the divine command theory** (for contemporary presentations, see **Adams, 1979**; **Wieranga, 1983**; Quinn, 2000).[33] 6.48

God is supposed to be an all-powerful, all-knowing, all-powerful, loving, and perfectly good being who is the creator of our universe. This fits roughly the descriptions of God given by the major monotheistic religions. This chapter will not take a stand on whether such a being exists. The focus will only be **whether God could be the source of moral standards if you presuppose that He exists.**[34] 6.49

Divine command theory and moral words

We first need to formulate divine command theory more carefully. The first option would be to understand the divine command theory as a 6.50

metaethical view of what moral words mean. According to this theory, when you say that "it is wrong to lie" all you mean is that God commands us not to lie.

6.51 It is not plausible that everyone means this when they use the word "wrong." Many people do not believe in God and other people think that many different gods exist. These people can't be talking about what God commands when they use moral language. Or, if you think that they are still talking about God's commands, then you would have to think that these people are badly conceptually confused. Despite their best attempts they keep talking about what God commands – even though they don't even believe in Him.

6.52 You could try to avoid this problem by claiming that the divine command theory is only about what religious people mean when they talk about right and wrong. This view would claim that when a believer claims that "it is right to rest on Sundays" she means that God commands us to rest on Sundays. This view would then have to give some other explanation of what other people mean when they talk about right and wrong.

6.53 Robert Merrihew Adams has shown that this is not what the divine command theorists should say (**Adams, 1979**).[35] First of all, you want to know just as much what **atheists** and **polytheists**[36] mean when they talk about right or wrong. The more serious problem is that this new proposal again fails to leave room for moral disagreements.

6.54 Consider the following exchange between Catholic Margaret and atheist James:

MARGARET: Premarital sex is wrong.
JAMES: No, premarital sex isn't wrong.

According to the version of the divine command theory under consideration, Margaret's claim means that God commands us not to have premarital sex. However, this view also claims that James's utterance doesn't mean that God isn't against premarital sex as he doesn't even believe in God. James must therefore be talking about something other than what God commands.

6.55 As a result, in this exchange Margaret would be talking about God's commands and James about something completely different. The problem is that this would make the previous exchange a lot like this:

MARGARET: The weather is fine.
JAMES: No, the traffic is bad.

In this case there's no disagreement between Margaret and James; they are talking about different things.

This case illustrates how you can't have a disagreement unless the words in your mouth mean the same as they mean for other people. Yet, in the previous case there was a disagreement between Margaret and James about whether premarital sex is wrong. Because of this, the divine command theory can't be a theory of what believers mean when they use moral words. 6.56

Divine command theory and moral properties

What is the divine command theory about, then, if it isn't about what moral words mean? The most charitable way to understand this theory is to see it as an account of the nature of moral properties. If an act is right, it has the property of being right. Divine command theory is a theory of what this property is like. This view is not interested in what the word "right" means, but rather what it is for an act to be right. This is a **metaphysical question**[37] about the world. 6.57

Robert Merrihew Adams has formulated an improved version of the divine command theory along these lines (**Adams, 1979**).[38] According to him, the divine command theory reveals the fundamental nature of moral properties. What moral properties consist of is, on this view, captured by the following type of claims: 6.58

- For an act to be right is for it to be an act which God commands us to do.
- For an act to be wrong is for it to be contrary to God's commands.

This proposal solves the problems of the previous versions of the divine command theory. Adams's view is neutral about what you mean when you say that an act is wrong. It can recognize that when believers, atheists, agnostics, Christians, Muslims, and polytheists discuss what is right and wrong they use the words "right" and "wrong" with the same meaning. Because of this, everyone will talk about the same topic and this in turn allows people to have genuine moral disagreements. 6.59

According to the resulting view, when you call an act "wrong," you mean that this act should not be done and that we should blame people for doing it. In fact, this is what everyone means when they talk about right and wrong. When you use the word "wrong" in this sense you also manage to refer to a certain property of acts in virtue of which the act should not be 6.60

done. The divine command theory is then supposed explain what this property is like. The quality of acts you pick out when you talk about wrong acts is that God commands us not to do these acts. If wrong acts were like this, then the wrongness of acts would explain why we should not do the wrong thing and why we should be blamed for acting wrongly.

6.61 This story allows Adams to say that even non-believers use moral words with the same meaning as religious people. Because of this, they need not be conceptually confused. Atheists might have mistaken beliefs about which acts are right and wrong and why, but this is no worse than someone having mistaken beliefs about many other things.

Advantages of divine command theory

6.62 The first good thing about the divine command theory is that it can explain nicely how you can know what is right and wrong. Because God is infinitely good and loving He reveals His commands to us through **revelation**.[39] God communicates to us what is right and wrong because He wants us to follow His commands. Of course, this still leaves us with many questions of divine revelation itself. How do we know how God's commands should be interpreted? How do we know which one of the conflicting religious texts is the unique source of divine revelations? These are, admittedly, pressing questions, but at least in principle the divine command theory can tell us a story of how we can know what is right and wrong.

6.63 Secondly, divine command theory can at least attempt to explain the so-called **normativity**[40] of moral properties. This quality of moral properties is difficult to pin down. J.L. Mackie famously argued that moral properties are magnetic (**Mackie, 1977, ch. 1, sect.** 7).[41] Acts which are right have "to-be-doneness" built into them, because you are required to do these acts by their very nature. Likewise, wrong acts have "to-be-avoidedness" built into them – there is a categorical requirement not to do these acts.

6.64 The divine command theory can explain why right and wrong acts have such normative "oomph." According to this theory, the to-be-doneness of right acts is based on our relation to God and, more specifically, on God's authority and the debt we owe to Him (**Swinburne, 2008**).[42] The suggestion is that you can understand our relationship to God by considering the relationship between parents and their children. Parents have authority over their young children. Young children should obey their parents because the parents know better, they love their children, and they are responsible for their existence and well-being.

Divine command theorists can use this model to explain how God has 6.65
authority over us and therefore also why His commands are normative for us in the same way. If God's commands are normative for us, then right and wrong must be normative for us too. This is even before we have said anything about Heaven and Hell. Admittedly, this story too raises difficult questions. We can ask how helpful the parenthood analogy is for understanding what our debt to God could be. We can also ask what the source of the requirement to repay our debts to God is. The answer to this question can't be that God just demands us to repay our debts to Him, or we face a vicious circle. But at the very least, the divine command theory has introduced a distinct way of thinking about normativity of moral properties that is recognizable from the familiar analogy of families.

The Euthyphro Dilemma*

The end of the previous section showed that the divine command theory 6.66
has many advantages. This final section will explain the most famous and powerful objection it. This objection is so good that even many believers reject the idea that morality is based on God's commands.

The Euthyphro dilemma was first formulated 2400 years ago by **Plato** 6.67
in a dialogue entitled ***Euthyphro***, which gives this objection its name (Plato, circa 380 BC).[43] You can also find discussions of similar arguments in the writings of **Gottfried Leibniz** and **Ralph Cudworth** (**Leibniz, 1686, sect. 2**; **Cudworth, 1731, book I, ch. 2**).[44] The following will be a sketch of how the objection is usually understood today. There is some **controversy**[45] about whether this is the argument which Plato had in mind in his original dialogue.

If you accept the divine command theory, you have to think that there 6.68
is a strong correlation between two properties. You are committed to the idea that all and only the acts which God commands us to do are right. Any act that is right is an act which God commands us to do, and any act that God commands us to do is right. So far, the divine command theory only says that two properties – right and what God commands – always come together. They are perfectly correlated.

6.69 This could not be merely a coincidence. We will need to explain why the correlation between the two properties holds. There are two alternatives. The first is:

A. God commands us to do certain acts because these acts are right.

The second alternative is to think that:

B. Some acts are right because God commands us to do them.

Therefore, either God's commands explain why certain acts are right (B), or facts about which acts are right explain what God commands us to do (A). The Euthyphro dilemma is **a dilemma**[46] because both of these alternatives are problematic for the divine command theory. Whichever way you explain the correlation between the two properties there is bad news for the view.

What is right explains what God commands*

6.70 Let us consider option (A) first. If you accept this option, you will think that God commands us to do certain acts because they are right. The problem is that this is not really faithful to the spirit of the divine command theory. You are now assuming that there are right and wrong acts first. You then think that God sees which acts are right and because of this He commands us to do them. However, in this case God is not a part of the explanation of what it is for acts to be right. After all, some acts are right independently of Him.

6.71 God could still be argued to serve an important function in ethics. It could be claimed that His commands offer us additional information about what is right and wrong. God could also give you additional incentives for doing the right thing. But as far as we focus on metaethics and the nature of moral properties, God would in this case play a lesser role.

God's commands explain what is right*

6.72 Your second alternative is to think that right acts are right just because God commands us to do them. On this view, we use facts about God's commands to explain what it is for some acts to be right. This fits how the divine command theory was formulated above. The suggestion was that for an act to be right just is for it to be what God commands you to do. On this alternative an act is right only because God commands you to do it.

Therefore, if you choose this horn of the dilemma, you must think that acts are not initially right or wrong at all. God then comes on the scene and commands us to do certain acts. As a result, some acts become the right thing to do and others the wrong thing to do. This horn of the dilemma leads to three famous problems (**Miller, C., 2013**).[47] 6.73

Problem 1: God's goodness First of all, this alternative makes God's own goodness a mystery (Alston, 1989, p. 255). Most people who believe in God think that He is perfectly good. If you believe in God, how should you understand this property of God if you think that things are good and right because of God's commands? 6.74

Some divine command theorists argue that the property of goodness exists independently of God even if right and wrong are based on God's commands. This more restricted divine command theory therefore relies on a separate theory of goodness that is not connected to what God commands. This leads to the question: if good is independent of God's commands, why couldn't right and wrong be independent of His commands too? 6.75

The second alternative is to accept that God's goodness too is based on God's commands. This would help you to understand good and right in the same way. However, it is not plausible that God is good because of God's commands. God can't be good because He commands Himself to be in a certain way. Because of this, there is no plausible way to understand God's goodness if you think that acts are right because God commands us to do them. 6.76

Problem 2: Anything could be wrong The second problem with thinking that acts are right because God commands us to do them is that any act could be right (Quinn, 2000, p. 70). Recall that according to this view, no act is right before God commands us to do it. God then commands us to do certain acts and as a result these acts become the right thing to do. If God had commanded us to do some other acts, then these acts would have been right. If He commanded us to boil newborn babies alive, then doing so would have been the right thing to do. 6.77

Some theist philosophers have accepted this implication. **St. Augustine** wrote in the ***City of God*** that murdering another person is the right thing to do when God commands you to do it (**St. Augustine, circa 420 AD, book I, ch. 21**).[48] For most of us this is too big a **bullet to bite**.[49] Surely 6.78

there are some acts that could not be morally right even if God commanded you to do them. Horrible acts like killing newborn babies for fun by boiling them alive could not be morally right even if God told you to do them.

6.79 *Problem 3: The reasons for God's commands* The final problem is that plausible answers to the previous objection lead only to further problems (Timmons, 2002, pp. 29–30). Suppose that someone claims that it is not the case that anything could be right or wrong because God could never act on a whim. As a perfectly rational being, He always acts and issues commands for good reasons. And given the reasons He has, certain things just had to become right and wrong. What's wrong with this response to the previous challenge?

6.80 The problem is that this response makes God's commands redundant. If God has good reasons to command you not to do certain acts because they are unfair or hurt others, then you already would have good reasons not to do these acts. You too should care about unfairness and avoiding hurting others for exactly the same reasons as God. Therefore whatever reasons God has to command certain acts, these reasons are also why you should act in those ways. This means that whatever reasons God has for His commands, these same considerations make it right for us to do the relevant acts. This means that if God has good reasons to issue His commands, He is no longer needed as the ultimate source of morality.

6.81 So, to summarize, acts can't be right *because* God commands you to do them because:

i. this would make God's own goodness mysterious;
ii. any act could be right if God commanded you to do it; and
iii. if God's commands are not mere whims, then his commands are redundant as we already share His reasons.

It is more plausible to believe that God commands us to do certain acts because they are right. The only weakness of this conclusion is that this doesn't allow you to use God's commands to explain what it is for acts to be right. Either way of looking at the divine command theory, it fails.

Summary and Questions

6.82 This chapter has explored three metaethical theories: subjectivism, relativism, and the divine command theory. The first two of these theories are attempts to explain what moral words mean. These views say that when you claim that an act is right you mean either that you approve of the act or that your society approves of it. These widely held views have many attractive features. They fit the idea that different people have different moral views, they make moral properties less mysterious, and they can also explain how we know what is right and why we care about this. A lot can be said for these views.

We then saw why most philosophers do not accept these metaethical views. First of all, they don't seem to fit our everyday moral experiences. We often come to be in favor of acts because we think that they are right. We also do not think that information about what people approve of is good evidence for what is right. Perhaps the most serious problem with these views, however, is that they do not leave room for ordinary moral disagreements. 6.83

The last sections of this chapter then investigated the divine command theory. This theory is not about the meaning of moral words but rather about what it is for acts to be right. This view too has many attractions, but you should only accept it if you can give a good response to the Euthyphro dilemma. 6.84

Based on the philosophical resources introduced in this chapter, consider the following questions: 6.85

1. Which basic idea motivates subjectivism, relativism, and the divine command theory? How plausible is this foundation?
2. How do subjectivists and relativists analyze the following claims:
   i. It is wrong to eat meat.
   ii. Mao should not have started the Great Leap Forward.
   iii. You should help the poor.
3. Use examples to explain why moral disagreements are a problem for subjectivists and relativists. Can you think of a response to this objection?
4. Does subjectivism or relativism fit better the idea that we usually want to do what we think is right?
5. How should divine command theorists attempt to tackle the Euthyphro dilemma?

Annotated Bibliography

Adams, Robert Merrihew (1979) "Divine Command Metaethics Modified," *Journal of Religious Ethics*, 7(1), 66–79, full text available at http://

commonsenseatheism.com/wp-content/uploads/2010/03/Adams-Divine-Command-Metaethics-Modified-Again.pdf, accessed March 3, 2014. An influential article in which Adams uses the tools of contemporary philosophy of language and metaphysics to formulate a new, attractive version of the divine command theory.

Alston, William (1989) "Some Suggestions for Divine Command Theorists," in *Christian Theism and the Problems of Philosophy*, ed. Michael Beaty (Notre Dame: University of Notre Dame Press), pp. 303–326. According to Alston, the divine command theory is only a theory about our obligations in terms of God's commands. However, he thinks that you can avoid the arbitrariness objection by assuming that God is perfectly good. God's goodness is then basic – something that cannot be explained in any way.

Anscombe, G.E.M. (1958) "Modern Moral Philosophy." See bibliography to Chapter 5 above.

Benedict, Ruth (1946) *Patterns of Culture* (New York: Penguin). A famous work in anthropology which uses empirical evidence to show that each culture has its own more or less consistent sets of values and moral constraints, which can only be understood holistically by taking part in the culture's way of life.

Boghossian, Paul (2006) "What is Relativism?," in *Truth and Relativism*, ed. Patrick Greenough and Michael Lynch (Oxford: Oxford University Press), pp. 13–37, full text available at http://as.nyu.edu/docs/IO/1153/whatisrel.pdf, accessed March 3, 2014. A very helpful attempt to clarify how relativist views in philosophy should be formulated and what the main problems with such views are.

Cudworth, Ralph (1731) *A Treatise concerning Eternal and Immutable Morality*, excerpts available at http://oll.libertyfund.org/?option=com_staticxt&staticfile=show.php%3Ftitle=2077&chapter=157715&layout=html&Itemid=27, accessed March 3, 2014. A short early book which has had a huge influence on the development of British moral philosophy in the intuitionist tradition. According to Cudworth, right and wrong exist as eternal, immutable, and self-subsisting ideas in God's mind. God did not create these ideas but merely communicates them to us. This work also contains a powerful formulation of the Euthyphro objection to voluntarist theological views.

Dreier, Jamie (1990) "Internalism and Speaker Relativism," *Ethics*, *101*(1), 6–26, full text available at http://www.brown.edu/Departments/Philosophy/onlinepapers/dreier/Internalism_and_Speaker_Relativism.pdf, accessed March 3, 2014. An influential paper which revived subjectivism in metaethics with a sophisticated formulation of the theory, which avoids many problems of the previous versions. Dreier uses the model of indexical words to understand how moral words function.

Fischer, Andrew (2011) *Metaethics: An Introduction* (Durham: Acumen). This is perhaps the clearest and most accessible textbook on metaethics at the moment.

Harman, Gilbert (1975) "Moral Relativism Defended," *Philosophical Review*, *84*(1), 3–22, full text available at http://www.jstor.org/stable/2184078?origin=crossref, accessed March 10, 2014. A classic defense of moral relativism, which argues that moral judgments are a type of inner judgments which are relative to the motives shared by the speakers.

Hart, H.L.A. (1961) *The Concept of Law* (Oxford: Clarendon Press). A classic work in philosophy of law, which is famous for its defense of legal positivism, according to which laws are manmade social rules.

Hobbes, Thomas (1660) *The Leviathan*. See the bibliography of Chapter 3 above.

Kirchin, Simon (2012) *Metaethics* (Basingstoke: Palgrave Macmillan). A reasonably accessible and opinionated metaethics textbook. Kirchin defends a view according to which values should be understood with the model of colors.

LaFollette, Hugh (1991) "The Truth in Ethical Relativism," *Journal of Social Philosophy*, *22*(1), 146–154, full text available at http://www.hughlafollette.com/papers/RELATIVE.HTM, accessed March 3, 2014. An accessible article which explains nicely the advantages of relativism in ethics.

Leibniz, G.W. (1686) *Discourse on Metaphysics*, full text available at http://www.webpages.uidaho.edu/mickelsen/texts/leibniz%20-%20discourse%20on%20metaphysics.htm#II, accessed March 3, 2014. A famous short and theoretical piece of early modern period rationalist metaphysics. Leibniz discusses the nature of physical substance, motion, and minds in the theistic framework. The first sections introduce and attempt to respond to the Euthyphro dilemma.

Mackie, J.L. (1977) *Ethics: Inventing Right and Wrong* (London: Penguin). Chapter 1 available at http://www2.arnes.si/~supmpotr/mackie.pdf, accessed March 3, 2014. A classic book in which Mackie defends moral error theory according to which moral claims are uniformly false.

Miller, Alexander (2013) *Contemporary Metaethics: An Introduction*, 2nd ed. (Cambridge: Polity). An advanced and comprehensive textbook on contemporary metaethics. Required reading for all serious students of the subject.

Miller, Christian (2013) "Euthyphro Dilemma," in *The International Encyclopedia of Ethics*, ed. Hugh LaFollette (Oxford: Wiley-Blackwell), pp. 1785–1791, full text available at http://users.wfu.edu/millerc/Euthyphro.pdf, accessed March 3, 2014. A very clear overview article on the Euthyphro dilemma and the main responses to it, which also contains a comprehensive bibliography for further reading.

Moore, G.E. (1922) "The Nature of Moral Philosophy," in his *Philosophical Studies* (London: Routledge & Kegan Paul), pp. 310–339, full text available at http://www.ditext.com/moore/nmp.html, accessed March 3, 2014. Moore's lecture on ethics for a general audience in which he discusses obligations and

Aristotle's views about happiness. The end of the article also contains an early formulation of the powerful disagreement argument against subjectivism and relativism.

Plato (circa 380 BC) *Euthyphro*, full text available at http://classics.mit.edu/Plato/euthyfro.html, accessed March 3, 2014. A classic dialogue on the nature of piety. Different definitions of piety are introduced by Euthyphro and then found wanting by Socrates. The dialogue is famous for its argument against theism in moral philosophy.

Pojman, Louis (2000) "Who's to Judge?," in *Vice and Virtue in Everyday Life: Introductory Readings in Ethics*, ed. Christina Sommers and Frederic Summers (San Diego: Hartcourt College Publishers), pp. 238–251, full text available at http://www.nyu.edu/classes/gmoran/POJMAN.pdf, accessed March 3, 2014. An accessible critical discussion of both relativism and subjectivism.

Quinn, Philip (2000) "Divine Command Theory," in *The Blackwell Guide to Ethical Theory*, ed. Hugh LaFollette (Oxford: Blackwell), pp. 53–73. An accessible overview discussion of the divine command theory.

Shafer-Landau, Russ (2004) *Whatever Happened to Good and Evil?* (Oxford: Oxford University Press). A wonderful short book defending moral realism against subjectivism, relativism, and other forms of nihilism. Very entertaining and requires no philosophical background. Highly recommended reading for this chapter.

St. Augustine (circa 420 ad) *The City of God*, full text available at http://www.newadvent.org/fathers/1201.htm, accessed March 3, 2014. A work of early theology which investigates Christianity's relation to other religions and secular powers. According to St. Augustine, we can distinguish between the state and the church, the love of the self and the love of God, and the resulting City of Man and City of God. Good Christians must serve the City of God. This book also contains interesting discussions of the Euthyphro problem and just war theory.

Swinburne, Richard (2008) "God and Morality," *Think*, *7*(20), 7–15, full text available at http://users.ox.ac.uk/~orie0087/pdf_files/General%20untechnical%20papers/God%20and%20Morality.pdf, accessed March 3, 2014. A fairly accessible attempt to explain why and how the existence of God affects what moral truths there are. Requires some background knowledge of metaethics.

Timmons, Mark (2002) *Moral Theory: An Introduction* (Lanham: Rowman & Littlefield). An advanced and thorough textbook on ethical theories which has very useful chapters on both the divine command theory and relativism.

Wieranga, Edward (1983) "A Defensible Divine Command Theory," *Noûs*, *17*(3): 387–407, full text available at http://www.commonsenseatheism.com/wp-content/uploads/2009/09/Wierenga-A-defensible-divine-command-theory.pdf, accessed March 3, 2014. According to Wieranga's view, we should not understand the divine command theory as an account of the meaning of moral words but rather as an account of what makes acts right and wrong. He then argues that the theory understood in this way can avoid many problems with the more traditional versions of the theory.

Online Resources

1 An overview article on metaethics: http://plato.stanford.edu/entries/metaethics/.
2 Another overview of metaethics: http://www.iep.utm.edu/metaethi/.
3 A great discussion on this question between David Enoch and Mark Schroeder: http://www.philostv.com/david-enoch-and-mark-schroeder-2/
4 Joshua Knobe's experimental work on whether ordinary people believe in objective moral facts: http://onthehuman.org/2010/12/objective-moral-truths/.
5 In her classic paper, Anscombe criticizes modern moral theories for using the moral law model without a law-maker: http://www.pitt.edu/~mthompso/readings/mmp.pdf.
6 A very basic explanation of subjectivism: http://www.bbc.co.uk/ethics/introduction/subjectivism.shtml.
7 A more thorough introduction of relativism: http://plato.stanford.edu/entries/moral-relativism/.
8 An explanation of divine command theories under the label "theological voluntarism": http://plato.stanford.edu/entries/voluntarism-theological/.
9 Jamie Dreier's article "Internalism and Speaker Relativism": http://www.brown.edu/Departments/Philosophy/onlinepapers/dreier/Internalism_and_Speaker_Relativism.pdf.
10 Life and works of Hobbes: http://plato.stanford.edu/entries/hobbes/ and Chapter 6 of his *Leviathan*: http://ebooks.adelaide.edu.au/h/hobbes/thomas/h68l/chapter6.html.
11 Some famous philosophers just love this example: http://www.philosophy.ox.ac.uk/__data/assets/word_doc/0016/1933/Crispin_Wright_paper.doc.
12 Christopher Hitchens trying waterboarding: http://www.youtube.com/watch?v=4LPubUCJv58.
13 An overview of philosophical discussions about moral motivation: http://plato.stanford.edu/entries/moral-motivation/.
14 A video of mink farming: http://www.youtube.com/watch?v=wbb9agOXGt8.
15 Interesting article on the moral conversion with regard to slavery: http://www.huffingtonpost.com/matt-j-rossano/religion-and-abolishing-slavery_b_951048.html.
16 An overview of ethics of cloning: http://repository.upenn.edu/cgi/viewcontent.cgi?article=1034&context=bioethics_papers.

17 James Rachels on subjectivism: http://tinyurl.com/p3pk7ue.

18 G.E. Moore's article "The Nature of Moral Philosophy": http://www.ditext.com/moore/nmp.html.

19 An overview article on moral relativism: http://plato.stanford.edu/entries/moral-relativism/, Gilbert Harman's "Moral Relativism Defended": http://www.jstor.org/stable/2184078?origin=crossref, and Hugh LaFollette's "The Truth in Ethical Relativism": http://www.hughlafollette.com/papers/RELATIVE.HTM.

20 Paul Boghossian discussing how moral relativism should be formulated: http://philosophybites.com/2011/10/paul-boghossian-on-moral-relativism.html and Boghossian's article "What is Relativism?": http://as.nyu.edu/docs/IO/1153/whatisrel.pdf.

21 You can even take part in such studies yourself online: http://www.yourmorals.org/.

22 As this PhD thesis by Heather M. Jeffers shows: http://cardinalscholar.bsu.edu/bitstream/123456789/196140/1/JeffersH_2012-3_BODY.pdf.

23 Explanation of cultural relativism: http://en.wikipedia.org/wiki/Cultural_relativism.

24 A guide to tipping in different countries: http://www.cntraveler.com/travel-tips/travel-etiquette/2008/12/Etiquette-101-Tipping-Guide.

25 Simon Blackburn discussing problems of relativism: http://philosophybites.libsyn.com/simon_blackburn_on_moral_relativism.

26 Wikipedia on female mutilation: http://en.wikipedia.org/wiki/Female_genital_mutilation.

27 Louis Pojman's article "Who's to Judge?": http://www.nyu.edu/classes/gmoran/POJMAN.pdf.

28 Interesting statistics about Armenians' attitudes towards gays: http://globalvoicesonline.org/2012/06/29/armenia-intolerant-society/.

29 Explanation of what saunas are: http://en.wikipedia.org/wiki/Sauna.

30 Finnish sauna traditions: http://www.bbc.co.uk/news/magazine-24328773.

31 Wikihow on how to use a sauna safely asks you to wear suitable attire: http://www.wikihow.com/Use-a-Sauna-Safely.

32 Wikipedia on God: http://en.wikipedia.org/wiki/God.

33 An overview article on divine command theory: http://www.iep.utm.edu/divine-c/, Robert Merrihew Adams's article "Divine Command Metaethics Modified Again": http://commonsenseatheism.com/wp-content/uploads/2010/03/Adams-Divine-Command-Metaethics-Modified-Again.pdf, and Edward Wieranga's article "A Defensible Divine Command Theory": http://www.commonsenseatheism.com/wp-content/uploads/2009/09/Wierenga-A-defensible-divine-command-theory.pdf.

34 An interesting debate between Shelly Kagan and William Lane Graig on this very topic: http://www.youtube.com/watch?v=SiJnCQuPiuo.

35 Link to Adams's article: http://commonsenseatheism.com/wp-content/uploads/2010/03/Adams-Divine-Command-Metaethics-Modified-Again.pdf.

36 Definition of atheism: https://en.wikipedia.org/wiki/Atheism and polytheism: https://en.wikipedia.org/wiki/Polytheism.

37 An overview of what metaphysics is: http://plato.stanford.edu/entries/metaphysics/.

38 Adams's article on divine command theory: http://commonsenseatheism.com/wp-content/uploads/2010/03/Adams-Divine-Command-Metaethics-Modified-Again.pdf.

39 Wikipedia on revelations: http://en.wikipedia.org/wiki/Revelation.

40 An overview of recent philosophical work on normativity: http://analysis.oxfordjournals.org/content/70/2/331.full.pdf?keytype=ref&ijkey=Q50DmwsULURmO5j.

41 Chapter 1 of Mackie's *Ethics: Inventing Right and Wrong*: http://www2.arnes.si/~supmpotr/mackie.pdf.

42 Richard Swinburne on God and the requirements of morality: http://users.ox.ac.uk/~orie0087/pdf_files/General%20untechnical%20papers/God%20and%20Morality.pdf.

43 Christian Miller's helpful overview article on the subject: http://users.wfu.edu/millerc/Euthyphro.pdf, the life and works of Plato: http://plato.stanford.edu/, and Plato's dialogue: http://classics.mit.edu/Plato/euthyfro.html.

44 The life and works of Leibniz: http://plato.stanford.edu/entries/leibniz/, his *Discourse on Metaphysics*: http://www.webpages.uidaho.edu/mickelsen/texts/leibniz%20-%20discourse%20on%20metaphysics.htm#II, the life and works of Ralph Cudworth: http://en.wikipedia.org/wiki/Ralph_Cudworth, and his *Treatise concerning Eternal and Immutable Morality*: http://oll.libertyfund.org/?option=com_staticxt&staticfile=show.php%3Ftitle=2077&chapter=157715&layout=html&Itemid=27.

45 A podcast on the Euthyphro dilemma which discusses this question too: http://www.partiallyexaminedlife.com/2011/11/16/episode-46-plato-on-ethics-religion/.

46 An explanation of what dilemmas are: https://en.wikipedia.org/wiki/Dilemma.

47 Christian Miller's article "Euthyphro Dilemma": http://users.wfu.edu/millerc/Euthyphro.pdf.

48 Information about St. Augustine: http://en.wikipedia.org/wiki/Augustine_of_Hippo, about the *City of God*: http://en.wikipedia.org/wiki/City_of_God_(book), and Book I of the book: http://www.newadvent.org/fathers/120101.htm.

49 A phrase many philosophers are fond of: http://en.wikipedia.org/wiki/Bite_the_bullet.

7

NATURALISM AND THE OPEN QUESTION ARGUMENT

For the reasons explained in the previous chapter, very few metaethicists are subjectivists, relativists, or divine command theorists. Most metaethicists reject the idea that the source of moral requirements is what people approve of or what God commands. If these views are not plausible, what other alternatives do you have? This chapter will discuss a metaethical theory called **moral realism** whereas the next chapter will discuss **expressivism**. 7.1

Moral Realism

If you didn't like the views discussed in the previous chapter, then you might accept that certain acts just are right in themselves. According to this view, acts are not right because you approve of them or because God tells you to do them. Instead, some acts just have the property of being right. In order to understand what this property is like, you shouldn't think about anything else other than the act itself and its basic qualities. **Moral realism**[1] is therefore the view in metaethics that right and wrong are mind-independent moral properties. To say that these properties are mind-independent means that whether an act is right or wrong doesn't depend on what anyone thinks of the act. 7.2

There are many other properties that do not depend on what you approve of or on what God commands you to do. Some objects are heavy, some move fast, and some are composed of carbon atoms. Likewise, some acts only last 7.3

This Is Ethics: An Introduction, First Edition. Jussi Suikkanen.

for ten seconds, some require a lot of effort, and others take place only in the evenings. None of this depends on what you think. Moral realists believe that moral properties similarly do not depend on what you think.

Naturalism vs. non-naturalism

7.4 **One fundamental debate in metaethics**[2] accepts this idea that some acts have the property of being the right thing to do exactly like some objects are composed of carbon atoms. Both of these properties exist, objectively speaking. The different sides in this debate disagree about the nature of these moral properties.

7.5 Both sides in this disagreement believe that all acts have a number of basic properties, which are often called **natural properties**. These properties include many familiar properties such as the ones mentioned above: acts last a certain length of time or they are typically done at a certain time of the day or by a certain group of people.

7.6 When philosophers talk about natural properties, they tend to talk about properties that have three distinguishing features (**Moore, 1903, ch. 2, sect. 26**; **Lewis, 1983, sect. 2**; **Copp, 2003**).[3] Natural properties can be:

i. observed empirically;
ii. studied scientifically;
iii. and the having of them can cause other things to happen.

Therefore, how long an act lasts is one of its natural properties: you can observe how long an act lasts, you can measure this by scientific instruments, and the duration of an act can, for example, cause you to be bored. It is worth adding that not all naturalists think that natural properties have all these three properties. Some naturalists think that a property is a natural property merely in virtue of being something we can observe. These philosophers do not think that natural properties must always be something you can study scientifically.

7.7 The so-called **naturalists in metaethics**[4] believe that moral properties like right and wrong are natural properties. According to naturalists, you can observe and study scientifically which acts are right and what it is for these acts to be right. Naturalists also think that right and wrong can make a real difference to what happens in the world. The wrongness of a public policy such as **slavery**[5] can, for example, cause people to protest against it (Sturgeon, 1988, p. 245).

Different naturalists defend different views about which natural proper- 7.8
ties rightness and wrongness are. Some naturalists, for example, believe that for an act to be right is for it to maximize the amount of happiness (**Mill, 1861, ch. 4, para. 9**).[6] Other naturalists believe that the rightness of an act consists of the fact that you would want to desire to do the act if you vividly imagined what would happen as a result (**Lewis, 1989**).[7] If these views were right, then you could learn which acts are right through empirical investigation. You could test empirically which acts tend to promote happiness and what you would want to desire if you vividly imagined the consequences of your actions.

In contrast, **non-naturalists in metaethics**[8] deny that moral properties 7.9
are natural properties (Dancy, 2006). They think that there are properties that are completely different in kind and that moral properties are that type of properties. It is easy to approach this view with the following illustration. Consider a situation in which **God creates a new universe**.[9] He first creates all the physical particles of the new world. This time God wants to create a clone of our own universe and so He creates in the new universe an identical twin for every atom of our universe. He also arranges these atoms in the same way as the atoms are arranged in our universe. After all this, God has a break.

At this point, the new universe will have its natural properties. It will 7.10
contain physical objects like tables, cars, and lions and these objects will have properties like a specific mass, an electric charge, and a size. However, according to the non-naturalists, nothing in this world will yet be right or wrong because so far God has only created the natural properties. They think that, after His break, God would have to add right and wrong to this world, because they are non-natural properties.

Most non-naturalists do not believe that the universe or its moral 7.11
properties were created by God. They think that moral properties just happen to exist as an additional part of our universe in the same way as **the Big Bang**[10] just happened. Non-naturalists also believe that these new non-natural properties are different in kind. They can't be empirically observed, you can't study them scientifically, and they can't cause anything to happen.

Pros and cons of non-naturalism

An example from Gilbert Harman illustrates the advantages of non- 7.12
naturalism nicely (**Harman, 1977**).[11] Imagine that you are walking home

from a party when you suddenly see a group of kids setting a cat on fire. You might be tempted to say that you could just see that this act is wrong, but this way of talking must be highly metaphorical. What you really see is the kids, the cat, the petrol, and the cat catching fire, but you do not see the wrongness of it all. **What you see just makes you think that the act in question is wrong.**[12]

7.13 The same goes for science. Scientific instruments like **the huge particle accelerators**[13] do not detect right and wrong and chemistry textbooks do not have chapters on moral properties. Moral properties do not seem to be needed in causal explanations either. Do you really need to explain why people protest against a policy by how unjust the policy is? It seems as though you could always find better and more basic explanations in these cases. Perhaps people protest against the policy because it discriminates arbitrarily against certain groups or because it makes so many people poor and these are things they don't want to happen. These are basic natural properties that seem to suffice for explaining why the protests happened. There's no need to mention any additional moral qualities of the protests (admittedly, some naturalists think that we should, exactly for this reason, think that moral properties just are natural properties of the type that can influence what happens).

7.14 Moral properties therefore seem to be very different from natural properties since it doesn't seem as if these properties cause anything to happen. Non-naturalists believe that this means that moral properties must be of their own unique kind (**Moore, 1903, ch. 1, sect. 15**).[14] This supports the idea that you can't use science to investigate what is right and wrong. Yet it is not enough to say that moral properties are not like natural properties. You want to know: what *are* they like, then?

7.15 Non-naturalists struggle to give an informative answer to this question. They often say that **normativity**[15] makes moral properties unique and special (Dancy, 2006, pp. 132–142). This is the idea that, unlike other properties, moral properties have a certain authority to require that you act in certain ways. For example, the fact that it is wrong to lie to other people requires you to not do so. But explaining what this ability to require consists of is equally difficult.

7.16 The best that philosophers have come up with has been to say that moral properties have unique **practical relevance** – they directly bear on what you are to do. In contrast, whether a natural property bears on what you are to do is always a further fact about the natural property on this view. If what you do is wrong, then you are not to act in that way, whereas if you are considering making other people laugh, this as such leaves it open what you are to do.

The second problem with non-naturalism is that it is mysterious 7.17
how you could ever know[16] what's right and wrong if these were non-natural properties. According to this view, moral properties don't cause anything to happen and they can't be empirically observed or studied scientifically. Therefore, how could you know which acts have these properties?

Before we tackle these problems of non-naturalism, let us first look 7.18
at G.E. Moore's hugely influential **Open Question Argument** *for* non-naturalism (**Moore, 1903, ch. 1, sect. 13**; Feldman, 2005).[17] This argument attempts to show that moral properties must be simple non-natural properties of their own kind. As will be explained below, this argument too has its problems. Despite these problems the argument continues to be important in metaethics since all theories must still be able to give an explanation of the powerful intuitions behind it.

The Open Question Argument

One simple distinction plays a crucial role in the Open Question Argu- 7.19
ment. On one side of this distinction is the world in which you live. It is populated by concrete objects such as **Barack Obama, the Eiffel Tower,**[18] and your teeth. The properties of these objects are also part of the world. Barack Obama is tall, the Eiffel Tower is made of iron, and your teeth can bite.

These worldly objects and their properties must be distinguished from 7.20
the language you use to describe them. The basic units of language are words and sentences. **These words and sentences have meaning and they refer to the objects and properties in the world.**[19] In philosophy it is extremely important to keep track of when you are talking about the world (and its objects and properties) and when you are talking about language (and its words and sentences).

Philosophers have devised a convention that helps you to keep track of 7.21
this. You should use quotation marks when you talk about words. It is therefore correct to write that the word "red" has three letters. Here I have mentioned the word "red" and described its quality of having three letters. In contrast, when you talk about the world you should not use quotation marks (except when you are quoting other people). Therefore, it is correct

to write that red is one of the three basic colors, but "red" is not colored – it is a word and thus has no particular color.

7.22 With this distinction in mind, we can return to **G.E. Moore**'s famous argument, which you can find in the first chapter of Moore's ***Principia Ethica***.[20] It is worth knowing that even if the Open Question Argument is usually attributed to Moore, many other philosophers before him had presented similar arguments against naturalism (**Price, 1758, ch. 1, sect. 1; Sidgwick, 1889, 480–483**).[21]

Stage 1: Words and properties

7.23 Moore's argument begins with an assumption about words. They have two essential properties – **meaning** and **reference**. The meaning of a word is roughly what you have in mind when you are using the word. When you use the word "ice-cream," you might have in mind an idea of a frozen dessert which is made out of dairy products and which you can buy from a van or a supermarket. This is what the word means according to this simple view (**Locke, 1690, book III, chs 1–2**).[22]

7.24 Words also have a reference. The reference of a word is an object, property, or substance which the word picks out. In Paris, there is a tall iron building which was constructed in 1889. This object is the reference of the words "the Eiffel Tower."

7.25 The basic assumption behind the Open Question Argument is that the meaning of a word determines what the word refers to. People have a certain idea in their mind when they use the word "snow": it's something cold and white and it falls from the sky in the winter. Because we have this idea in mind when we use this word, it refers to a certain substance that covers the ground in the winter. The reference of a word is thus whatever satisfies the idea we have in our mind when we use the word.

7.26 This assumption has an implication which is the first premise of Moore's argument:

> Premise 1: Two seemingly different properties are in fact one and the same property only if two words that are used to talk about these properties have the same meaning.

To see the point of this premise, consider the word "grandmother," which means the same as the words "mother's or father's mother" because you have the same ideas in mind when you use these words. This is why "mother's or father's mother" is the correct definition of the word "grandmother." Moore's first premise then says that, because of this, the properties of being a grandmother and being a mother's or father's mother must be one and the same property.

Moore thought that this premise follows from the earlier assumption. If you assume that what words refer to is determined by what you have in mind when you use them, then it is easy to think that if you have two different ideas in mind when you use two words then these words must stand for different things. Likewise, if you have the same idea in mind when you use two different words, then presumably these words must refer to the same thing. 7.27

Stage 2: Moral words and moral properties

The first stage of Moore's argument has an important consequence for ethics. It means that: 7.28

> Premise 2: A moral property such as the property of being good can be a natural property only if the word "good" means the same as some words which we use to talk about natural properties.

It follows from this premise that the property of being good can be a natural property only if the word "good" means the same as the words "whatever maximizes the amount of happiness" or "whatever you want to desire in the circumstances in which you vividly imagine the consequences of your options" or the like. In terms of definitions, the second premise of Moore's argument states that the property of being good is a natural property only if the word "good" can be correctly defined by using words which pick out natural properties.

Stage 3: The open question test

The third stage of Moore's argument gives you a test which you can use to see whether two words mean the same thing or not. If a good definition captures the correct meaning of the analyzed word, then this is also a test for the correctness of definitions. The Open Question Argument bears the name of this test. 7.29

Imagine that someone claims that the words "brother" and "male sibling" mean the same. Here is how Moore's test is supposed to work. You are 7.30

supposed to first take an object that satisfies the suggested definition. So let us assume that Richard is your male sibling. Moore then suggested that in this situation you should consider the question: "Richard is your male sibling, but is he your brother?"

7.31 Can you begin to consider how you should answer this question? Moore thought that if you can't, then this question is closed. He then claimed that if this question is closed then the words "brother" and "male sibling" must mean the same. The explanation for this is that when you use the words "male sibling" in the first part of the question you attach one idea to Richard in your mind – namely, that he is your male sibling. You then can't begin to think about whether Richard is your brother because when you apply the word "brother" to Richard you have that very same idea in your mind again. You are in effect asking, "Richard is my male sibling but is he my male sibling?" which must be a closed question.

7.32 When the words in question mean something different, the corresponding questions will be open. Consider someone who wants to define the word "dessert" as "something sweet." We can then consider an object which satisfies this definition, say a banana. Moore says that you should then consider the question: "A banana is sweet, but is it a dessert?"

7.33 You can begin to consider how to answer this question and therefore it is an open one. You can eat a banana for a dessert, but is it the case that whenever you have a banana you are having a dessert? This is debatable. Because the question is an open question, according to Moore the words "dessert" and "something sweet" cannot mean the same and so you cannot define one of them in terms of the other.

7.34 Moore's third premise can then be formulated like this:

> Premise 3: The words "A" and "B" mean something different if and only if the question "X is A, but is it B?" is an open question. A question is open if you can begin to consider how to answer it and closed if you can't.

Stage 4: Moral words and open questions

7.35 Let us then return to the word "good." In this last stage of the argument, Moore argues that the open question test shows that the word "good" doesn't mean the same as any other words that are used to talk about natural properties. Take the utilitarian who claims that "good" means "whatever maximizes general happiness." Let us assume that your act of reading this book makes more people happy than anything else you could do. Ask yourself then: "Reading this book maximizes general happiness, but is it good?"

Moore claimed that questions like this are always open. Being able to correctly describe an act with words that refer to natural properties always leaves room for considering whether that act is good. That something maximizes happiness or is what you desire to desire never fully settles whether the act in question is good. You can always begin to think whether acts that maximize happiness or ones you desire to desire are good. Even if later on you come to the conclusion that they are, this isn't true merely on the basis of the meaning of the words. 7.36

This led Moore to the next premise of his argument: 7.37

> Premise 4: Questions of the form "X is N, but is X good?," where N stands for a word used to talk about a natural property, are always open questions.

Stage 5: Putting the argument together

From Premises 3 and 4, Moore concluded that moral terms like "good" and words that refer to natural properties like "what maximizes happiness" can never mean the same thing. Moore thus denied that there are correct definitions of moral words using only words that stand for natural properties. 7.38

If you then return to the Premise 2, you can see how the Open Question Argument forms a strong argument against naturalism. The second premise says that a moral property can be a natural property only if the corresponding moral word means the same as some words which you can use to talk about natural properties. Therefore, good can be a natural property only if the word "good" means the same as words used to talk about natural properties. 7.39

Moore has just concluded that the word "good" never has the same meaning as words used to talk about natural properties. From this and the second premise, he can conclude that: 7.40

> Conclusion: Moral properties (like the property of being good) are not natural properties.

This conclusion led Moore to believe that goodness must be a non-natural property of its own kind.

Responses to the Open Question Argument

7.41 Moore's argument has been hugely influential. Most research in metaethics is still done under the shadow of the Open Question Argument (**Darwall, Gibbard, and Railton, 1992**).[23] Despite this, no one really thinks that the argument works in the traditional form explained above. The following section will consider three reasons for this.

Response 1: Begging the question

7.42 **William Frankena** made one of the first objections to the Open Question Argument (**Frankena, 1939**).[24] He accused Moore of **begging the question** against naturalism. Philosophers use **this phrase**[25] in a different and more precise way than other people.

7.43 Consider first an example of this phrase as typically used. Imagine that a politician announces a plan to raise taxes. One thing a commentator might say in response is, "This policy begs the question: will many people who earn a lot move to other countries where the taxes are lower?" Here the commentator is using the words "begs the question" to mean that the given policy invites an obvious question.

7.44 You can't use this phrase in philosophy in the same way, because in philosophy you beg the question with an argument when you use your conclusion as one of your premises. If you are trying to give an argument for the conclusion that God exists, your premises cannot already rely on His existence or you are begging the question in the philosophical sense. Arguments that beg the question like this are no good because they don't give any new reasons to believe in God. Only someone who already believes in God can use them to conclude that God exists.

7.45 If we understand begging the question in this way, then Frankena claimed that when Moore made the Open Question Argument against naturalism he was already assuming that naturalism is false as one of his premises. You would already need to be a non-naturalist to accept Moore's argument against naturalism, which is just as silly as assuming that God exists in an argument for His existence.

7.46 You can see the force of this objection from the perspective of a naturalist. Imagine that you are absolutely certain that for an act to be good is for it to maximize general happiness. You then meet Moore, who tells you that even if an act maximizes happiness you can begin to consider whether it is a good act. You should protest at this point. Given how certain you are, this is a closed question for you. The answer is so obvious that you can't begin to consider how to answer the question.

Because of this, it looks from your perspective as though Moore has just 7.47
assumed that "good" and "whatever maximizes general happiness" do not mean the same thing. This assumption that relies on the truth of non-naturalism is what makes him think that you must be confused if you don't think that the relevant question is an open question. In this case the Open Question Argument doesn't give you any new reasons to give up your naturalism. Moore has therefore begged the question. He has assumed his conclusion, non-naturalism, as one of his premises.

Despite the appeal of this objection, Moore wasn't merely assuming that 7.48
questions like "this act maximizes general happiness, but is it good?" are open. He had evidence that a lot of normal people begin to consider questions like this. You can go out and ask people and you are unlikely to meet people who think questions like this are silly. This is why Moore was entitled to say that "good" does not mean "whatever maximizes general happiness" in our shared language. As a result, when he said that the crucial questions are open he wasn't merely relying on his personal dislike of naturalism, and therefore it doesn't seem as though he was begging the question.

Response 2: Making know-how explicit

The second response to the Open Question Argument challenges the argu- 7.49
ment's hidden assumption according to which it is always easy to know whether or not two words mean the same thing (Soames, 2003, pp. 46–48). You can use the open question test to see whether two words mean the same only if this assumption is true. For example, because it is transparent that "grandmother" and "mother's or father's mother" mean the same, you can't begin to consider how to answer the question "Ann is my mother's mother, but is she my grandmother?" You know that you have the same idea in mind when you use these two expressions and for this reason you can't consider how to answer the question.

The second objection points out that it's not always easy to know whether 7.50
two words mean the same (Smith, 1994, pp. 37–38). Because of this, you can sometimes use two words that mean the same without knowing it. In these cases, the relevant questions in Moore's test would feel open for you even if the words in the question meant the same. This would mean that

the open question test would not work as a test of sameness of meaning and so the whole Open Question Argument would fail.

7.51 Let's make this objection more concrete with an example. There is a difference between skills and more theoretical knowledge. Skills are abilities to do things. If you can ride a bike, you know how to ride one – you have the skill. We call such skills "know-how." In contrast, theoretical knowledge consists of knowing that such and such is the case. You might know that $2 + 2 = 4$ and that John F. Kennedy was the President of the United States.

7.52 The second objection suggests that when you learn a new word you don't do this by learning facts but rather by learning a new skill of how to classify things under a label. When you learned to use the words "green" and "blue," you learned how to separate green things from blue things. When you acquired this skill, you didn't learn any definitions. You just came to know how to react with words to things that resemble one another in a certain way.

7.53 The second response to the Open Question Argument applies this thought to moral language. When you grow up, you see others categorize acts under labels such as "good" and "bad." At some point, you begin to attempt to do the same. In the beginning you might get things wrong in the same way as a baby might call a cow "a horse." When this happens, other people will correct you. Gradually you will learn the skill of calling acts "good" and "bad" in a way that is acceptable to others.

7.54 When you have acquired the relevant linguistic skills, you don't just randomly call things "blue" or "bad." In your mind, you use some implicit standards for making these distinctions. You might call certain objects "books" because they are pages of paper bound together even if you have never explicitly thought about this before. In this case you mean many pages of paper bound together whenever you use the word "book" even if this might not be obvious to you.

7.55 In response to the Open Question Argument the naturalist can then argue that the fact that the relevant questions of that argument are open doesn't show that moral words don't mean the same as other words. The naturalist can insist that the correct definition of "good" ("whatever maximizes general happiness" or "whatever you desire to desire when you vividly imagine things" or…) captures explicitly the principle which we use implicitly to classify acts as "good." Even if you may not know it, this is what you have in mind when you call an act "good."

7.56 This would explain why we can always ask whether an act that maximizes happiness is good. When you ask whether such acts are good, you are first relying on your implicit ability to classify acts as "good" on the grounds that they maximize general happiness. At this point, you are not using your explicit knowledge about what the word means. This is why you can begin to wonder whether acts that maximize general happiness are good. As a result, "good" can mean "whatever maximizes general happiness" despite the open question. This would be enough to save naturalism from the Open Question Argument.

There is one potential problem with this response. Even if what you mean by different words isn't always easy to know, this cannot be completely hidden from you either (Baldwin, 1993, p. xix). When you think about it hard enough, you should be able to tell which principles you use implicitly when you apply different words. First of all, you can test the suggested principles against what you think of different cases. If the principle doesn't agree with your judgments, then it isn't the one you are using. Secondly, you can think about how natural the principle feels. Is it something you could have in mind when you apply the word? 7.57

If you like the Open Question Argument, you can use these ideas to argue against the naturalist definitions of "good." Whenever a naturalist gives you a definition of the word "good," you can argue that it doesn't fit the way you are using the word or that it feels too alien to be the principle you are using. If you can do this in enough cases, then you are entitled to think that moral words can't be defined by using other words which are about natural properties. 7.58

Response 3: The sense/reference distinction

The third objection attacks the first premise of the Open Question Argument: two seemingly different properties can in fact be one and the same property only if the words we use to talk about these properties mean the same thing. According to this premise, the properties of being a vixen and being a female fox are one and the same property because the words "vixen" and "female fox" mean the same thing. 7.59

The third objection says that what a word means – that is, what you have in mind when you use the word – does not determine what the word refers to (Kripke, 1980). If this is right, then contrary to what Moore believed, words that have different meanings can still refer to one and the same property. 7.60

Two famous examples illustrate this. Consider first the names **"Evening Star" and "Morning Star."**[26] When you use these words, you have in your 7.61

mind the star first seen in the evening and the star last seen in the morning. However, the fact that you have these different ideas in mind when you use these words doesn't mean that the words refer to different objects. It turns out that both of these names pick out the planet **Venus.**[27] This illustrates how words that do not mean the same can be names for the same object.

7.62 Another famous example is about scientific identity-statements and water. Water consists of H_2O molecules. If the liquid in your bottle has any other chemical constitution, then it isn't water. In other words, there is just one substance here and we have two different names for it: "water" and "H_2O." These two words refer to the same substance even if they don't mean the same. When you use the word "water," you have in your mind the idea of a transparent, tasteless, and odorless liquid that falls from the sky and fills the seas. In contrast, when you use the word "H_2O," you are thinking of hydrogen and oxygen atoms in a certain formation. Despite this difference in what you have in mind, these two words still pick out the same substance from the world.

7.63 These examples illustrate that words that have different meanings can refer to the very same thing. Moore was therefore wrong when he claimed that two seemingly different properties can be one and the same property only if the words we use to talk about these properties mean the same thing. There is no reason why the words "good" and "whatever maximizes general happiness" could not refer to the same property of acts even if these words do not have the same meaning. This is why the Open Question Argument fails to show that good is not a natural property.

7.64 This response led to the development of the **contemporary forms of metaethical naturalism.**[28] The earlier forms of naturalism were **analytic**[29] forms of naturalism. According to these views, moral properties are natural properties because moral language can be fully understood in terms of non-moral and naturalist language.

7.65 In contrast, according to the new, **synthetic** forms of naturalism, moral words do not mean the same thing as words we use to talk about natural properties; and yet moral words can still pick out natural properties, as the previous response showed. These views then recommend that you should empirically investigate which natural properties moral words pick out (**Boyd, 1988**).[30] In the same way as it was a cosmological discovery that the words "Evening Star" and "Morning Star" refer to Venus and a chemical discovery that water is H_2O, we need to empirically investigate to see which natural property good is. This requires focusing on which natural properties best explain when we use moral words.

This response to the Open Question Argument failed to settle the debate because Moore's defenders have formulated new versions of the argument that can deal with the objection.[31] We must, however, move on. There is one last thing which still needs to be explored in this chapter. Moore concluded from the Open Question Argument that good is a simple, non-natural property of its own unique kind. You can't observe this property empirically or study it scientifically. How then did Moore think we could ever know about what's good? 7.66

Intuitionism in Metaethics*

One traditional answer to this question is called **intuitionism**.[32] We have already discussed one form of intuitionism in Chapter 5. Ross's theory of prima facie duties is called intuitionism in normative ethics because he believed that there are many moral duties that do not have a single source. Ross also accepted the more **epistemological**[33] form of intuitionism which will be discussed in this section (see Huemer, 2005; Zimmermann, 2010, ch. 4; Kaspar, 2012). Here, intuitionism is a theory of how you know which acts have non-natural moral properties. 7.67

The problem of knowledge*

When you investigate the world you should aim at knowledge. Knowledge is the gold standard because when you know something you get things right in a reliable way. What knowledge is more precisely is an interesting and difficult question. 7.68

According to **the traditional theory of knowledge**,[34] knowing something requires three things. Consider the fact that Paris is the capital of France. Knowing that Paris is the capital of France first requires that you *believe* that Paris is the capital of France. If you don't believe that it is, then you just don't know that this is a fact. Secondly, knowing this fact also requires that it is *true* that Paris is the capital of France. You can't know that Marseilles is the capital of France because it isn't. 7.69

Even if you believe something that is true, this isn't enough for you to know. You might believe that it will be sunny tomorrow just because you really want to play tennis then. In this case, even if it turns out to be sunny tomorrow, you didn't *know* that it would be. This is because you just got lucky – you didn't have any real evidence. As a result, it is often said that 7.70

your true belief counts as knowledge only if you have justification for that belief. According to the traditional view, you know that p when:

i. you believe that p;
ii. it is true that p; and
iii. you are justified in believing that p.

7.71 The debate about how you could know what is good if goodness is a non-natural property has focused on the last condition: justification. Clearly we have moral beliefs and, if we are lucky, perhaps at least some of these beliefs are true. Yet in order to know what is good and bad, you would in addition need to have justification for your true moral beliefs. The challenge for the non-naturalist is to explain what could justify our moral beliefs given that most of our other beliefs are justified by what we see and hear.

7.72 One answer to this challenge relies on **inferential justification**.[35] Your belief is inferentially justified when it is supported by your other justified beliefs. Your belief that Max is at home is inferentially justified when it is supported by your other beliefs that he just picked up the phone and that he could have done so only if he were at home.

7.73 Intuitionists argue against the idea that all our moral beliefs could be inferentially justified. They claim that all your moral beliefs can't be justified because they are supported your other justified beliefs. Intuitionists claim that the inferential justification requirement leads either to **a vicious regress or a vicious circle**[36] (BonJour, 1985, pp. 17–25).

7.74 The inferential justification view says that justified beliefs must always be supported by your other justified beliefs. We can then ask: what justifies these supporting beliefs? According to the view we are discussing, these beliefs too must be supported by some other justified beliefs. What justifies those beliefs? This leads to an infinite chain of justifying beliefs. However, as a finite being, you can't have an infinite number of beliefs that support one another.

7.75 To avoid this problem you could argue that the mutually supporting beliefs form **a network of beliefs**[37] in which every single belief is supported by some other beliefs in the network. This is no good either. Different people can have different networks of mutually supporting beliefs. Consider a scientist and **a scientologist**[38] who hold internally consistent but mutually conflicting beliefs. It would be odd to think that their beliefs are equally justified. Furthermore, it would be strange to think that no matter how wacky a view is, the beliefs of that view are justified just as long as they are consistent.

Foundationalism to the rescue*

One traditional solution to this problem of knowledge is called 7.76
foundationalism.[39] According to this view, not all justified beliefs need to be justified by some other justified beliefs. Some foundationalists have argued that some basic beliefs are justified because we are directly acquainted with the objects of these beliefs (**Russell, 1911**).[40] You might, for example, be justified in believing that you are hot now because you are acquainted with how you feel at the moment. Other foundationalists claim that some of our basic beliefs can be justified because they are produced by a reliable mechanism.

Intuitionists in metaethics are foundationalists in this broad sense. They 7.77
too deny that all justified moral beliefs need to be supported by some other beliefs. Many other views in metaethics can accept this type of foundationalism too. What makes intuitionism a special form of foundationalism, however, is that they have introduced a distinct way in which some basic moral beliefs could be justified even if they are not justified by other justified beliefs. They argue that you are justified to believe certain moral propositions because these propositions are "self-evident" (**Ross, 1930, ch. 2, para. 27**).[41] This doesn't mean that these propositions will necessarily seem obviously true to you. Rather, intuitionists argue that understanding and attentively considering a self-evident proposition is sufficient for being justified to believe it (Shafer-Landau, 2003, p. 247).

Intuitionists argue that some basic moral propositions are self- 7.78
evident in this sense. These propositions might include the following propositions:

- Pain and suffering is bad.
- It is wrong to kill innocent people in ordinary situations.
- Other things being equal, you should keep your promises.

If (i) you understand the concepts used in these propositions and (ii) you carefully consider these propositions in a calm and unbiased way, then you are justified to believe these things irrespective of what else you believe. Note that here neither understanding the concepts nor carefully considering the proposition on its own justifies the given moral belief. Rather, both conditions need to be satisfied at the same time. If this is the case, then you do not need to give any further reasons for why you believe these propositions to be true. Just understanding and accepting them after careful consideration justifies your belief in itself.

7.79 This becomes less mysterious if you consider the following basic propositions:

- Nothing can be both red and green all over.
- $2 + 2 = 4$.
- The existence of grandchildren is impossible without at least three generations.

If you understand these propositions, you are justified to believe them to be true even if you cannot give any further reasons for why these propositions are true. They just are true and you are justified to believe this. Intuitionists then argue that some basic moral propositions are exactly like this too.

Misconceptions and objections*

7.80 *Misconception 1: The role of experience and emotions* Intuitionism in metaethics has often been misunderstood. First of all, even if intuitionists argue that you don't need any external justification for some of your basic moral beliefs, they can also emphasize the importance of experiences, emotions, and education. Intuitionists can claim that without the right experiences, feelings, and upbringing you could not properly understand the relevant propositions or consider them carefully enough.

7.81 For example, without having been upset because someone has cheated on you, you might not understand what it means to say that cheating is wrong. In this way, even if experiences and emotions do not directly justify your moral beliefs, perhaps our moral beliefs would not be justified without them.

7.82 *Misconception 2: What seems self-evident to you* Secondly, the self-evident basic beliefs need not be obvious to you or be based on quick moral reactions. Coming to accept the relevant propositions may often require a lot of time, effort, and serious thinking. This is why many moral propositions that seem self-evident to you at first may turn out not to be self-evident in the end. These seemingly obvious beliefs can be based on our emotional and selfish biases. This is why you can't object to intuitionism on the grounds that the suggested moral propositions do not seem self-evident to you. The claim is only that if you eventually come to accept these propositions when you fully understand them and consider them carefully, your beliefs will be justified. A quick emotional reaction doesn't show that you have understood the proposition.

Objection 1: People who understand but don't agree A more serious problem is that not everyone who understands the relevant propositions (like that pain is bad) believes these propositions to be true. Consider Fred, who thinks that suffering is good because it makes people appreciate the small pleasures in life. In this case, you would want to say that Fred perfectly well understands the proposition that suffering is bad but he just doesn't agree with it. Shouldn't this undermine the idea that you can have justification for believing that suffering is bad merely by understanding the concepts in question and considering the proposition carefully (Nowell-Smith, 1954, p. 48)? What should the intuitionists say about people like Fred? 7.83

Many critics have missed the point that intuitionism itself is neutral about cases like Fred. It only says that, if you understand and believe the proposition that suffering is bad after careful consideration, then you are justified to have that belief. This has no consequences for the cases in which people like Fred do not believe that suffering is bad. Some people just are so convinced about the truth of their own views that there is nothing you can do to change their mind. Because of this, you can't require intuitionists to be able to do so either. 7.84

Even if this response can deal with the objection itself, it is still not perfect. Intuitionists should be able to say something more informative about Fred. The basic question is: what kind of a mistake does Fred make if he doesn't accept that pain is bad? What is it about him that prevents him from accepting the belief that would justify itself? Does he not understand the words in question after all? Does he fail to consider the proposition carefully enough? Or, is he just not required to accept this belief even if he understands the proposition and considers it carefully? Many people think that intuitionism should be able to answer these questions as this would be the best way to explain the difference between people who hold justified moral beliefs and those who don't. Yet even if the intuitionists fail to answer these questions, they can still argue that normal people who are not like 7.85

Fred – people who understand and accept the proposition that pain is bad – are justified to hold this belief.

7.86 *Objection 2: Dogmatism* You will probably not be happy with this answer. It seems objectionably **dogmatic**[42] to ignore people who disagree with your view. It also seems too conservative to say that our own current moral beliefs are unique in the sense that only these beliefs can justify themselves.

7.87 However, intuitionists are not committed to ignoring other people's views or to saying that only they know what is right and wrong. Intuitionists can accept that disagreement between carefully reflecting people is a reason to doubt the seemingly self-evident moral propositions. Whatever beliefs seem self-evident to you at one moment may turn out to be a mistake later on. What seems self-evident to us can therefore later on fail to be self-evident in the required way. Intuitionists who understand this need not be guilty of pushing their own prejudiced beliefs on others.

Summary and Questions

7.88 This chapter has explored different versions of moral realism according to which there are objective moral facts. All these views accept that acts have moral properties independently of what we think of these acts. The main disagreement between realists, therefore, is about whether moral properties are just like all other properties or whether they are properties of their own unique kind.

7.89 Naturalists in metaethics believe that moral properties are just like all other properties. They believe that you can observe and scientifically study moral properties, which also can cause things to happen. For example, you can use people's moral qualities to explain their behavior. According to this view, you can say that Mother Teresa helped so many people because she was so kind. Naturalists therefore attempt to make moral properties a part of our scientific worldview.

7.90 In contrast, non-naturalists defend the idea that moral properties are of their own unique kind, because they are *normative* properties. That these properties have practical significance is built into these properties themselves, which makes them unique.

7.91 The main bulk of this chapter then investigated Moore's influential argument against naturalism. According to it, moral properties can't be natural properties because even if you know what natural properties an act has you can still always meaningfully ask whether the act is good. Understanding this argument and the responses to it is essential for understanding much of moral philosophy today.

The very last part of this chapter considered how you could know about moral properties if they were non-natural properties. The traditional non-naturalist response to this challenge is a theory called intuitionism, which relies on the notion of self-evident truths. According to this view, there are some basic moral propositions which you are entitled to believe merely in virtue of understanding them. 7.92

Based on the philosophical resources introduced in this chapter, consider the following questions: 7.93

1. What do moral realists believe? How plausible do you find the view?
2. What are the differences between natural and non-natural properties supposed to be?
3. How would you explain the Open Question Argument to your friends?
4. Consider the second objection to the Open Question Argument. How do the defenders of this objection and Moore disagree about what goes on in your mind when you use words?
5. How do intuitionists explain moral knowledge? Is this explanation satisfactory?

Annotated Bibliography

Baldwin, Thomas (1993) "Editor's Introduction," in G.E. Moore, *Principia Ethica*, rev. ed. (Cambridge: Cambridge University Press), pp. ix–xxxvii. An accessible and charitable introduction to *Principia Ethica*, which also contains a helpful discussion of the Open Question Argument.

BonJour, Laurence (1985) *The Structure of Empirical Knowledge* (Cambridge: Cambridge University Press). A classic text in epistemology in which BonJour begins from the epistemic regress problem and then argues against foundationalism and for coherentism.

Boyd, Richard (1988) "How to Be a Moral Realist," in *Essays on Moral Realism*, ed. Geoffrey Sayre-McCord (Ithaca: Cornell University Press), pp. 181–228, full text available at http://commonsenseatheism.com/wp-content/uploads/2010/09/Boyd-How-to-be-a-moral-realist.pdf, accessed March 5, 2014. A classic defense of synthetic naturalist realism which attempts to understand moral properties with the model of other scientific identity statements.

According to Boyd, the reference of moral words is determined by what causally regulates the use of these words in our linguistic community.

Copp, David (2003) "Why Naturalism?," *Ethical Theory and Moral Practice*, 6, 179–200, full text available at http://ethik.univie.ac.at/fileadmin/user_upload/inst_ethik_wiss_dialog/Copp__D_2003_Why_Naturalism.pdf, accessed March 5, 2014. One of the best articles on what the distinction between naturalism and non-naturalism is supposed to be.

Dancy, Jonathan (2006) "Nonnaturalism," in *Oxford Handbook in Ethical Theory*, ed. David Copp (Oxford: Oxford University Press), pp. 122–145. An illuminating article which attempts to clarify what makes non-natural moral properties unique and why we should believe in such properties.

Darwall, Stephen, Allan Gibbard, and Peter Railton (1992) "Toward fin de siècle Ethics: Some Trends," *Ethics*, *101*(1), 115–189, full text available at http://www.jstor.org/stable/2185045?origin=crossref, accessed March 11, 2014. Exceptional overview of the metaethical landscape which explains the huge influence Moore's Open Question Argument has had on the contemporary debates.

Feldman, Fred (2005) "The Open Question Argument: What It Isn't; And What It Is," *Philosophical Issues*, *15*, 22–43. A clear overview of different interpretations of Moore's argument. According to Feldman, most interpretations read more into Moore's argument than he actually had in mind.

Frankena, W.K. (1939) "The Naturalistic Fallacy," *Mind*, *48*(192), 464–477, full text available at http://www.jstor.org/stable/2250706, accessed March 5, 2014. A thorough early critical discussion of Moore's Open Question Argument.

Harman, Gilbert (1977) "Ethics and Observation," in his *The Nature of Morality* (Oxford: Oxford University Press), pp. 3–10, full text available at http://www-personal.umich.edu/~lormand/phil/teach/intro/readings/Harman%20-%20Ethics%20and%20Observation.htm, accessed March 11, 2014. In this famous paper, Harman objected to moral realism on the grounds that objective moral properties do not play a role in good causal explanations and therefore we should not believe in them.

Horgan, Terence and Mark Timmons (1992) "Troubles for the New Wave Moral Semantics: The 'Open Question Argument' Revived," *Philosophical Papers*, *21*(3), 153–175, full text available at http://thorgan.faculty.arizona.edu/sites/thorgan.faculty.arizona.edu/files/Troubles%20for%20New%20Wave%20Moral%20Semantics.pdf, accessed March 5, 2014. One of the series of important metaethical articles in which Horgan and Timmons use the Moral Twin Earth thought experiment to create a new and improved version of the Open Question Argument against the new forms of naturalism.

Huemer, Michael (2005) *Ethical Intuitionism* (Basingstoke: Palgrave Macmillan). A passionate defense of non-naturalist realism and intuitionism in metaethics.

Kaspar, David (2012) *Intuitionism* (London: Bloomsbury). A useful textbook on intuitionism in moral epistemology. Kaspar explains the view very clearly on the basis of the most recent work on the topic and he also covers the main objections to intuitionism and the view's broader consequences in moral philosophy.

Kripke, Saul (1980) *Naming and Necessity* (Oxford: Blackwell). One of the most important philosophy books of the twentieth century. Kripke argued that a prioricity, necessity, and analycity are distinct categories and he also introduced the idea that the reference of many words is fixed by causal chains of use rather than by what people think.

Lewis, David (1983) "New Work for a Theory of Universals," *Australasian Journal of Philosophy*, *61*(4), 343–377, full text available at http://xa.yimg.com/kq/groups/19143263/487058615/name/New+Work+for+a+Theory+of+Universals.pdf, accessed March 5, 2014. A landmark article in which Lewis defends the view that properties are sets of possible things.

Lewis, David (1989) "Dispositional Theories of Value," *Proceedings of the Aristotelian Society*, Supplement *63*, 113–137, full text available at http://www.colorado.edu/philosophy/heathwood/pdf/lewis_dtv.pdf, accessed March 5, 2014. In this classic article Lewis argued that we can give a naturalist account of the meaning of value-talk by considering what human beings are disposed to desire to desire under certain conditions of imaginative acquaintance.

Locke, John (1690) *An Essay Concerning Human Understanding*, full text available at http://oregonstate.edu/instruct/phl302/texts/locke/locke1/contents3.html, accessed March 5, 2014. Locke's empiricist masterpiece in which he explains how we come to know things through sense-perception. According to Locke, moral knowledge must always be inferred from other truths.

Mill, John Stuart (1861) *Utilitarianism*. See the bibliography of Chapter 1 above.

Moore, G.E. (1903) *Principia Ethica*. See the bibliography of Chapter 3 above.

Nowell-Smith, P.H. (1954) *Ethics* (Oxford: Blackwell). A slightly old-fashioned book on ethics but Nowell-Smith expresses nicely the worry which many people have about intuitionism: if moral properties were objective and we had a reliable access to them, you would expect there to be more general agreement about moral questions.

Price, Richard (1758) *A Review of the Principle Questions in Morals*, full text available at http://oll.libertyfund.org/?option=com_staticxt&staticfile=show.php%3Ftitle=2077&chapter=157683&layout=html&Itemid=27, accessed March 10, 2014. In this short manuscript Price defends rationalism – the view that moral distinctions are part of the genuine character of actions. He also argues against Hutcheson's sentimentalism. According to Price, our understanding can help us to recognize what is right and wrong.

Ross, W.D. (1930) *The Right and the Good*. See the bibliography of Chapter 4 above.

Russell, Bertrand (1911) "Knowledge by Acquaintance and Knowledge by Description," *Proceedings of the Aristotelian Society*, *11*, 108–128, full text available at http://selfpace.uconn.edu/class/percep/RussellKnowAcquaint.pdf, accessed

March 5, 2014. A classic article in which Russell introduced the distinction between two different forms of knowledge. We know some basic things by being directly aware of them and then we can expand our knowledge by making inferences from what we already know directly.

Shafer-Landau, Russ (2003) *Moral Realism: A Defence* (Oxford: Oxford University Press). Perhaps the best recent defense of non-naturalist realism in metaethics. Shafer-Landau provides strong arguments against all the other alternatives and defends non-naturalism against the best objections to the view. The three chapters on moral knowledge are especially useful.

Sidgwick, Henry (1889) "Some Fundamental Ethical Controversies," *Mind*, *14*(56), 473–487, full text available at http://www.henrysidgwick.com/2247121%20some%20fundamental%20ethical%20controversies.pdf, accessed March 10, 2014. A discussion of free will, which also includes an early formulation of the open question argument.

Smith, Michael (1994) *The Moral Problem* (Oxford: Blackwell). One of the core texts in metaethics. At the beginning of the book Smith helpfully maps the different views in metaethics and he then goes onto defend an analytic form of naturalist realism.

Soames, Scott (2003) *Philosophical Analysis in the Twentieth Century*, Vol. 1 (Princeton: Princeton University Press). A thorough textbook on early twentieth-century analytic philosophy. The chapter on Moore's ethics provides a useful explanation of Moore's main arguments from a philosophy of language perspective.

Sturgeon, Nicholas (1988) "Moral Explanations," in *Essays on Moral Realism*, ed. Geoffrey Sayre-McCord (Ithaca: Cornell University Press), pp. 229–255. A classic article in which Sturgeon tries to defend naturalist realism in metaethics by arguing that moral properties can be used in the best causal explanations.

Zimmerman, Aaron (2010) *Moral Epistemology* (London: Routledge). The most up-to-date textbook on moral knowledge. Explains different alternatives clearly and discusses their pros and cons with exciting examples.

Online Resources

1 An overview article of moral realism: http://plato.stanford.edu/entries/moral-realism/.

2 An overview of the naturalism vs. non-naturalism debate in metaethics: http://plato.stanford.edu/entries/moral-non-naturalism/.

3 Chapter 2 of Moore's *Principia Ethica*: http://fair-use.org/g-e-moore/principia-ethica/chapter-ii, David Lewis's article "New Work for a Theory

of Universals": http://xa.yimg.com/kq/groups/19143263/487058615/name/New+Work+for+a+Theory+of+Universals.pdf, and David Copp's "Why Naturalism?": http://ethik.univie.ac.at/fileadmin/user_upload/inst_ethik_wiss_dialog/Copp__D_2003_Why_Naturalism.pdf.

4 An overview of naturalism in metaethics: http://plato.stanford.edu/entries/naturalism-moral/.

5 Timeline of protests against slavery: http://www.ushistory.org/more/timeline.htm.

6 Chapter 4 of Mill's *Utilitarianism*: http://www.gutenberg.org/files/11224/11224-h/11224-h.htm#CHAPTER_IV.

7 David Lewis's article "Dispositional Theories of Value": http://www.colorado.edu/philosophy/heathwood/pdf/lewis_dtv.pdf.

8 An overview of non-naturalism in metaethics: http://plato.stanford.edu/entries/moral-non-naturalism/.

9 An animation of the Creation: http://www.youtube.com/watch?v=0oR1v0DpTcs.

10 Information about the beginning of the universe: http://www.bbc.co.uk/science/space/universe/questions_and_ideas/big_bang/.

11 Harman's "Ethics and Observation": http://www-personal.umich.edu/~lormand/phil/teach/intro/readings/Harman%20-%20Ethics%20and%20Observation.htm. Harman uses the example to argue against moral realism.

12 In David Hume's words: http://www.iwise.com/2w29w.

13 Information about the Large Hadron Collider: https://en.wikipedia.org/wiki/Large_Hadron_Collider.

14 The section in which Moore states his conclusion: http://fair-use.org/g-e-moore/principia-ethica/s.15.

15 Brief explanation of normativity: http://en.wikipedia.org/wiki/Normative.

16 See Matt Bedke's argument from 60:44 onwards: http://www.philostv.com/matt-bedke-and-walter-sinnott-armstrong/.

17 Tristram McPherson's clear explanation of the Open Question Argument: http://filebox.vt.edu/users/tristram/Docs/McPherson-OpenQuestion-RoutledgeEncyclopedia.pdf and Moore's original presentation: http://fair-use.org/g-e-moore/principia-ethica/s.13.

18 A wax version of President Obama at the Eiffel Tower: http://www.telegraph.co.uk/news/newstopics/howaboutthat/5691077/Barack-Obama-spotted-in-Eiffel-Tower-in-wax.html.

19 What words mean and how they refer are interesting philosophical questions: http://www.iep.utm.edu/lang-phi/.

20 The life and works of G.E. Moore: http://plato.stanford.edu/entries/moore/ and the *Principia Ethica*: http://fair-use.org/g-e-moore/principia-ethica.

21 Price's *Review of the Principal Questions in Morals*: http://oll.libertyfund.org/?option=com_staticxt&staticfile=show.php%3Ftitle=2077&chapter

=157683&layout=html&Itemid=27 and Sidgwick's "Some Fundamental Ethical Controversies": http://www.henrysidgwick.com/2247121%20some%20fundamental%20ethical%20controversies.pdf.

22 Book III of Locke's essay: http://oregonstate.edu/instruct/phl302/texts/locke/locke1/Book3a.html#Chapter I.

23 An overview of the history of metaethics which focuses on the influence of the Open Question Argument:http://www.jstor.org/stable/2185045?origin=crossref.

24 The life and works of Frankena: http://en.wikipedia.org/wiki/William_Frankena and his "The Naturalistic Fallacy": http://www.jstor.org/stable/2250706.

25 Clear explanation of what it is to beg the question: http://www.fallacyfiles.org/begquest.html.

26 Quick explanation of the so-called Frege's Puzzle and Frege's solution to it: http://whyalmost50.blogspot.co.uk/2013/03/freges-puzzle.html.

27 Wikipedia on Venus/Evening Star/Morning Star: http://en.wikipedia.org/wiki/Venus.

28 Overview of contemporary forms of metaethical naturalism: http://plato.stanford.edu/entries/naturalism-moral/#ConNat.

29 Explanation of analysis: http://plato.stanford.edu/entries/analysis/.

30 Richard Boyd's article "How to Be a Moral Realist": http://commonsenseatheism.com/wp-content/uploads/2010/09/Boyd-How-to-be-a-moral-realist.pdf.

31 The souped-up Open Question Arguments use the so-called Moral Twin Earth thought experiment: http://www.public.iastate.edu/~geirsson/pdf/mte-intuitive.pdf (the footnotes also provide a useful list of the literature). For Horgan and Timmons' original, see "Troubles for the New Wave Moral Semantics: The 'Open Question Argument' Revived": http://thorgan.faculty.arizona.edu/sites/thorgan.faculty.arizona.edu/files/Troubles%20for%20New%20Wave%20Moral%20Semantics.pdf. This advanced material is hard and yet very cool stuff!

32 Concise explanation of intuitionism in metaethics: http://kant1.chch.ox.ac.uk/rlfrazier/intuit/.

33 Overview of epistemology in philosophy: http://plato.stanford.edu/entries/epistemology/.

34 Explanation of the tripartite theory: http://www.theoryofknowledge.info/what-is-knowledge/the-tripartite-theory-of-knowledge/.

35 Explanation of inferential justification: http://www.theoryofknowledge.info/epistemic-justification/.

36 Michael Huemer's clear exposition of the Pyrrhonian Problematic: http://spot.colorado.edu/~huemer/note434b.pdf.

37 Overview of coherentism: http://plato.stanford.edu/entries/justep-coherence/.
38 Description of scientology: http://en.wikipedia.org/wiki/Scientology.
39 Overview of foundationalism: http://plato.stanford.edu/entries/justep-foundational/.
40 Russell's "Knowledge by Acquaintance and Knowledge by Description": http://selfpace.uconn.edu/class/percep/RussellKnowAcquaint.pdf.
41 See paragraph beginning "Something should be said…": http://www.ditext.com/ross/right2.html.
42 Dictionary definition: http://www.thefreedictionary.com/dogmatic.

8

MORAL MOTIVATION AND EXPRESSIVISM

The previous two chapters focused mainly on moral properties. Chapter 6 investigated whether moral properties depend on what we think or what God commands. Chapter 7 then considered realist views according to which moral properties are either natural or non-natural properties of their own right. 8.1

Some metaethicists think that the whole focus of the previous chapters has been wrong. They believe that you should forget about moral properties and instead begin metaethical investigation from the nature of moral *thought*. We should first figure out what kind of mental state you are in when you sincerely and genuinely accept a moral sentence like "torture is wrong." You can call this mental state a **moral judgment**. 8.2

When you start to think about the nature of moral judgments, it is useful to begin from the observation that **genuine moral judgments influence how people behave**[1]: people who think that eating meat is wrong rarely eat meat. Some people in metaethics think that when you fully recognize this practical role of moral judgments, you will be able to see what's wrong with the views discussed in the previous chapters. The problem is that, according to those views, when you make a moral judgment you're attempting to form a true belief about the moral reality. 8.3

The metaethical views discussed in this chapter argue against this idea. They claim that the previous picture makes moral thinking too theoretical. It makes ethics scientific and cold, something which you need not care about. As a result, **expressivists**[2] want to understand moral thinking in a very practical way. They believe moral deliberation is planning how to live. 8.4

This Is Ethics: An Introduction, First Edition. Jussi Suikkanen.

This planning serves a useful practical purpose because it helps you to live and work with other people. Once we recognize this point of moral thinking, the whole question of the nature of moral properties goes away.

8.5 The first part of this chapter will focus on the **Argument from Motivation**, which is the main argument for understanding moral thinking in this new way. This argument has two premises: the **Humean Theory of Motivation** and **Moral Judgment Internalism**. Both of these theses will be discussed in detail below. The middle parts of the chapter will then discuss some of the main counterexamples to Moral Judgment Internalism. Finally, the last sections will explain the resulting view – expressivism – in more detail. The chapter then concludes with a discussion of the most serious problem with expressivism, the so-called **Frege–Geach problem**.

The Argument from Motivation

8.6 The Argument from Motivation is often ascribed to David Hume on the basis of the following passages from the *Treatise*:

1. "Reason is the discovery of truth or falsehood [...] As reason is nothing but the discovery of this connection, it cannot be by its means that the objects are able to affect us." (**Hume, 1739–1740, book II, ch. 2, sect. 3**)[3]
2. Morality "is supposed to influence our passions and actions [...] And this is confirmed by common experience, which informs us that men are often governed by their duties, and are deterred from some actions by the opinion of injustice, and impelled to others by that of obligation." (**Hume, 1739–1740, book III, ch. 1, sect. 1**).[4]

From these two premises Hume concluded:

3. "When you pronounce any action or character to be vicious, you mean nothing, but that from the constitution of your nature you have a feeling or sentiment of blame from contemplation of it." (Ibid.)

8.7 You should be able to see what Hume is getting at here. The argument seems to be that because morality moves us to act and reason doesn't, reason is not responsible for our moral judgments but rather these judgments are more like emotional reactions. When you think that an act is wrong, you are feeling something rather than believing that something is the case (for an alternative interpretation of the argument, see **Sayre-McCord, 2008**).[5]

Instead of discussing the details of Hume, it is perhaps more useful to 8.8
focus on a more modern formulation of the argument. The modern version of Hume's first premise is called the **Humean Theory of Motivation**, the modern version of the second premise **Moral Judgment Internalism**, and the modern understanding of his conclusion **expressivism**. The following two sections will explore the two premises of this argument, after which we will return to the structure of the argument and its conclusion.

The Humean Theory of Motivation

The first premise of the Argument from Motivation is based on the idea 8.9
that there are only two categories of mental states to which any mental state you take belongs (Smith, 1994, pp. 7–9). Some mental states are called **cognitive states**. These states include mainly beliefs but also suppositions and other belief-like states. The rest of our mental states are **non-cognitive states**. Desires, plans, intentions, wishes, wants, goals, approvals, and other desire-like states belong to this category.

Directions of fit

This distinction between cognitive belief-like states and non-cognitive 8.10
desire-like states is often explained in terms of different **directions of fit**.[6] Belief-like states are said to have a **mind-to-world direction of fit** whereas desires have a **world-to-mind direction of fit**. Let me try to illustrate this idea with a simple example from **Elizabeth Anscombe**[7] (Anscombe, 1957, sect. 32).

Imagine that Michael goes to a grocery store with a shopping list that 8.11
reads "milk, cheese and chocolate." Michael occasionally takes a look at his list and then puts the corresponding items – milk, cheese, and chocolate – into his basket. Michael is also being followed by a reporter called Frank. As Michael is putting his items into his basket, Frank writes down on a piece of paper "milk, cheese, and chocolate." As a result, Frank's list contains exactly the same words as Michael's list.

Michael's and Frank's lists are in one respect very different from one 8.12
another. Using the terminology of directions of fit, Michael's list has the

basket-to-list direction of fit. The role of this list is satisfied when the items in Michael's basket fit the list. Frank's list has the opposite list-to-basket direction of fit. The purpose of this list is satisfied when the list fits what Michael puts in his basket.

8.13 You can then use this analogy to understand the difference between cognitive belief-like states and non-cognitive desire-like states. Consider your own intention to finish reading this book. The role of this state is satisfied when the world fits the content of your mental state: when you have finished reading this book. This is why non-cognitive desire-like states like intentions have the world-to-mind direction of fit. Cognitive belief-like states are different. Take the belief that **Ceylon tea comes from Sri Lanka**.[8] The role of this state is fulfilled when the mental state fits how things are in the world. This is why this state and other belief-like states have the mind-to-world direction of fit.

8.14 **Michael Smith**[9] has offered a useful test which you can use to see which direction of fit a given mental state has (Smith, 1994, pp. 111–119). According to him, if you are in a belief-like state with the mind-to-world direction of fit, then that state tends to go out of existence when you have evidence that the world is not like how the state represents it as being. You therefore *believe* that it is sunny outside because you would cease to be in this state if you saw people coming inside wet. In contrast, desire-like states do not tend to go out of existence when we have evidence against their truth. Your desire to travel will continue to exist no matter how much evidence you have that you are home at the moment. Note that this test has at least one central weakness. It says that your beliefs only *tend* to go out of existence when you are presented with evidence of their falsity. This leaves room for you to continue to have some irrational beliefs even if you have evidence that says that these beliefs are false. Smith's test unfortunately doesn't really specify how to distinguish these wayward beliefs from desires.

The role of beliefs and desires

8.15 The distinction between the two directions of fit is the foundation of the Humean Theory of Motivation (Smith, 1987). This theory claims that belief-like and desire-like mental states play very different roles in our lives. Only belief-like states with the mind-to-world direction of fit can be said to be true or false. These states aim at fitting the world, at representing it correctly. If beliefs achieve this goal successfully they are true, and if they fail to achieve it they are false. You can't say the same about desires. Your desire to have ice cream cannot be true or false because it's not even trying to fit the world.

Even more important is the idea that only desire-like states with the world-to-mind direction of fit can move us to act, whereas beliefs are supposed to be motivationally inert. Consider a situation in which you believe that you have **the ingredients of a stir-fry in your refrigerator**.[10] Unless you *want* to have a stir-fry this belief in itself will not get you cooking. The belief only aims at fitting the world and therefore it lacks the practical oomph required for moving you. You will start preparing the meal only if you want to eat a stir-fry. 8.16

To summarize: according to the Humean Theory of Motivation, all mental states are either cognitive belief-like states or non-cognitive desire-like states. Only the belief-like states with the mind-to-world direction of fit can be true or false, and only the desire-like states with the world-to-mind direction of fit can motivate you to act. 8.17

Moral Judgment Internalism

Hume's second premise above claimed that morality influences our actions and passions. He based this premise on the observation that "**men are often governed by their duties**."[11] This is why Hume asserted that "**morals excite passions, and produce or prevent actions**."[12] This thesis is today known as **Moral Judgment Internalism**.[13] It claims that there is *a necessary connection* between moral judgments and motivation: if you make a moral judgment that acting in a certain way is right, then you will have motivation to act in that way. 8.18

The denial of Moral Judgment Internalism is of course called **Moral Judgment Externalism** (Brink, 1989, ch. 3). It claims that there is no necessary connection between moral judgments and motivation. According to this view, if you make a moral judgment that acting in a certain way is right, you will not be motivated accordingly unless you already have an additional desire that connects your judgment to the given act. 8.19

To make externalism clearer, it is useful to consider non-moral beliefs of which externalism is true. Consider again your belief that you have the ingredients of a stir-fry in your refrigerator. This belief will not move you to act unless you have the additional desire to eat a stir-fry. Externalists understand moral judgments and their role in action just like 8.20

this. According to them, your belief that helping other people is good will not move you to act unless you already have a general desire to do good things.

8.21 How should we decide whether internalism or externalism is true? The standard method for doing this relies on our intuitions about cases. You first describe individual cases in which people seem to make moral judgments and have certain motivations to act. The question then is which one of the views best explains what we would say about these cases: have the people in them made genuine moral judgments or not? How this method has been applied in the debate between internalists and externalists will be described below. The discussion will start from a very strong form of internalism and a case that seems to support that view. It will then go through some of the cases that externalists have used to argue against internalism and how they have led to weaker and weaker forms of internalism. We should, however, remember that behind this debate is a larger question about whether morality is (i) a practical discipline aimed at solving everyday problems or (ii) a theoretical discipline aiming at figuring out what the moral reality is like. If you find the former picture of morality attractive, then you will probably find internalism more plausible. In contrast, if you like the latter understanding of morality more, then externalism will probably seem more appealing to you.

Very Strong Internalism

8.22 A lot has been written on internalism and externalism (Björklund *et al.*, 2012; Kahn, 2013). In order to evaluate their plausibility with cases, it is easiest to start from the strongest possible form of internalism:

> **Very Strong Internalism**: If you judge that you morally ought to do an act, you will necessarily do that act unless some external force prevents you from acting in that way. (See **Stevenson, 1937, p. 16**)[14]

This thesis would mean that if you think that you ought to help old people across the street you will do this unless someone blocks your way or puts a gun to your head.

8.23 The reason why some people have accepted Very Strong Internalism is that it can easily explain the way we think about **hypocrisy**.[15] Consider Mary who always goes on about the evils of eating meat. Imagine then that you see Mary happily eating a large juicy steak. In this case you would probably think that Mary has been a hypocrite. You would think she didn't genuinely believe that eating meat is wrong but rather she was only acting as if she thought this.

Very Strong Internalism can explain why you would think this. According to it, making a genuine moral judgment requires acting accordingly. In contrast, if externalism were true, agents could make moral judgments and act in the completely opposite way. So if externalism were true, you would have no reasons to doubt Mary's sincerity. There would be nothing wrong on that view with Mary first railing against eating meat and then eating steaks, as the connection between moral judgments and motivation is merely an accidental one according to externalists. In contrast, Very Strong Internalism makes sense of the fact that we often *do* question other people's sincerity in this type of case – when we think their behavior is hypocritical. 8.24

Weakness of will

Despite this, not many people accept Very Strong Internalism. This is because most people want to leave room for **weakness of will.**[16] At least some of the time you give in to temptation and act against your better judgment. There must be room for people who think that **adultery**[17] is wrong even if they cannot resist the temptation to cheat on their partners. Very Strong Internalism would make this impossible, because it says that moral judgments require acting accordingly unless external forces come into play and stop you. 8.25

In the cases of weakness of will you act against your better judgment even without external forces stopping you. Because the adulterer has judged that adultery is wrong, he still has *some* motivation not to cheat. When he cheats, he also has a sexual desire which has a disproportionally strong ability to move him. Perhaps the adulterer wants excitement. Even if the adulterer thinks that excitement isn't all that important, this desire can become stronger than his motivation to act morally. 8.26

Strong Internalism

Because internalists want to leave room for weakness of will, they usually move from Very Strong Internalism to Strong Internalism (**Hare, 1952, ch. 11, sect. 2**):[18] 8.27

> **Strong Internalism**: If you make a genuine moral judgment that you morally ought to act in a certain way, then you will necessarily have at least some motivation to act in that way.

This thesis allows that moral motivation can be overridden by other stronger desires in the cases of weakness of will. Strong Internalism still requires that when you act against your best moral judgment you must suffer from an internal conflict. In the relevant cases you must be torn between acting morally and giving into the temptation.

8.28 Let us return to the case of Mary, who claims that eating meat is wrong and yet eats it. Strong Internalism claims that even if her desire to eat meat is winning, Mary must still have at least some motivation not to eat meat, otherwise she has not made a genuine moral judgment. If Mary really has judged that eating meat is wrong, she must feel torn when she eats meat. Perhaps she suffers from **anemia**[19] and her doctor has ordered her to eat meat. As a result, Mary feels pangs of shame when she does what her doctor has told her to do. If you can understand Mary in this way, then she is not a counterexample to Strong Internalism.

Counterexamples to Strong Internalism

8.29 Strong Internalism has many advantages: it can make sense of both hypocrisy and weakness of will. Despite this, there are serious objections to it too. This section considers the three counterexamples to Strong Internalism: **amoralists**, bad people, and certain individuals who suffer from clinical depression. It will then introduce an even weaker form of internalism, which is supposed to be able to deal with these cases.

Amoralists

8.30 **Sigrún Svavarsdóttir**'s example introduces amoralists (**Svavarsdóttir, 1999, pp. 176–183**).[20] Suppose that Virginia has asked Patrick to help a politically persecuted stranger. Svavarsdóttir then describes the case like this:

> Patrick rather wearily tells her that he has no inclination to concern himself with the plight of strangers. Virginia then appeals to explicit moral considerations: in this case, helping strangers is a moral obligation and a matter of

> fighting enormous injustice. Patrick readily declares that he agrees with her moral assessment, but nevertheless cannot be bothered to help. Virginia presses him further, arguing that the effort required is minimal and, given his position, will cost him close to nothing. Patrick responds that the cost is not really the issue, he just does not care to concern himself with such matters. Later he shows absolutely no sign of regret for either his remarks or his failure to help. (Svavarsdóttir, 1999, p. 176)

In this case, Patrick is supposed to be an amoralist: he makes a genuine 8.31
moral judgment but has no motivation at all to act accordingly. Patrick can quote Homer Simpson: "**just because I don't care doesn't mean that I don't understand**."[21] Yet, according to Strong Internalists, amoralists like Patrick should not be possible, because on their view you can't make a moral judgment without having at least some motivation. Strong Internalists must therefore explain why **so many of us mistakenly think that amoralists are possible.**[22]

In response, R.M. Hare suggested that the alleged amoralists make 8.32
moral judgments in inverted commas (**Hare, 1952, ch. 11, sect. 1**).[23] In Svavarsdóttir's case, Patrick is only saying that "it would be 'morally obligatory' to help the persecuted," and by this he means that most people would consider doing so obligatorily. Patrick can say this without committing himself to acting in the required way. He doesn't really mean that you ought to help the persecuted. Therefore, because Patrick has not made a genuine moral judgment, Strong Internalism can allow that he lacks any motivation to act accordingly.

Bad people

Consider next bad people who are motivated to do things precisely 8.33
because they are bad and wrong. **St. Augustine**[24] wasn't a bad person but Gunnar Björnsson has still used him nicely to illustrate this point: "St. Augustine confesses that, in his youth, he and some friends once stole pears from a neighbor, *just because it was wrong*; they had no interest whatsoever in the pears and could get much tastier fruit along morally acceptable and less strenuous routes"(**Björnsson, 2002**, p. 339).[25] Here St Augustine seems to judge that stealing a pear would be wrong and this judgment seems to make him want to steal it. In contrast, Strong Internalists claim that this judgment always comes with some motivation not to steal attached to it.

8.34 Strong Internalists must therefore explain why and how St. Augustine must have been conflicted even in this situation. They can argue that it is precisely the motivational pull of the moral judgment – that he doesn't want to steal the pear – that makes stealing the pear so exciting. It is exactly this motivational force of the moral judgment that makes pursuing the forbidden fruit attractive. If St. Augustine overcomes his desire not to steal in Björnsson's case, then cases like this are not counterexamples to Strong Internalism either.

A case of depression

8.35 Finally, let us consider a case concerning an individual who suffers from clinical depression. Before we think about this case, a warning is in order. The point of the following case is not to rely on a suspect stereotype of mentally ill people. The claim is not that depressed people are generally indifferent to their moral judgments. Rather, the idea is only that the following individual case from **Al Mele**[26] seems possible:

> Consider an unfortunate person – someone who is neither amoral nor wicked – who is suffering from clinical depression because of the recent tragic deaths of her husband and children in a plane crash. Seemingly, we can imagine that she retains some of her beliefs that she is morally required to do certain things [. . .] while being utterly devoid of motivation to act accordingly. She has aided her ailing uncle for years, believing herself to be morally required to do so. Perhaps, she continues to believe this but now is utterly unmotivated to assist him. (Mele, 2003, p. 111)

According to Strong Internalism, even individual cases like this should not be possible. It could not be that the clinically depressed mother is making a genuine moral judgment that she should help her uncle and yet has no motivation to do so. Despite this, you will probably find Mele's description of the case plausible. There are two ways in which Strong Internalists can respond to this objection.

8.36 Firstly, Strong Internalists can argue that the mother must have at least some motivation to help her uncle. Perhaps she is feeling a bit guilty for failing to do so, or maybe if she only had to push a magic button to help her uncle, she would do so. If one of these options were true of the mother, then this case wouldn't be a counterexample to Strong Internalism either. Some motivation could still be required for making a genuine moral judgment.

At this point, you could also move from Strong Internalism to the following weaker version of the thesis (Smith, 1994, p. 61): 8.37

Weak Internalism: If you judge that you morally ought to act in some way, then you will have at least some motivation to act in that way or you are practically irrational.

This thesis is immune to the previous counterexamples. You can always argue that amoral, bad, and depressed people are all practically irrational in some way and for this reason they do not pose a problem for Weak Internalism.

Despite this, Weak Internalism still has many of the advantages of the 8.38
stronger forms of internalism. For example, it can still explain why you would doubt the sincerity of Mary's moral judgments when she rails against eating meat in public and at the same time enjoys steaks in private. Weak Internalism still requires that she must have some motivation not to eat meat in this situation, unless she is suffering from impairing conditions such as clinical depression which can block the motivating power of her moral judgment. Otherwise she just doesn't genuinely think that there is anything wrong with eating meat.

Finally, Weak Internalism too holds on to the basic idea, which moti- 8.39
vates all forms of internalism. This is the insight that morality is in the end a very practical way of thinking. Unlike, for example, scientific inquiry, it is directly related to what we do in everyday life. We take part in moral debates precisely for the reason that we hope that by convincing other people of our views we can change how they behave. The truth of even the weaker forms of internalism can explain this practice.

Expressivism

We now have the two premises of the Argument from Motivation on the 8.40
table: the Humean Theory of Motivation and Moral Judgment Internalism. This helps us to rephrase the argument in the following way:

1. All mental states are either cognitive belief-like states with the mind-to-world direction of fit or non-cognitive desire-like states with the world-to-mind direction of fit.

2. Only the non-cognitive desire-like states with the world-to-mind direction of fit can motivate us.

These two premises are a more accurate statement of the Humean Theory of Motivation. We can then add to them the following Weak Internalism thesis:

3. Necessarily, if you make a genuine moral judgment that you morally ought to act in a certain way, then you have at least some motivation to act in that way or you are practically irrational.

From these three premises it follows that:

4. Moral judgments are desire-like states with the world-to-mind direction of fit.

8.41 Why does this follow? Well, according to Premise 2, beliefs lack a necessary connection to motivation: they only move you if you happen to have additional desires. However, Premise 3 tells us that there *is* a necessary connection between moral judgments and motivation. These judgments motivate you unless you are practically irrational. If this is true, then moral judgments can't be beliefs but rather they must be desire-like non-cognitive states instead.

8.42 Expressivism is the theory which endorses this surprising conclusion. (For an overview, see **Christman, 2011**[27]; for a textbook, see Schroeder, 2010; and for main expressivist texts, see Blackburn, 1993, 1998a; Gibbard, 1990, 2003.) This view is named after the idea that the meaning of moral words is given by their role: we use these words to *express* what we are planning to do. The rest of this section outlines some of the features and advantages of this theory.

The core claims of expressivism

8.43 Most expressivists accept the following three core ideas:

- *Core Claim about Moral Judgments*: When you make a genuine moral judgment, you do not form a belief but rather you are in a non-cognitive desire-like state.

- *Core Claim about Moral Language*: You can understand the meaning of moral words by considering what kind of mental states people are in when they use moral language.
- *Core Claim about Moral Properties*: Science offers a complete description of the world and this description does not include any moral properties or facts. Instead, moral facts and properties are our attitudes projected onto the world.

Let us then consider these claims in turn.

Claim 1: Moral judgments I'm sure you agree that it is wrong to lie. What mental state are you in when you make this judgment? According to expressivists, if you think that lying is wrong, you are thereby planning to avoid lying whenever you can (Gibbard, 2003, ch. 3). If this is the state you are in when you make a moral judgment, then you are in a non-cognitive desire-like mental state against lying. In this case you are motivated not to lie insofar as you are a rational person who acts according to her plans. This is why expressivism fits nicely with the conclusion of the Argument from Motivation. 8.44

Expressivism also provides a plausible explanation of our intuitions behind the Open Question Argument (**Darwall, Gibbard, and Railton, 1992, pp. 117–119**).[28] As you can recall, Moore believed that questions of the form "this act is N, but is it good?" are always open questions no matter which natural property we substitute in for N. According to expressivists, these questions are open because thinking that an act has a natural property doesn't commit you to plan to do anything. When you then ask yourself whether an act that has certain natural properties is good, you are considering whether to adopt a plan to act in a certain way. The natural properties of the object always leave this open. 8.45

Despite these advantages of expressivism, merely planning to do something isn't sufficient for a moral judgment. Imagine that Susan loves **Justin Bieber**[29] and therefore plans to listen to him whenever she can. This doesn't mean that, according to her, you are morally required to listen to Bieber. Susan only plans to do so because she happens to like him. Expressivists therefore must be able to distinguish moral judgments from personal preferences (Miller, 2013, pp. 39–42). 8.46

In response to this challenge, Simon Blackburn has suggested that moral judgments are networks of connected plans (Blackburn, 1998a, pp. 8–14). 8.47

If you think that lying is wrong, in addition to having a plan not to lie you also need to plan:

i. to criticize and blame other people who lie;
ii. to praise other people who do not lie;
iii. to feel guilty if you lie yourself;
iv. to help other people to plan not to lie;
v. to keep on planning not to lie and so on.

8.48 Blackburn claims that if you have this whole network of plans, then we can distinguish moral judgments from personal preferences. Susan has not made a moral judgment, because she has no plans for whether other people are to listen to Bieber too. In contrast, if you think that lying is wrong, you must also be planning about what other people are to do. Expressivists therefore think that moral judgments are more complicated sets of plans than mere personal preferences. Funnily enough, Blackburn's response to the previous objection means that if a **belieber**[30] has the right kind of network of plans (if they criticize and blame others for not listening to Bieber and so on), they do count as making a moral judgment that you should listen to Bieber!

8.49 *Claim 2: Moral language* In order to understand what expressivists say about moral language, we first need to return to subjectivism. Recall that according to subjectivists, when you say that "lying is wrong" you are describing the mental state you are in. You are **reporting** that you are planning not to lie. This report is true if you really have that plan and false otherwise.

8.50 As we saw in Chapter 6, subjectivism makes moral disagreements impossible. If you say "lying is wrong" and Joe says "no, lying is all right," according to subjectivism you are reporting that you are planning not to lie, whereas Joe is saying that he doesn't have this plan. These reports can both be true at the same time. As a result, you wouldn't be disagreeing with Joe, which is pretty implausible.

8.51 This means that expressivists can't think that moral utterances report our plans. Instead they say that the purpose of moral utterances is to **express** our plans (Schroeder, 2010, pp. 70–74). You can express your plans in many different ways. You could, for example, express your plan not to lie by just saying "lying!" with a special condemning tone of voice. This too would indicate to your audience that you are planning not to lie.

Expressivists think, roughly, that uttering the sentence "lying is wrong" expresses your plan not to lie in exactly the same way as the previous **ejaculation** (**Ayer, 1936, p. 137**).[31] That you can express your plan not to lie by uttering the word "wrong" explains what this word means.

What then does it mean to say that moral utterances express plans? 8.52
Expression here isn't **a causal relation**[32] like in other contexts. Wincing, for example, often *expresses* pain because pain *causes* you to wince. A distinguishing feature of such causal expression is that if you are not in pain you are not really wincing but rather only acting. This means that whenever one thing (wincing) causally expresses another thing (pain), what is expressed (pain) must be there to cause the expression (wincing).

Moral utterances can't express plans like this because you can make 8.53
insincere moral utterances (**Schroeder, 2008a, sect. 3.2**).[33] These utterances express the same plans as sincere moral utterances even if the plans that get expressed do not exist when these utterances are made. When the actor Sean Connery utters "Blofeld must die," he expresses James Bond's plan to kill Blofeld even when no one actually has such a plan. This is why the relationship between this utterance and the expressed plan isn't the same as the one between pain and the wincing caused by the pain.

This is easy to see in the non-moral cases. Expressivists claim that non- 8.54
moral utterances express ordinary beliefs. When you are lying, you can utter the sentence "it's raining" to express your belief that it is raining even when you actually believe that it's sunny. By making this dishonest utterance you can express beliefs which you want others to believe you have. The best way to manipulate other people is to deceive them about what you are really thinking.

The same applies to moral utterances. According to expressivists, when 8.55
you say "we should all help other people" you express a plan to help others even when you have no intention of doing so. This can happen, for example, when you attempt to make others more generous by making them think that you are planning to help other people too. In this case, a plan to help other people is not causing you to say that "we should all help other people" because you don't even have that plan. Because of this, your utterance can't express your real plans in the same way as wincing expresses your pain.

A better way to think about expression here is to think that a sentence 8.56
expresses the mental state which you would have to be in if you were to utter the sentence sincerely (Schroeder, 2008a, sect. 5). On this view, the sentence "it's raining" expresses the belief you would have to have if you

were to say it sincerely. You can only say this sentence sincerely if you believe that it is raining. This is why the sentence "it's raining" expresses the belief that it is raining.

8.57 Similarly, you can say sincerely that "we should all help other people" only if you are planning to help others yourself. This is why this sentence expresses a plan to help others even when you don't actually have the plan yourself. More generally then, moral sentences always express plans you would have to have if you were to say these sentences sincerely. According to expressivists, you can understand what moral words mean if you know what plans they express.

8.58 This story about the expression helps expressivists to avoid the problems of subjectivism. Expressivists think that when you say "lying is wrong" and Joe says "no, lying is all right," you are expressing your plan not to lie whereas Joe is expressing his plan to lie. In this situation, you and Joe do not have conflicting beliefs but you still arguably **disagree in planning** (**Stevenson, 1937, sect. 5**).[34]

8.59 Consider a case in which you are planning that we go to a Mexican restaurant, whereas I want us to go to an Italian restaurant instead. In this case there is a real disagreement between us: we disagree about what we will do. Expressivists understand moral disagreements in the same way. In the same way you and I have a disagreement about where to eat, you and Joe have conflicting plans about whether to lie or not. In both cases, there is a disagreement in planning because the plans we have can't be satisfied at the same time.

8.60 *Claim 3: Moral properties* Finally, expressivists tend to understand moral properties with the model of **disgusting things**.[35] The property of being disgusting is not a real property: it's not a way in which some things are in themselves. For one, what is disgusting for you might actually be quite likable for others. Instead, what certain things are like creates a reaction of disgust in you. When you talk about disgusting things you then color the world on the basis of this reaction. You **project** your reaction of disgust on to the world by saying that the thing which disgusts you is disgusting.

8.61 Expressivists understand moral properties with this model (Blackburn, 1984, pp. 170–171). They believe that there are only the concrete objects and properties which can be fully understood by science. That expressivists do not need any other properties is an important advantage of the view. Some features of the world make you plan to do certain things. The idea is that **you project your planning on to the world**[36] by talking about right and wrong. As properties, right and wrong are therefore only shadows of what you are planning to do.

Responses to two common objections

Objection 1: Truths and facts You might think that expressivism can't be right because we often talk about moral facts and truths. Surely right and wrong can't then be merely projections of our attitudes? Expressivists, however, think that it's perfectly fine for us to continue to talk about moral facts and truths (Blackburn, 1998a, p. 79). Consider the following utterances: 8.62

- Torturing people is wrong.
- Torturing people has the property of being wrong.
- It is true that torturing people is wrong.
- It is an objective mind-independent fact that torturing people is wrong.

According to expressivists, all these utterances say the same. They are just different ways of expressing your plan not to torture other people. Adding fancy words like "property," "true," "objective," and "fact" makes no difference to what you really mean. Many of these words are philosophical jargon anyway and as such rarely used in real life. When they are so used, perhaps they are used for additional emphasis: for saying how strongly behind your plan you stand. The expressivists insist, however, that they don't add any more substantial content to the moral claims we make. Of course, the expressivists need to tell us more about how exactly this is possible. How can it be that seemingly meaningful words like "property" and "objective fact" don't really, at the end of the day, mean anything much at all?

Objection 2: Mere attitudes Expressivists also insist that the expressions of our plans should be taken seriously (Blackburn, 1998b, pp. 196–197). The critics of expressivism sometimes ridicule expressivism because it says moral utterances are "mere" expressions of our plans. They argue that there must be more to morality than this. 8.63

In response, expressivists point out that your plans reflect what you most deeply care about. They say that there is nothing "mere" about your plan not to kill other people or your plan to help your sick friends. These concerns define you as a person. Expressivists also add that if we couldn't 8.64

peacefully coordinate what we do, we would barely survive. This is why we need to be able to project our plans onto the world so that we can make these plans fit together. The moral discussions we all have about what is right and wrong are ideal for this purpose, according to expressivists.

8.65 Finally, expressivists don't have to think that all plans and expressions are equally good. They can say that some attitudes are cruel and morally obnoxious. Of course, when you say this, you are again expressing your own concerns. However, you don't have to think that your own concerns are the best possible ones either. Your attitudes too could be better if they were more sensitive, coherent, and informed. According to expressivists, when we say this we are again expressing our plans to have new and improved plans.

The Frege–Geach Problem

8.66 We'll finish this chapter by looking at the main problem with expressivism. Under different guises, it is called **the Frege–Geach problem** or **the embedding problem**.[37] The discussions of this objection can get technical but the basic problem is simple enough (see Schroeder, 2010, chs 6–7).

Embedded claims

8.67 All examples of moral sentences in this chapter have so far been simple: "torturing people is wrong," "lying is wrong," and "we should all help other people." These sentences are called **subject–predicate sentences**. The subject term of these sentences picks out a group of acts, and the predicate then says something about those acts. You can easily understand these sentences in the expressivist way because when these sentences are uttered it is plausible that you must have some motivation to act accordingly. It is a short step from this to think that these sentences just express our plans.

8.68 The problem is that we also use moral words in more complicated sentences all the time. Consider the following utterances you can make:

- Is it wrong to have an abortion?
- Joe believes that tax evasion is wrong.
- If Nancy should give money to charity, then she should give to Red Cross.

- I don't think that it is wrong to lie, but I might be mistaken. In fact, I often wonder whether it is wrong to lie.

You can sincerely utter these sentences without having any particular plans, and for this reason these sentences can't express planning. Sincerely asking whether it is wrong to have an abortion doesn't require having any plans either to have an abortion or not to have one. Similarly, you can say that Joe believes tax evasion is wrong no matter what your tax plans are. In the third case, even if you are against giving money to charity, you can agree that *if* Nancy should give money to charity, giving to Red Cross would be a good option. Finally, you can sincerely say that you are uncertain about whether lying is wrong without having decided your plans with respect to lying. 8.69

Because these more complex moral sentences can be sincerely uttered without the corresponding plans, in these sentences the moral words are not expressing our plans. This leads to several problems for expressivists. First of all, expressivists owe you a story of what moral words mean in these complex embedded contexts (**Geach, 1960**).[38] In normal sentences these words are meant to express our plans. Here these words must mean something different, but what? 8.70

Secondly, the idea that moral words mean different things in different sentences is problematic. When you learn to speak a language you first learn to use a word in one situation and then you start to use it in other sentences too. You don't need to learn what a word means in different sentences separately. However, expressivism now seems to be saying that in simple sentences the meaning of moral words is given by the plans they express, whereas in other sentences they mean something else. When did we all learn this? 8.71

Valid inferences*

The next problem is that you can use moral words in good reasoning only if these words mean the same things in different sentences (Geach, 1960). Consider the following bad instance of reasoning: 8.72

1. Sally lives near a bank [a river bank].
2. If Sally lives near a bank [a monetary institution], then it is easy for her to get money.
3. It is easy for Sally to get money.

8.73 The word "bank" is ambiguous in this inference. What is inserted in brackets tells you what this word means in the two premises. This makes it easy to see why this inference is no good. That Sally lives near a river doesn't make it any easier for her to get money. The inference is not **valid** because the work "bank" means different things in the two premises. Really we are guilty of **equivocating**. Consider then the following piece of reasoning:

1. You should give more money to charity [a plan to give money to charity].
2. If you should give more money to charity [???], then you should give more money to Red Cross [???].
3. You should give more money to Red Cross [a plan to give more money to Red Cross].

8.74 If you ignore what's in the brackets, this is a valid inference because the conclusion necessarily follows from the two premises. The problem is that the expressivists can't easily explain why this is the case as for them this inference is just like the previous inference about Sally. The words "should give more money to charity" express a plan in the first premise. However, you can sincerely endorse the second premise without having any plans about giving to charity at all – the meaning of "should give money to charity" thus must mean something different. The upshot is that, if expressivism is right, this argument about giving to charity is just as fallacious as the bad reasoning about banks. But surely this is wrong – the moral argument is valid, and it's expressivism that's getting things wrong.

The negation problem*

8.75 Recently an even harder version of this problem has emerged (Unwin, 1999; **Schroeder, 2008b, pp. 710–714**[39]; Schroeder, 2010, ch.7). Consider the following statements:

1. Max thinks that helping other people is good.
2. Nina doesn't think that helping other people is good.
3. Olly thinks that not helping other people is good.
4. Pete thinks that helping other people is not good.

Max, Nina, Olly, and Pete all think something different in this situation. According to expressivists, they must therefore have different plans. The question then is what plans do Max, Nina, Olly, and Pete need to have for these four claims to be true of them? 8.76

The first three cases are easy. The first three claims must be true because: 8.77

A. Max is planning to help other people.
B. Nina is not planning to help other people.
C. Olly is planning not to help other people.

The problem must then be Pete. What is he planning to do for the fourth claim to be true? He can't lack a plan to help other people or have plan not to do so, because he must be thinking something different than Nina or Olly. This is why expressivists can't understand the mental state Pete is in in terms of planning at all.

This has led some expressivists to suggest that Pete has a special attitude of being neutral between helping and not helping. This, unfortunately, leads to a further problem. Max and Pete clearly disagree about something. Max thinks that helping other people is good whereas Pete thinks that it isn't. The new suggestion seems unable to explain this disagreement: Max is planning to help other people and Pete is only neutral between helping and not doing so. Are they really disagreeing, then? You can be neutral between watching television and surfing the Internet and yet you don't disagree with someone who is planning to surf the Internet. 8.78

The real challenge, then, for the expressivists is to explain what attitudes Pete must have for statement 4 to be true such that 8.79

i. these attitudes explain why Pete doesn't think the same as Nina and Olly; and
ii. they also explain why Pete disagrees with Max.

Whether expressivists can give an account of Pete's attitudes that can explain all of this still remains very much an open question.

Summary and Questions

This chapter has focused on the nature of moral judgments. The first part investigated the Argument from Motivation, which attempts to show that 8.80

moral judgments are not beliefs aiming at truth but rather non-cognitive attitudes of planning.

8.81 The Argument from Motivation has two premises. According to the first premise – the Humean Theory of Motivation – all mental states are either belief-like or desire-like states. Belief-like states are sensitive to evidence because they aim at being true representations of reality. This is why they have a mind-to-world direction of fit. Desire-like states, in contrast, motivate us to act as they aim at changing the world to fit themselves. This is why these states have a world-to-mind direction of fit. The Humean theory then claims that mere beliefs are never enough to motivate us.

8.82 The second premise of the Argument from Motivation is Moral Judgment Internalism, which claims that there is a necessary connection between moral judgments and motivation to act. You have not made a genuine moral judgment on this view unless you have some motivation to act accordingly. We then went through some of the alleged counterexamples to different versions of this thesis.

8.83 The Argument from Motivation is a powerful argument for expressivism, according to which moral judgments are states of planning. If you think that it is wrong to eat meat, then you have a plan not to eat it, to blame those who do, to keep on planning not to eat meat, to help others to plan not to eat meat, and so on. We then considered what expressivists say about moral language (its purpose is to express plans) and moral properties (they are projections of our plans onto the world).

8.84 The last section of the chapter introduced the Frege–Geach objection to expressivism. It points out that expressivists also need to explain what moral words mean when they are embedded in more complex sentences. Such explanations make it hard for expressivists to explain why certain pieces of reasoning are good and how to deal with the negation problem.

8.85 Based on the philosophical resources introduced in this chapter, consider the following questions:

1. Are all mental states really either belief-like states or desire-like states? Consider sensations (seeing blue, pain, hearing a C note played on a piano) and emotions (anger, feeling blue, jealousy, courage). Can these states be classified into beliefs, desires, or some combinations of them?
2. Humeans think that motivation to do an act must always consist of both a desire and a belief. Why is this true? Consider what mental states you must have in order to take a bus home. Are there cases in which beliefs or desires could motivate us to act on their own?

3. What is the motivation for internalist views about moral judgments? How good are the counterexamples to Strong Internalism and do the internalist responses to these cases work?
4. What are the three core commitments of expressivism?
5. Simon Blackburn has claimed that we can deal with the problem of valid inferences with a hierarchy of disapproving attitudes. How is this proposal supposed to work and what is wrong with it (**see Schroeder, 2008b, pp. 708–710**)?[40]

Annotated Bibliography

Anscombe, G.E.M. (1957) *Intention* (Oxford: Basil Blackwell). A landmark book in the philosophy of action, which investigates how practical reason is related to action. The focus is on how we should understand intentional action and intentions. Even if Anscombe never used the terminology of different directions of fit herself, she provided the best illustration of this distinction in this book.

Ayer, A.J. (1936) *Language, Truth and Logic*, full text available at http://archive.org/details/AlfredAyer, accessed March 5, 2014. A radical book in which the young Ayer defended logical positivism under the influence of the Vienna Circle. Chapter 6 is famous for its early emotivist theory of ethics.

Björklund, Fredrik, Gunnar Björnsson, John Eriksson, Ragnar Olinder Francén, and Caj Strandberg (2012) "Recent Work on Motivational Internalism," *Analysis*, *72*(1), 124–137. This overview article clearly distinguishes between different forms of internalism and also discusses the main arguments for and against these views. In addition, it contains the most comprehensive bibliography of the literature on the topic.

Björnsson, Gunnar (2002) "How Emotivism Survives Immoralists, Irrationality, and Depression," *Southern Journal of Philosophy*, *40*(3), 327–344, full text available at http://people.su.se/~gbjorn/327-344Bjornsson.pdf, accessed March 5, 2014. This article aims at showing that internalist views survive the alleged counterexamples to them. Björnsson discusses different types of immoral and listless people.

Blackburn, Simon (1984) *Spreading the Word* (Oxford: Oxford University Press). This book was written as an opinionated textbook in philosophy of language. Blackburn also constructs a model for how expressive domains of language (like moral and modal language) function. This includes showing how expressivists can deal with valid arguments and talk about moral truths.

Blackburn, Simon (1993) *Essays in Quasi-Realism* (Oxford: Oxford University Press). A collection of Simon Blackburn's best articles defending and developing expressivism. These articles have had a huge influence on the recent debates in metaethics.

Blackburn, Simon (1998a) *Ruling Passions* (Oxford: Oxford University Press). One of the main expressivist texts, in which Blackburn shows how expressivism helps us to locate practical reason in the naturalist and scientific worldview. It also contains important discussions of the Frege–Geach problem, thick ethical concepts, and game theory.

Blackburn, Simon (1998b) "Moral Relativism and Moral Objectivity," *Philosophy and Phenomenological Research*, *68*(1), 195–198. A review of Gilbert Harman and Judith Thompson's book on moral relativism and objectivity in which Blackburn defends his expressivism against some of the most popular objections to the view.

Brink, David (1989) *Moral Realism and the Foundations of Ethics* (Cambridge: Cambridge University Press). A systematic early attempt to develop naturalist realism further. Brink's book is also famous for its powerful defense of Moral Judgment Externalism.

Christman, Matthew (2011) "Ethical Expressivism," in *The Continuum Companion to Ethics*, ed. Christian Miller (London: Continuum), full text available at http://www.philosophy.ed.ac.uk/people/full-academic/documents/Chrisman%20-%20Ethical%20Expressivism%20for%20Continuum%20-%20penultimate.pdf, accessed March 5, 2014. A clear overview article which focuses on the motivations for expressivism, the Frege–Geach problem, the problem of creeping minimalism, and the most recent formulations of expressivism.

Darwall, Stephen, Allan Gibbard, and Peter Railton (1992) "Toward fin de siècle Ethics: Some Trends," *Ethics*, *101*(1), 115–189, full text available at http://www-personal.umich.edu/~sdarwall/Fin de siecle.pdf, accessed March 18, 2014. See the bibliography of Chapter 7 above.

Geach, Peter (1960) "Ascriptivism," *Philosophical Review*, *69*, 221–225, full text available at http://www.hist-analytic.com/Geach2.htm, accessed March 5, 2014. An influential article in which Geach first introduced the embedding problem. Because Geach acknowledged the influence of Frege's work on assertions, this objection came to be known as the "Frege–Geach objection."

Gibbard, Allan (1990) *Wise Choices, Apt Feelings* (Cambridge, MA: Harvard University Press). Gibbard's earlier formulation of expressivism. According to this view, moral judgments consist of judging when it is rational to experience moral emotions such as guilt and blame, where this judgment is understood in terms of acceptance of norms that govern these moral emotions.

Gibbard, Allan (2003) *Thinking How to Live* (Cambridge: Cambridge University Press). One of the most sophisticated expressivist works, in which Gibbard introduced the idea that "ought" claims express complicated planning states.

This helped him to construct a complex semantic theory to make sense of embedded normative claims and their logical relations.

Hare, Richard (1952) *The Language of Morals* (Oxford: Oxford University Press). Available at http://www.ditext.com/hare/lm.html, accessed March 5, 2014. An important and influential work of early metaethics in which Hare understood moral claims with the model of universal prescriptions.

Hume, David (1739–1740) *A Treatise of Human Nature*. See the bibliography of Chapter 1 above.

Kahn, Leonard (2013) *Moral Motivation* (London: Bloomsbury). A useful textbook on the internalism vs. externalism debate. Kahn uses the resources of cognitive science and empirical moral psychology throughout the book.

Mele, Al (2003) *Motivation and Agency* (Oxford: Oxford University Press). In this book, Mele creates a comprehensive view about human agency by focusing on motivation. He defends the Humean Theory of Motivation and argues that human actions can be causally explained by the agent's motivational base, which consists of desires and intentions. Chapter 5 is very good on the internalism debate.

Miller, Alex (2013) *Contemporary Metaethics: An Introduction*. See the bibliography of Chapter 6 above.

Sayre-McCord, Geoffrey (2008) "Hume on Practical Morality and Inert Reason," *Oxford Studies in Metaethics*, 3, 299–320, full text available at http://philosophy.unc.edu/people/faculty/geoffrey-sayre-mccord/on-line-papers/Hume%20on%20Practical%20Morality%20and%20Inert%20Reason.pdf, accessed March 18, 2014. In this article, Sayre-McCord argues that Hume himself never put forward the Argument from Motivation and that he wasn't an expressivist either.

Schroeder, Mark (2008a) "Expression for Expressivists," *Philosophy and Phenomenological Research*, *72*(1), 86–116, full text available at http://www-bcf.usc.edu/~maschroe/research/Schroeder_Expression.pdf, accessed March 5, 2014. An illuminating article on how the expression relation should be understood.

Schroeder, Mark (2008b) "What Is the Frege–Geach Problem?," *Philosophy Compass*, *3*(4), 703–720, full text available at http://www-bcf.usc.edu/~maschroe/research/Schroeder_Frege-Geach_Problem.pdf, accessed March 5, 2014. An accessible and thorough introduction to both the history of the Frege–Geach problem and the contemporary debates.

Schroeder, Mark (2010) *Noncognitivism in Ethics* (London: Routledge). The most up-to-date and comprehensive textbook on different forms of non-cognitivism in metaethics and their problems.

Smith, Michael (1987) "The Humean Theory of Motivation," *Mind*, *96*, 36–61. In this classic paper, Smith clarifies the distinction between desires and beliefs and argues that motivating reasons must be desire–belief pairs because this helps us to use motivating reasons to explain actions and to understand motivation as the pursuit of a goal.

Smith, Michael (1994) *The Moral Problem*. See the bibliography of Chapter 7 above.

Stevenson, Charles (1937) "The Emotive Meaning of Ethical Terms," *Mind*, *46*(181), 14–31, full text available at http://www.jstor.org/stable/2250027, accessed March 18, 2014. A classic article in which Stevenson defended prescriptivism, according to which the purpose of ethical statements is to change and influence other people's attitudes. In this paper, Stevenson also introduced the idea of "disagreements in interest" to deal with the disagreement problem.

Svavarsdóttir, Sigrún (1999) "Moral Cognitivism and Motivation," *The Philosophical Review*, *108*(2), 161–219, full text available at http://makowski.wdfiles.com/local–files/wprowadzenie-do-analizy-metaetycznej/svavarsottir.pdf, accessed March 5, 2014. In this article Svavarsdóttir defends the externalist view that there is no necessary connection between moral judgments and what you are motivated to do. According to her, moral judgments motivate only if they are accompanied by additional desires. Svavarsdottir defends this view with a large number of good examples.

Unwin, Nicholas (1999) "Quasi-Realism, Negation and the Frege–Geach Problem," *Philosophical Quarterly*, *49*(196), 337–352. A critical investigation of Simon Blackburn's earlier attempts to solve the Frege–Geach problem, which is the first clear formulation of the objection in the modern negation problem form.

Online Resources

1. An overview of the debates about moral motivation: http://plato.stanford.edu/entries/moral-motivation/.
2. Expressivist views are also called non-cognitivist theories. An overview of different theories in this family: http://plato.stanford.edu/entries/moral-cognitivism/.
3. *Treatise*, Book II, chapter 2, section 3: http://www.gutenberg.org/files/4705/4705-h/4705-h.htm#link2H_4_0075.
4. *Treatise*, Book III, chapter 1, section 1: http://www.gutenberg.org/files/4705/4705-h/4705-h.htm#link2H_4_0085.
5. Sayre-McCord on how to read Hume: http://philosophy.unc.edu/people/faculty/geoffrey-sayre-mccord/on-line-papers/Hume%20on%20Practical%20Morality%20and%20Inert%20Reason.pdf.
6. Wikipedia on directions of fit: http://en.wikipedia.org/wiki/Direction_of_fit.
7. The life and works of Anscombe: http://plato.stanford.edu/entries/anscombe/.

8 Information about tea in Sri Lanka: https://en.wikipedia.org/wiki/Tea_production_in_Sri_Lanka.
9 Michael Smith's homepage: http://www.princeton.edu/~msmith/.
10 Stir-fry ingredients: http://www.bbc.co.uk/food/stir-fries.
11 *Treatise*, Book III, chapter 1, section 1: http://www.gutenberg.org/files/4705/4705-h/4705-h.htm#link2H_4_0085.
12 *Treatise*, Book III, chapter 1, section 1: http://www.gutenberg.org/files/4705/4705-h/4705-h.htm#link2H_4_0085.
13 Gunnar Björnsson's PhD thesis on this topic: http://www.phil.gu.se/gunnar/morint.pdf. See the introduction for an explanation and history of this thesis.
14 Charles Stevenson's "The Emotive Meaning of Ethical Terms": http://www.jstor.org/stable/2250027.
15 Explanation of hypocrisy: http://en.wikipedia.org/wiki/Hypocrisy.
16 An overview of the notion of weakness of will: http://plato.stanford.edu/entries/weakness-will/.
17 An article on people like this: http://www.guardian.co.uk/theobserver/2010/mar/07/polly-vernon-infidelity-betrayal-help-relationships.
18 Chapter 11 of Hare's *The Language of Morals*: http://www.ditext.com/hare/lm11.html.
19 Explanation of anemia: http://en.wikipedia.org/wiki/Anemia.
20 Svavarsdóttir's homepage: https://philosophy.osu.edu/people/svavarsd%C3%B3ttir and her "Moral Cognitivism and Motivation": http://makowski.wdfiles.com/local–files/wprowadzenie-do-analizy-metaetycznej/svavarsottir.pdf.
21 The Homer quote: http://weknowmemes.com/2012/08/just-because-i-dont-care-doesnt-mean-i/.
22 Studies on how many of us believe in amoralists: http://dingo.sbs.arizona.edu/~snichols/Papers/PsychopathsFinal.pdf.
23 The relevant section from Hare's *The Language of Morals*: http://www.ditext.com/hare/lm11.html.
24 Information on Augustine of Hippo: http://en.wikipedia.org/wiki/Augustine_of_Hippo.
25 Björnsson's "How Emotivism Survives Immoralists, Irrationality, and Depression": http://people.su.se/~gbjorn/327-344Bjornsson.pdf.
26 Al Mele's homepage: http://myweb.fsu.edu/amele/almele.html.
27 Christman's overview: http://www.philosophy.ed.ac.uk/people/full-academic/documents/Chrisman%20-%20Ethical%20Expressivism%20for%20Continuum%20-%20penultimate.pdf.
28 An explanation of how expressivists can use the Open Question Argument to their advantage: http://www-personal.umich.edu/~sdarwall/Fin%20de%20siecle.pdf.
29 Some Justin Bieber: http://www.youtube.com/watch?v=Ys7-6_t7OEQ.

30 The definition of a belieber: http://www.urbandictionary.com/define.php?term=Belieber.

31 Explanation of the term: http://en.wikipedia.org/wiki/Ejaculation_(grammar) and Chapter 6 of Ayer's *Language, Truth and Logic*: http://www.colorado.edu/philosophy/heathwood/pdf/ayer.pdf.

32 Overview of philosophy of causation: http://plato.stanford.edu/entries/causation-metaphysics/.

33 Schroeder's article "Expression for Expressivists": http://www-bcf.usc.edu/~maschroe/research/Schroeder_Expression.pdf.

34 Stevenson's classic disagreement in attitude view: http://www.jstor.org/stable/2250027.

35 Fascinating information about disgust: http://en.wikipedia.org/wiki/Disgust.

36 Overview of projectivism: http://plato.stanford.edu/entries/moral-anti-realism/projectivism-quasi-realism.html.

37 Mark Schroeder's article "What Is the Frege-Geach Problem?": http://www-bcf.usc.edu/~maschroe/research/Schroeder_Frege-Geach_Problem.pdf and overview of the embedding problem: http://plato.stanford.edu/entries/moral-cognitivism/#EmbPro.

38 Geach's classic article "Ascriptivism": http://www.hist-analytic.com/Geach2.htm.

39 Schroeder's "What is the Frege–Geach Problem?": http://www-bcf.usc.edu/~maschroe/research/Schroeder_Frege-Geach_Problem.pdf.

40 Schroeder's "What is the Frege–Geach Problem?": http://www-bcf.usc.edu/~maschroe/research/Schroeder_Frege-Geach_Problem.pdf.

Part Four

ETHICAL QUESTIONS

9

MORAL RESPONSIBILITY

This book has so far covered three broad areas of moral philosophy. The first part focused on pleasure, happiness, well-being, and the meaning of life. The second part introduced ethical theories that investigate how you should treat other people. Finally, the previous part explored metaethics, which studies the nature of moral properties, moral language, and moral judgments. 9.1

This last part will return to more concrete ethical questions. This chapter discusses moral responsibility: the important question of when it is appropriate to blame and praise other people for what they do. This question is discussed because it nicely illustrates how seriously we take it when other people do morally bad and wrong things, and how philosophical arguments can at times seem to threaten this fundamental part of how we live and relate to other people. The final chapter will then consider two of the most pressing ethical questions of our times: population growth and global warming. These ethical questions will illustrate both the resources which philosophical theories offer for solving important ethical problems and also the theoretical problems we face when we try to apply these theories in practice. 9.2

What Is Moral Responsibility?

This chapter considers what **moral responsibility**[1] is and what it takes for you to be morally responsible for what you do. These are very abstract 9.3

This Is Ethics: An Introduction, First Edition. Jussi Suikkanen.

and general questions, which is why they should be approached from something more concrete. For this reason, it is useful to follow **Peter Strawson**[2] and to start from the idea that we all *hold* other people morally responsible all the time (**Strawson, 1962, sect. 3**).[3] When you hold someone morally responsible for what they have done, you react to their actions with **reactive attitudes**.[4] If someone does something bad to you, you blame, resent, and condemn that person for what she has done. You similarly praise and feel gratitude, respect, and love toward people who treat you well. When you react in these concrete ways to other people's actions, you are thereby holding them responsible. If someone accidentally harms or benefits you, you don't blame or praise them exactly for the reason that they were not responsible for what was sheer good or bad luck.

9.4 These reactions are essential for how we relate to other people. They enable us to form important relationships such as friendships, parental relationships, and romantic relationships. By praising, respecting, and loving other people, we can bond with them. In contrast, the negative reactive attitudes enable us both to show that we personally care about what others do (which often can bring us closer) and to distance ourselves from others (which can help us to burn bridges). If you never react in these ways to what other people do, then it seems as though other people are just mere strangers to you.

9.5 We know then what it is to hold another person morally responsible. We must, however, recognize that *holding* someone responsible is not sufficient for *judging* that they are responsible. This is easy to illustrate with an example. If your dog soils your carpet, you might blame it for this and thus in a sense you are holding your dog responsible for what it did. Despite this, you would probably deny that your dog really was morally responsible for its behavior. This is because when you judge that someone is responsible for what they have done you are judging that it is *appropriate* to have the reactive attitudes toward them (Wallace, 1994, p. 91). In the case of your dog, you might blame it but ultimately you would not think that this really is appropriate. The dog just couldn't help it. This fits well with the idea that you are morally responsible for what you do when it is appropriate for other people to adopt reactive attitudes toward you. If you are morally responsible for your actions, we are also entitled to ask you for reasons for why you have behaved in the way you have (Oshana, 1997). It makes no sense to ask your dog why it soiled your carpet.

Causal responsibility and attributability

Moral responsibility in this sense should be distinguished from both **causal responsibility** and **attributability**. You are causally responsible for an outcome simply in virtue of bringing about that outcome. In contrast, when the movements of your body are attributable to you as an action, they are something that you do rather than a mere chain of events that happens to you. 9.6

In order to understand this distinction, consider again your dog soiling a carpet. Firstly, it is clear that your dog is causally responsible for the wet carpet. It initiated a chain of events that led to this result. Secondly, wetting the carpet can also be attributed to your dog as an action. Perhaps your dog did this in order to mark its territory. Admittedly, there could also be cases in which a dog is causally responsible for wetting a carpet even if this cannot be attributed to the dog as an action. Dogs too can have accidents! In any case, we don't think that the dog is morally responsible for wetting the carpet even if this is something the dog does. As we saw above, even if we blame your dog for the wet carpet, we don't thereby necessarily think that it was morally responsible. 9.7

The important conclusion to draw from this is that you can be causally responsible for a bad outcome and this act can even be correctly attributed to you even if you are not morally responsible for the act and its bad consequences (Watson, 1996). Imagine that you are **blackmailed**[5] to forge an official document in your role as a public servant. If you don't agree to forge the document, your family will be killed. If you then make the forgery, you are causally responsible for the forgery and the act of forging the document can be attributed to you. Despite this, you might not be morally responsible for what you have done, because it doesn't seem appropriate to blame you. 9.8

You probably don't think that inanimate objects, animals, or very young children are morally responsible for their actions. As the previous case shows, even you are not always morally responsible for what you do. The crucial question then is: when are you morally responsible (for overview, see Fischer, 1999)? When is it appropriate to have reactive attitudes like blame and praise toward other people? 9.9

The agency condition

The first necessary condition for being morally responsible is called the **agency condition**. It states that you can be morally responsible for what you do only if you are an agent. What does this require from you? 9.10

9.11 First of all, in order to be an agent you must have goals that lead you to act (Smith, 1987). Without goals, you can't intentionally pursue outcomes, and if you are not pursuing outcomes you are not doing anything. Without goals, things only happen to you. In order to be an agent, you must also have some idea of the situation you are in. If you do not believe that you have the ingredients of a stir-fry in your fridge, then your goal to make one will not get you anywhere. In order to be an agent you must therefore have goals, an idea of the situation you are in, and these goals and beliefs must lead you to behave the way you do.

9.12 This first requirement for being morally responsible explains why **volcanoes**[6] are not morally responsible for the damage they cause. Volcanoes are not agents, because they don't have goals or beliefs about the situation they are in.

9.13 We need to add two further elements to this agency condition. Consider a case in which you come home and switch on the lights by flipping a switch. Sadly, in this case your flat has been wired wrong. When you flip the switch this causes **an explosion**[7] in your neighbor's kitchen which kills the whole family.

9.14 In this case, you are causally responsible for killing your neighbors. However, there are two reasons why you are not morally responsible for this. Firstly, you had no idea that switching the lights on would cause the explosion and you could not have been expected to know this either. This suggests that you are only morally responsible for what you know will happen as a result of what you do (and perhaps also for what you could have known would happen, had you tried to find out more about the situation you were in).

9.15 This case also illustrates that you can be held morally responsible only if you can control what happens. The previous case included too many accidents. It was an accident that the wires were connected wrongly and that the short circuit caused the explosion. Perhaps there was a one in a million chance that this would happen. Thus it would be unreasonable to blame you for killing your neighbors.

9.16 The agency condition for moral responsibility claims that you are morally responsible for what you do only if:

i. what you do flows from your goals and your beliefs about your situation;
ii. you know what will happen as a result of your actions or at least you could know this fairly easily; and
iii. what happens is under your control.

But, even if satisfying the agency condition is a necessary condition for 9.17
being morally responsible, it isn't a sufficient condition for moral responsibility. This is shown by the fact that in the previous blackmail case, you satisfied the agency condition even if you weren't morally responsible for the forgery. For this reason, there are other more interesting conditions which you must also satisfy in order to be morally responsible for what you do.

Freedom and real selves

Philosophers who work on moral responsibility usually focus on the 9.18
following two further conditions for moral responsibility (Kane, 2005, pp. 6–7):

> **The freedom principle**: You are morally responsible for what you have done only if you could have done something else instead (also known as the principle of alternative possibilities).

> **The deep attributability principle**: You are morally responsible for what you have done only if acting in that way was up to your real self.

Sadly, there is no uncontroversial way to motivate the first principle with 9.19
a concrete example, but here's a case that should illustrate the basic idea behind it. Imagine again that someone points a gun at you and says that she will shoot you unless you forge an official document in your public role. Intuitively, in this case you can't be blamed for making the forgery. Some people would say that this is because there is nothing else you could have done. Your only alternative would have been death, which they say is no alternative at all. Because you therefore didn't have any other alternatives, it is not appropriate to blame you. Other people reject this example because they think you do have an alternative in this case. You could take the bullet instead of making the forgery, which is then said to be enough for you to be morally responsible for your actions. As we will see later on in this chapter, it is very hard to find cases in which we genuinely lack alternatives and, furthermore, our intuitions about such cases aren't always very clear. But I hope that the previous case gives you some idea of the basic thought behind the freedom principle.

The deep attributability principle can be motivated by moving the trigger 9.20
of the previous case inside the agent. Imagine **a heroin addict**[8] whose life is unbearable if she doesn't get more drugs. She might not want to be an

addict, but she just can't bear the withdrawal symptoms. In this case, even if we might blame the addict for having the addiction, perhaps we should not blame her for taking the drug, because she can't help it. In this case, the addict's **real self** is not responsible for the addict's actions, and for this reason we should not blame her. This simple example motivating the deep attributability principle has its problems too. You might think that we should consider the addict's addictions as a genuine part of who she is. This would make the real self of the person irrelevant for what the person is responsible for. Later on, we will return to the question of when we should consider addictions as a part of the addict's real self.

9.21 In any case, these two conditions for moral responsibility are of paramount importance in our ethical thinking – we base our decisions about when to punish people for their actions on them. This chapter will explore these conditions further. We will first look at the freedom principle and the way in which it has been used to undermine our moral responsibility. We will then consider Harry Frankfurt's counterexamples to it. The last sections of the chapter will explore the debates about how the deep attributability principle should be understood.

The Freedom Principle: A Threat for Moral Responsibility

9.22 The freedom principle states that you can be morally responsible for what you do only if you could have done otherwise. Many people find this principle plausible. If you can't help but act in some way, then how could you be blamed for acting in that way? Because you don't have any other options, judging you for what you do seems unfair. This section will first look at how the freedom principle can be used to undermine moral responsibility, together with a general thesis about our world called determinism. It will then consider how considerations based on luck and the role of our character in our actions can also be used to undermine moral responsibility.

The consequence argument

9.23 The problem is that if the freedom principle is true, then the truth of **determinism**[9] seems to mean that you can never be morally responsible for any of your actions. **Determinism**[10] is the thesis that everything that happens is determined by how things were at the beginning of the universe and by the laws of nature. Given the distant past and the laws of nature, things couldn't be different from what they are now. More formally, **determinism** is the thesis that a statement of the laws of nature and a complete description of the facts about the world at the beginning of the universe entail all other truths.

You get a powerful argument against moral responsibility if you accept 9.24
two further premises. They are:

Premise 1: You can't now change the distant past.
Premise 2: You can't now change the laws of nature.

These two premises together entail:

Conclusion: You can't now change the distant past or the laws of nature.

Determinism was the claim that the distant past and the laws of nature determine everything else that takes place. What you do is part of this "everything else." This means that what you do is also something you can't change: it is determined by the distant past and the laws of nature, which are beyond your control. This is why determinism means that you can never do otherwise than what you actually do (van Inwagen, 1983, p. 16 and ch. 3).

This is the so-called **consequence argument**[11] to the conclusion that 9.25
determinism rules out alternative possibilities. If alternative possibilities are a necessary condition for moral responsibility as the freedom principle says, then this argument means that you are never morally responsible for what you do.

The problem of luck

Perhaps things would be easier if **indeterminism**[12] were true. The best 9.26
theory in physics to describe the smallest building blocks of our universe is called **quantum mechanics.**[13] According to many interpretations of quantum mechanics, the quantum world contains events that aren't completely determined by the laws of nature and the past. The laws of quantum mechanics only talk about how probable it is that something will happen. What then ends up happening is a genuinely open question.

9.27 You might then think that, if indeterminism were true, you would have alternative possibilities and therefore you could be morally responsible. Sadly, things are not so simple (Mele, 2006, pp. 6–9). Let's assume that indeterminism is true and that there are genuinely random events. Assume that in this situation you weigh your options and decide that **you shouldn't lie to your friend when he asks about his new haircut**.[14] You intend to say that it looks awful. In this situation where there are random occurrences, you can still end up saying "it looks nice," despite the fact that you intended to say exactly the opposite.

9.28 The problem is that in indeterministic situations you no longer have control over what you do and therefore you can't be held responsible for your actions. After all, even if you decide to do something, you might still end up doing something different. What you do is thus more a matter of luck than being up to you. Indeterminism also means you aren't responsible for your actions.

Galen Strawson's argument against moral responsibility

9.29 Both determinism and indeterminism therefore seem to undermine moral responsibility. Either you lack alternative possibilities, or what you do is down to luck. There is also another good reason to doubt that you can be morally responsible for what you do. This argument has been presented most clearly by **Galen Strawson (Strawson, 1994)**.[15]

9.30 **Strawson**[16] first draws a distinction between being **truly responsible** and being responsible in some weaker sense. True responsibility is a notion strong enough to support decisions about who should be punished and who rewarded – think of God evaluating your actions and deciding whether you deserve to go to Heaven or Hell. Strawson also assumes that you are morally responsible in the weaker everyday sense only if you are also truly responsible. The idea here seems to be that if you don't deserve blame from God, you don't deserve it from anyone else either. In other words, if you are not willing to dish out the ultimate punishment to people, then you shouldn't judge them at all. Strawson therefore sets the standards for moral responsibility high from the very beginning.

9.31 Strawson's argument against moral responsibility starts from the plausible idea that what you do is a consequence of your character. You might decide to help your friend because that's the kind of person you are. This means that in order for you to be truly responsible for what you do, you must also be truly responsible for your character from which your actions flow. Your character, after all, explains what you do.

The next step of the argument states that in order for you to be truly responsible for your character: 9.32

i. you must have done something in the past that made you who you are; and
ii. you must have been truly responsible for this act too.

If it is an accident that you become a kind person, then you can't be truly responsible for your character or the kind actions that flow from it. If you are not truly responsible for your character, then we should not praise you for your kind acts, because they are just fortunate coincidences.

You can now see where this is going: we get to a vicious regress. Having a character for which you are truly responsible requires that you did earlier something that made you the person you are and that you were responsible for these self-forming acts. These self-forming acts, too, were a consequence of your earlier character. You could have been truly responsible for these self-forming acts only if you were truly responsible for your earlier character from which *they* flowed. In order for you to have been truly responsible for your earlier character, that character too should have been a consequence of even earlier acts of self-formation for which you were responsible. Those acts too had to be a consequence of an even earlier character for which you were responsible, and so on. 9.33

The problem is that, in the case of a normal person, you can't have an infinite regress of self-forming acts and new characters. You were born at some point in the past, which is why at some point in the past you just happened to develop a character that led to your first acts. You could not have been truly responsible for this first character, because it was given to you by both nature and nurture. As a result, you weren't responsible for the acts that flowed from this character and thus you weren't responsible for the ways in which you have shaped your characters later on. This means that you can't be truly responsible for anything you do. 9.34

You might think that this argument is pretty similar to the consequence argument above. To a degree this is true, but there is one important difference between these two arguments. Unlike the consequence argument, Strawson's argument does not rely on determinism. It works equally well both in situations in which determinism is true and in situations in which 9.35

it isn't. Either way, you can't be responsible for your initial character and all the rest that follows from it. Strawson's argument, however, also has its flaws. The main problem with this argument is that the notion of being *truly responsible* is difficult to make sense of. Can you genuinely consider whether other people should go to Heaven or Hell? Furthermore, is it true that we are not entitled to hold other people morally responsible in the ordinary sense unless we are willing to judge whether they should go to Heaven or Hell? If you find the notion of true responsibility objectionable, then you have reason to challenge Strawson's clever argument.

The Frankfurt Cases

9.36 So far, we have looked at some of the arguments against moral responsibility. We have assumed that alternative possibilities are a necessary condition for moral responsibility. This is why determinism turned out to be a problem for moral responsibility – it says that we never have any alternative possibilities. But what if alternative possibilities were irrelevant to moral responsibility? **Harry Frankfurt** argues this in his famous article "**Alternate Possibilities and Moral Responsibility**" (Frankfurt, 1969; see also Fischer, 2002; Kane, 2005, ch. 8; and Mele, 2006, ch. 4).[17] Here's the original case he used:

> Suppose someone – Black let us say – wants Jones to perform a certain action. Black is prepared to go to considerable lengths to get his way, but he prefers to avoid showing his hand unnecessarily. So he waits until Jones is about to make up his mind what to do, and then he does nothing unless it is clear to him (and Black is an excellent judge of such things) that Jones is going to decide to do something other than what he wants him to do. If it does become clear that Jones is going to decide to do something else, Black takes effective steps to ensure that Jones decides to do, and he does do, what he wants him to do. Whatever Jones's initial preferences and inclinations, then Black will have his way. (**Frankfurt, 1969, p. 835**)[18]

9.37 Imagine that Black wants a politician to be assassinated. Black has built a device that can manipulate Jones's brain in a very specific way. If Black believes that Jones will decide not to kill the politician, he will switch the device on and this will make Jones decide to shoot the politician. However, Jones too wants the politician to be killed. After weighing his options, he decides to shoot him and then acts accordingly. Black, therefore, never has to switch his device on. But because he had both the ability to predict Jones's actions and the device in place, Jones did not have any other alternatives than to shoot the politician, which is what he did anyway.

Frankfurt thinks that in this case you can blame Jones for the murder of the politician even if he could not have done anything else. As a result, freedom to do otherwise cannot be a necessary condition for moral responsibility. This would enable you to be morally responsible even if determinism were true. This position is a version of **compatibilism**.[19] Compatibilism seems to offer us a way of protecting moral responsibility from the worries expressed in the previous section. 9.38

Objections and responses*

Objection 1: Flicker of freedom The first problem of Frankfurt's argument is that Jones seemed to have an alternative – **a flicker of freedom** – in the described scenario (Fischer, 1994, p. 134). He could have decided not to shoot the politician, in which case Black's device would have made him kill the politician. Because Jones had this alternative, you can hold him responsible for the murder since he did this without Black's interference. This alternative would be enough to save the freedom principle from the objection. 9.39

Objection 2: A dilemma Frankfurt's example also leads to a dilemma (Widerker, 1995). Either determinism or indeterminism is true. Consider Frankfurt's case, then, in both deterministic and indeterminist situations. 9.40

In a world where everything is determined by the past and the laws of nature, Jones is predetermined to act in the way he does. To assume that he is responsible for killing the politician when Black doesn't interfere is to beg the question against those who think that moral responsibility requires alternative possibilities. It is to assume that compatibilism is true even before you start to think about the case. In this situation, the case serves no purpose. 9.41

This means that the example must take place in an indeterministic situation in which there are genuinely random occurrences. The problem is that, in this situation, Black cannot predict in advance what Jones will do. If Black switches the device on too early when Jones could still change his mind, Black will be responsible for the murder. If Black switches the device on after Jones has fully decided to kill the politician, Jones would have had 9.42

alternative possibilities before this and he is therefore responsible for the murder. Either way, the example doesn't work in this situation.

9.43 *Response 1: Mele and Robb* At this point, the debate about Frankfurt's cases tends to get technical. One sophisticated response to these objections has been given by Al Mele and David Robb (Mele and Robb, 1998). In their souped-up example, Black implants a new type of device in Jones's brain in an indeterministic world. This new device will have a timer, and so Black does not need to make any predictions. He sets this new device to work in parallel with Jones's ordinary brain processes, and so the new process doesn't interfere with anything else that happens in Jones's brain except at certain crucial moments.

9.44 You can think of the events that lead Jones to kill the politician as a series of choices – a choice to decide to kill the politician, a choice to buy a gun, and, finally, a choice to fire the gun. The device's parallel process is timed so that always, at the very last moment, the device makes Jones choose to do what Black wants unless Jones has already chosen to do this anyway. This means that Black doesn't need to make any predictions about Jones's choices even if they are not predetermined by anything. This timer device does not, therefore, offer Jones any flickers of freedom like Frankfurt's original case. This is because, when needed, the device overrides Jones's decisions at exactly the same moment when Jones has the last chance to make the decision himself.

9.45 If Jones keeps making the choices Black wants, then these choices preempt the parallel process of Black's device. In this case, the device is redundant. But Jones could not have chosen differently at any point in the chain of choices. Exactly at the moment when he would have done so, Black's device was set to interfere. If you still want to hold Jones responsible for killing the politician in this case, then you reject the idea that alternative possibilities are a necessary condition for moral responsibility.

9.46 *Response 2: Dennett* Admittedly, Mele and Robb's case threatens to be too technical to be a very effective case against the freedom principle. The case is so gimmicky that it is hard to have clear intuitions about it. Perhaps your intuitions about the case are sharper. In any case, many people do find a simpler case from **Daniel Dennett**[20] more compelling (Dennett, 1984, p. 133). It is about **Martin Luther**,[21] who was a sixteenth-century monk and a Church reformer. Luther believed that faith is a personal gift from God and therefore it doesn't require the intermediation of the Catholic

Church. He also claimed that the Catholic Church was corrupt and in desperate need of radical reform. Luther defended these revolutionary ideas in a number of writings.

In 1521, Luther was invited to appear in the front of the **Diet of Worms** 9.47
(a general assembly of the Estates of the Holy Roman **Emperor Charles V** which met in the town of Worms).[22] At this meeting, Luther was asked whether he stood by the ideas that were printed in his books. Luther cared so much about his faith that he reportedly replied, "Here I stand, I can do no other." Scholars now believe that Luther in fact never said this, but let's imagine that he did. As a result, the Diet banned Luther's works.

Luther's refusal to recant was based on his most fundamental concerns. 9.48
Without them, he literally would not have been the same person. Given his identity, Luther had no other options but to stand behind his works. Despite this, we want to hold him morally responsible. If the Catholic Church was as corrupt as Luther believed, then we really should praise him for his efforts. This case fits the idea that freedom to do otherwise is not a necessary condition for moral responsibility – you can be responsible for something that your character compels you to do.

The Deep Attributability Principle

If freedom to do otherwise is not a necessary condition for moral respon- 9.49
sibility, this leaves you with the two other necessary conditions. First of all, you must be an agent. What this requires was briefly discussed at the beginning of this chapter. The second condition, called the deep attributability principle, requires that your actions must also be up to your real self. This important principle will be discussed in the remainder of this chapter. When do your actions flow from your real self in a way that makes you morally responsible for them?

The deep attributability principle is often motivated by thinking about 9.50
the constraints on your actions that are internal to you. These constraints consist of psychological conditions like **addictions, compulsions, obsessions, phobias, neuroses, and various other mental health problems.**[23]

People who suffer from these conditions often satisfy the other require- 9.51
ments for moral responsibility, and yet we don't want to hold them morally responsible for what they do. For example, it isn't always appropriate to blame addicts for what they do, because it isn't up to them. This is why addictions illuminate what is required for moral responsibility.

Frankfurt's higher-order desire theory

9.52 Harry Frankfurt introduced us to three addicts who all desire to take drugs and who are also unable to resist this desire (**Frankfurt, 1971, sect. 2**).[24] The first of these addicts is **an unwilling addict**.[25] Even if he desires to take the drug, he also badly wants to quit to save his marriage. In Frankfurt's terminology, this addict has **a second-order desire** for his first-order desire not to move him to act. Sadly, this unwilling addict can't resist his desire for more drugs and so his addiction forces his hand: his behavior is therefore compulsive. According to Frankfurt, for this reason you shouldn't hold this addict morally responsible. This person's addiction isn't a part of his real self, which explains why he isn't responsible for the consequences of his addiction.

9.53 Compare the unwilling addict to **a willing addict**.[26] The willing addict doesn't care about his marriage, but rather loves getting high and also endorses the drug-loving counter-culture. He has a genuine second-order desire for his first-order desire for drugs to be effective. Even if this second addict is just as addicted as the unwilling addict, you should hold him responsible because he has the desires he wants to have and he therefore stands by his addiction. This is why this addict's addiction is part of his real self.

9.54 Here Frankfurt uses the second-order desires to account for why the unwilling addict is not responsible and the willing addict is. Behind this thesis is the idea that it's your second-order desires that make you the person you are. If you have second-order desires to have the desires that move you to act, then you are behind your actions as a person; and if you are behind what you do, then you can be held responsible.

9.55 Frankfurt also uses the higher-order desires to explain why animals are not morally responsible for what they do, even if they satisfy the other conditions for moral responsibility. Animals have goals and an awareness of their environment, and for this reason they satisfy the agency condition for moral responsibility. Animals can't, however, think about what they want to desire: they lack the capability for rational self-evaluation because they just act on their instincts. This is why we don't hold animals morally responsible.

9.56 This leads us to Frankfurt's third addict: the **wanton**[27] who is an extremely spontaneous human being. The wanton addict will have all kinds of basic first-order desires, and one of them is his strong desire to take drugs. The wanton can't resist this desire even if he tries. Because the wanton is so spontaneous, he never considers his own desires. He neither endorses them nor desires not to have them. According to Frankfurt, this addict would be more like an animal acting on its instincts than a person whom you should hold responsible.

This makes Frankfurt conclude that moral responsibility requires an 9.57 appropriate hierarchy of desires. In order for you to be responsible for what you do, you must want to want to do that thing. If you don't want your desires to move you, but they do so anyway, you can't be held responsible for your actions because these actions can't be deeply attributed to you. In this case, your real self isn't behind what you do but rather your addiction is making you do things. This shows how Frankfurt thinks that the real self of the person is her higher-order desires.

The idea that you are not responsible for what you do unless your real 9.58 self stands behind your actions is attractive. However, what exactly constitutes your real self has turned out to be a controversial question. The rest of this chapter will look at how the real self should be best understood so as to help us to understand who it is appropriate to blame and praise for their actions.

The Real Self

The flaws of Frankfurt's higher-order desire theory of the real self were 9.59 revealed quickly. There are no good reasons to give your second-order desires a privileged status when it comes to who you really are (Double, 1991, p. 35). Let's consider Jackie, who is a willing addict. She desires her first-order desire to take drugs to move her.

Jackie is also a wanton with respect to her second-order desires. She 9.60 never considers which desires she wants to desire to have: she just comes to desire to have certain desires. The original wanton was the addict who had a strong desire for drugs but no higher-order desire to have this desire. Frankfurt claimed that the wanton is not morally responsible for his drug taking because of this.

The problem is that there is no reason why Jackie should be any more 9.61 responsible than the original wanton. According to Frankfurt's own view, Jackie is not morally responsible for her higher-order desire because she doesn't desire to have it. It is then mysterious how a higher-order desire for which Jackie is not responsible could make her responsible for her desire to take drugs and the actions that flow from this desire.

9.62 Frankfurt can't respond to this problem by saying that in order to be responsible Jackie would need a third-order desire to have a second-order desire to desire to take drugs. No one has artificial desires like this and this response would only move the problem one step back. To avoid the previous problem, Frankfurt has suggested that Jackie could either:

A. identify with her second-order desire to desire drugs; or
B. exclude this higher-order desire as an external force within her psychological makeup.

If Jackie chooses A and welcomes her second-order desire as a central part of who she is, this can make Jackie morally responsible for her actions, according to Frankfurt.

9.63 This leads to two questions. Firstly, why should we focus on the second-order desires? Why can't you directly welcome your normal desires as who you are in the same way as Jackie can commit herself to her second-order desire directly? Why can't you, for example, adopt your desire to raise a family as a central part of who you are? If you can make this normal desire directly a part of who you are, then your real self will be behind your project of building a family without the need for any higher-order desires.

9.64 The second problem is that it is not clear how you could make a desire part of you in this way. We wanted to know which desires are your real self. To merely say that you must welcome the given desire or identify with it or be committed to it isn't very helpful, and it also seems to already rely on a pre-existing real self to explain what it is to identify with a desire.

9.65 Frankfurt himself later on gave two accounts of what you need to do to make a desire yours in a strong sense. His first proposal was that you have wholeheartedly to endorse the desire. This means standing behind it without any ambivalence or conflict of will (**Frankfurt, 1998**).[28] He has also suggested that only the desires that are based on what you love are an element of your real self (**Frankfurt, 2004**).[29] Instead of these views, let's look at **Gary Watson**'s more plausible suggestion (**Watson, 1975**).[30]

Watson's theory of the real self

9.66 When it comes to who we really are, Watson too emphasizes the importance of **reflective self-evaluation**. Consider why the willing addict is responsible for his actions even if the unwilling and wanton addicts are not. The basic difference between these cases is that the willing addict endorses his addiction in his own deliberation. Unlike the unwilling and wanton addicts, he stands behind his actions and for this reason it is appropriate to hold him responsible.

Watson, however, claims that Frankfurt has misunderstood what reflective self-evaluation is. For Frankfurt, reflective self-evaluation is a matter of whether or not you want to have the desires you have, but this only led to the previous problems. Watson argues that we should instead consider practical reason and its ability to make evaluative judgments. 9.67

According to Watson, when it comes to moral responsibility it is important *why* you have the desire on which you act. In some cases, you have used your practical reason to conclude what the best course of action is. As we saw in the previous chapter, usually you then want to act in that way. 9.68

Watson suggests that your practical reason is your real self. If your practical reason and the evaluative judgments it makes are responsible for your desires, then these desires are representative of your real self. Therefore, because the willing addict judges that taking drugs is the best option for him, it is appropriate to hold him responsible. In contrast, because the unwilling addict judges that it would be best not to take drugs, his desire to take drugs isn't a part of who he really is and therefore we should not hold him responsible. 9.69

The time-slice problem

Watson's theory is elegant in many ways, but it has at least two problems. The first problem is that, like Frankfurt's theory, his view is **a time-slice theory** (Christman, 1991). According to Watson, for you to be morally responsible when you act, your desires and evaluative judgments must match. You must want to do what you think is best. This view says nothing about how the evaluative judgments need to be formed before the time of action. 9.70

This creates a problem. Imagine that before yesterday you had no intention of being faithful to your partner: you believed that there is nothing good about exclusive sexual relationships. Your partner then hires a hypnotist. Last night when you were sleeping the hypnotist hypnotized you. You don't remember this, but you are still under **the hypnosis**.[31] Because of the hypnosis you now want to be faithful, and your practical reason endorses this desire. 9.71

9.72 Most people think that you should not be praised for your faithfulness in this situation. This is a problem for the time-slice view. Currently your psychological makeup satisfies all the suggested standards for moral responsibility: you want to do what you think is the best course of action. Despite this, you are not responsible for your behavior because your psychological makeup was brought about **in a wrong way**.[32] This means that you can be morally responsible for what you do only if you come to have your desires and evaluative judgments in an appropriate way. This condition must rule out hypnosis and brainwashing, but not the ordinary ways in which we come to have our desires and evaluative judgments.

Responsiveness to reasons

9.73 Susan Wolf has given another reason for why it is not enough for moral responsibility that your actions merely flow from your real self (Wolf, 1990, chs 2 and 4). There are people whose actions flow from their real self, but who are not capable of figuring out what they should do. **A psychopath**[33] can genuinely come to the conclusion that she ought to kill other people, because she just can't understand that other people's lives matter. Yet we don't think that such psychopaths are necessarily morally responsible for what they do. Instead of blaming the psychopaths, we want to treat them and protect other people from their actions.

9.74 Susan Wolf's explanation for this is that you are not morally responsible for what you do unless you are capable of finding out what you ought to do and acting accordingly. According to her, moral responsibility therefore requires normative competence: in order to be responsible, you must be able to recognize what you have reasons to do. For being responsible, in addition to making evaluative judgments you also need the ability to get at least some of these judgments right. Morally responsible agents must be sensitive to reasons.

9.75 This explains why psychopaths are not morally responsible even if their actions flow from their real selves. The problem is that psychopaths lack the ability to recognize the moral reasons they should be acting on: they can't see that other people's pain is a reason not to hurt them. Because they lack this skill, it would be unfair to hold them responsible.

9.76 The shortcoming of this view is that it makes it difficult for bad people to be morally responsible for their actions. Some bad people recognize what is wrong but do it anyway. These people act against their best judgments and therefore they suffer from weakness of will. It is hard to blame these people, because they aren't really in control of what they do. Others fail to see what is wrong and thus do what they mistakenly think is the best thing to do. According to Wolf, they are not responsible because they lack the required normative competences. But, then, how could you blame anyone who acts badly?

Summary and Questions

This chapter clarified the notion of moral responsibility. It is useful to begin from the reactive attitudes, which include guilt, blame, praise, admiration, gratitude, forgiveness, and so on. If you react to what others do with these attitudes, then you are holding them morally responsible for their actions. People are morally responsible if it is appropriate for you to react to their actions with these attitudes. 9.77

The chapter then discussed three necessary conditions for moral responsibility. According to the first one, you should only hold responsible those agents who have goals and a conception of the situation they are in. The second condition is called the freedom principle, which says that you are responsible for what you do only when you have alternative possibilities. If everything is determined by the laws of nature and the past, then this condition threatens to rule out moral responsibility altogether. 9.78

Compatibilists like Harry Frankfurt argue that you can be morally responsible for what you do even if determinism is true and you don't have alternative possibilities. Frankfurt used the famous Black and Jones example to argue for this conclusion. In this case, Black has built a device into Jones's brain which is supposed to interfere only if Jones is about to do something other than what Black wants. Even if this device seems to rule out alternative possibilities, we still hold Jones responsible for what he does independently. 9.79

The last sections of the chapter discussed the third condition, the deep attributability principle. According to it, you are morally responsible for your actions only if they flow from your real self. Harry Frankfurt then suggested that your real self consists of a hierarchical structure of desires. You are what you desire to be motivated by. This view can't quite explain why, specifically, the second-order desires would be so important for who you are. The chapter then concluded by discussing Gary Watson's theory, according to which who you are is intimately tied to your judgments about what is good. 9.80

9.81 Based on the philosophical resources introduced in this chapter, consider the following questions:

1. What is the difference between holding a person responsible and that person being responsible?
2. Formulate Galen Strawson's argument against moral responsibility as a set of numbered premises and a conclusion. Which premise should we give up?
3. Do Frankfurt's and Dennett's examples show that moral responsibility does not require alternative possibilities?
4. What is your real self? Are there cases in which you can be responsible for actions that do not flow from your real self?
5. I have written this chapter without mentioning the notion of free will. Some people believe that there is no difference between being morally responsible and having a free will. Others think that even if we are morally responsible, we can still lack a free will. If you are morally responsible in the sense described in this chapter, could something more be required for having a free will? If so, what?

Annotated Bibliography

Christman, John (1991) "Autonomy and Personal History," *Canadian Journal of Philosophy*, *21*(1), 1–24. A wonderful paper in which Christman explores self-governance as an aspect of freedom and responsibility. On his view, self-governance requires not only that your values guide your actions, but also that these values are formed in a way you could accept.

Dennett, Daniel (1984) *Elbow Room: The Varieties of Free Will Worth Wanting* (Cambridge, MA: MIT Press). Dennett argues that when we are worried about free will, we are really worried about our dignity as responsible agents. This requires being able to control ourselves in the light of our goals and expectations. Dennett shows how this understanding of ourselves is compatible with thinking of ourselves as biological beings.

Double, Richard (1991) *The Non-Reality of Free Will* (Oxford: Oxford University Press). Double argues that judgments about moral responsibility and free will are evaluative judgments. He contends that, given that there are no objective evaluative facts, the truth of incompatibilism and compatibilism becomes relative to your evaluative perspective.

Fischer, John Martin (1994) *The Metaphysics of Free Will* (Cambridge: Blackwell). In this book Fischer argues that moral responsibility is based on "guidance control." According to this view, responsibility requires sufficient responsiveness to reasons. Most importantly, Fischer convincingly argues that guidance control does not require alternative possibilities.

Fischer, John Martin (1999) "Recent Work on Moral Responsibility," *Ethics*, *110*(1), 93–139. A very thorough overview of the recent philosophical work on moral responsibility. It also contains an extensive bibliography on the topic.

Fischer, John Martin (2002) "Frankfurt-type Examples and Semi-Compatibilism," in Robert Kane (ed.), *Oxford Handbook of Free Will* (Oxford: Oxford University Press), pp. 281–308. A comprehensive summary of different reactions to Frankfurt's cases against the principle of alternative possibilities.

Frankfurt, Harry (1969) "Alternative Possibilities and Moral Responsibility," *The Journal of Philosophy*, *66*(23), 829–839, full text available at http://www.unc.edu/~dfrost/classes/Frankfurt_PAP.pdf, accessed March 11, 2014. The famous article in which Frankfurt used different versions of the Black and Jones case to argue for compatibilism.

Frankfurt, Harry (1971) "Freedom of the Will and the Concept of a Person," *The Journal of Philosophy*, *68*(1), 5–20, full text available at http://www.sci.brooklyn.cuny.edu/~schopra/Persons/Frankfurt.pdf, accessed March 11, 2014. Another influential argument in which Frankfurt first introduced his hierarchical account of desires to offer a compatibilist account of moral responsibility and free will. The different forms of addiction are used to great effect.

Frankfurt, Harry (1998) "Identification and Wholeheartedness," in his *The Importance of What We Care About* (Cambridge: Cambridge University Press), 159–176, full text available at http://web.mit.edu/holton/www/courses/moralpsych/i&wh.pdf, accessed March 11, 2014. Frankfurt's attempt to fix the problems of the higher-order desire account by using the idea of wholeheartedness. On this view, an agent's real self consists of the desires they hold without a conflict.

Frankfurt, Harry (2004) *Taking Ourselves Seriously* and *Getting It Right*, Tanner Lectures on Human Values, full text available at http://tannerlectures.utah.edu/_documents/a-to-z/f/frankfurt_2005.pdf, accessed March 11, 2014. More recent lectures from Frankfurt in which he gives an account of who we are and what reasons we have on the basis of what we love.

Kane, Robert (2005) *A Contemporary Introduction to Free Will* (Oxford: Oxford University Press). An accessible and illuminating textbook on contemporary philosophy of free will and moral responsibility. Highly recommended reading.

Mele, Alfred (2006) *Free Will and Luck* (Oxford: Oxford University Press). In this book, Mele argues that it is more likely that either libertarianism or compatibilism is true than that we are never morally responsible. In the end, Mele sides with compatibilism because of the problems libertarians have with luck.

Mele, Alfred and David Robb (1998) "Rescuing Frankfurt-style Cases," *Philosophical Review*, *107*, 97–112. An article in which Mele and Robb formulate an improved version of the traditional Frankfurt cases that can avoid the main problems with the original cases. Very interesting, but technical in places.

Oshana, Marina (1997) "Ascriptions of Responsibility," *American Philosophical Quarterly*, *34*(1), 71–83. According to Oshana, we should approach moral responsibility from when it is appropriate to demand of people that they explain their actions.

Smith, Michael (1987) "The Humean Theory of Motivation." See the bibliography of Chapter 8 above.

Strawson, Galen (1994) "The Impossibility of Moral Responsibility," *Philosophical Studies*, *75*(1/2), 5–24. A strong argument to the conclusion that we cannot be morally responsible for our actions, because our first self-forming actions had to be based on our initial character for which we were not responsible.

Strawson, Peter (1962) "Freedom and Resentment," *Proceedings of the British Academy*, *48*, 1–25, full text available at http://www.ucl.ac.uk/~uctytho/dfwstrawson1.htm, accessed March 11, 2014. A classic article, which defends the view that we are morally responsible for what we do. Strawson shows how we should approach moral responsibility by considering our relationships, reactive attitudes, and the ways in which we hold others responsible.

van Inwagen, Peter (1983) *An Essay on Free Will* (Oxford: Oxford University Press). In this book, van Inwagen uses the consequence argument to argue that determinism and moral responsibility are not compatible with one another. He then claims that, because we are in all likelihood responsible for our actions, we should reject determinism.

Wallace, Jay (1994) *Responsibility and the Moral Sentiments* (Cambridge, MA: Harvard University Press). Wallace develops the Strawsonian approach, which begins from our practices of holding each other responsible, into a full-blown theory of moral responsibility. According to him, moral responsibility is based on the powers of reflective self-control, where this requires being able to assess your actions in the light of moral considerations.

Watson, Gary (1975) "Free Agency," *The Journal of Philosophy*, *72*(8), 205–220, full text available at http://www.shef.ac.uk/polopoly_fs/1.101506!/file/Watson-Free-agency.pdf, accessed March 11, 2014. An important article in which Watson criticizes Frankfurt's hierarchical view of the real self and proposes an alternative based on evaluative judgments and values.

Watson, Gary (1996) "Two Faces of Responsibility," *Philosophical Topics*, *24*(2), 227–248. Watson defends the idea that real-self views can shed light on which actions are attributable to us, whereas accountability may require additional normative competences.

Widerker, David (1995) "Libertarianism and Frankfurt's Attack on the Principle of Alternative Possibilities," *Philosophical Review*, *104*, 247–261. An article in which Widerker develops the famous dilemma objection to the Frankfurt-style cases.

Wolf, Susan (1990) *Freedom within Reason* (Oxford: Oxford University Press). Wolf argues that being able to act autonomously and in accordance with your real self isn't enough for you to be morally responsible for what you do. Instead, you also have to be able to act in accordance with your reason. This requires an ability to do the right thing for the right reasons.

Online Resources

1 *Stanford Encyclopedia of Philosophy* on moral responsibility: http://plato.stanford.edu/entries/moral-responsibility/.

2 Stanford Encyclopedia of Philosophy on Peter Strawson: http://plato.stanford.edu/entries/strawson/.

3 An overview of philosophy of moral responsibility: http://plato.stanford.edu/entries/moral-responsibility/, the life and works of Peter Strawson: http://plato.stanford.edu/entries/strawson/ and his classic article "Freedom and Resentment": http://www.ucl.ac.uk/~uctytho/dfwstrawson1.htm.

4 Jeannette Kennett discussing reactive attitudes and Strawson's famous paper: http://media.philosophy.ox.ac.uk/uehiro/TT13US_JK.mp3.

5 An article on cases like this: http://www.nytimes.com/2013/06/18/world/asia/true-or-faked-dirt-on-chinese-fuels-blackmail.html?pagewanted=all&_r=0.

6 A volcano erupting: http://www.youtube.com/watch?v=5hE2DZdl0IA.

7 Similar case: http://www.dailymail.co.uk/news/article-2327039/Newark-blast-Was-fatal-explosion-caused-father-trying-fit-new-central-heating.html.

8 Video interview with an addict: http://www.usatoday.com/videos/news/2013/06/25/2456893/.

9 Historical explanation of determinism: http://www.informationphilosopher.com/freedom/determinism.html.

10 An overview of causal determinism: http://plato.stanford.edu/entries/determinism-causal/.

11 A concise explanation of the consequence argument: http://plato.stanford.edu/entries/compatibilism/#4.1.

12 Explanation of indeterminism: http://www.informationphilosopher.com/freedom/indeterminism.html.

13 Overview of quantum mechanics from a philosophical perspective: http://plato.stanford.edu/entries/qm/.

14 This is a tricky question: http://uk.answers.yahoo.com/question/index?qid=20121101120322AAT8vK9.

15 Wikipedia on Strawson: http://en.wikipedia.org/wiki/Galen_Strawson and Strawson's article "The Impossibility of Moral Responsibility": https://

philosophy.as.uky.edu/sites/default/files/The%20Impossibility%20of%20Moral%20Responsibility%20-%20Galen%20Strawson.pdf.

16 An interesting interview with Strawson on the topic: http://www.naturalism.org/strawson_interview.htm.

17 Wikipedia on Frankfurt: http://en.wikipedia.org/wiki/Harry_Frankfurt and his classic article: http://www.unc.edu/~dfrost/classes/Frankfurt_PAP.pdf.

18 Frankfurt's classic paper: http://www.unc.edu/~dfrost/classes/Frankfurt_PAP.pdf

19 Overview of compatibilism: http://plato.stanford.edu/entries/compatibilism/.

20 Wikipedia on Dennett: http://en.wikipedia.org/wiki/Daniel_Dennett.

21 Wikipedia on Martin Luther: https://en.wikipedia.org/wiki/Martin_Luther.

22 Wikipedia on the Diet of Worms: http://en.wikipedia.org/wiki/Diet_of_Worms and on Charles V: http://en.wikipedia.org/wiki/Emperor_Charles_V.

23 The American Psychological Association's classification codes for mental health problems: http://en.wikipedia.org/wiki/DSM-IV_codes.

24 Frankfurt's "Freedom of the Will and the Concept of a Person": http://www.sci.brooklyn.cuny.edu/~schopra/Persons/Frankfurt.pdf.

25 Bubbles from the Wire: http://www.youtube.com/watch?v=9oboLF5XBdc.

26 Cypress Hill's "I Want to Get High": http://www.youtube.com/watch?v=hsojt7iEcTQ.

27 Urban Dictionary on "wantons": http://www.urbandictionary.com/define.php?term=wanton even if this isn't a philosophically accurate definition.

28 Frankfurt's "Identification and Wholeheartedness": http://web.mit.edu/holton/www/courses/moralpsych/i&wh.pdf.

29 Frankfurt's Tanner Lectures on love: http://tannerlectures.utah.edu/_documents/a-to-z/f/frankfurt_2005.pdf.

30 Gary Watson's web page: http://weblaw.usc.edu/contact/contactInfo.cfm?detailID=68897 and his "Free Agency": http://www.shef.ac.uk/polopoly_fs/1.101506!/file/Watson-Free-agency.pdf.

31 Hypnotizing video: http://www.youtube.com/watch?v=WBFEsc3ebHY.

32 A court in Denmark has disagreed: http://www.whale.to/b/janus1.html.

33 The famous case of David Berkowitz: https://en.wikipedia.org/wiki/David_Berkowitz.

10

POPULATION GROWTH AND CLIMATE CHANGE

Let's start with a few **illuminating statistics**[1] about how many people have 10.1
lived on Earth at different times. The figures about the distant past are not necessarily reliable, but it has been estimated that between 8000 years BC and 4000 years BC roughly 5 million people lived at any one time. This was just after the **development of agriculture**.[2] Before this happened, the human population never exceeded a million people.

The closer we get to the present time, the more accurate the estimates 10.2
get. Between 150 and 300 million people lived 2000 years ago. The population remained at that level for the following 1000 years. The population then grew during the sixteenth century to between 400 and 500 million people. About 600 million people lived in the 1600s at any one time; around 1 billion people in the 1800s; 1.6 billion people in 1900; and in 1950 there were 2.5 billion people. The figure of 3 billion people was exceeded in 1960, 4 billion in 1975, 5 billion in the late 1980s, 6 billion in 2000, and 7 billion was finally achieved in 2012. It has been estimated that there will be about 9 billion people by 2050.

If you draw a graph of these figures, it will look like that shown in 10.3
Figure 10.1.

It is easy to spot **a trend**[3] from this graph. The human population was pretty stable until it began to **grow exponentially**[4] fairly recently.

Similar "**hockey stick**" graphs **are familiar** from the debates about 10.4
global warming.[5] Here are some of the headline figures. For the past 500,000 years, the concentration of **carbon dioxide**[6] (CO_2) has varied between 200 and 300 parts per million (ppm) by volume. For the last 10,000

This Is Ethics: An Introduction, First Edition. Jussi Suikkanen.

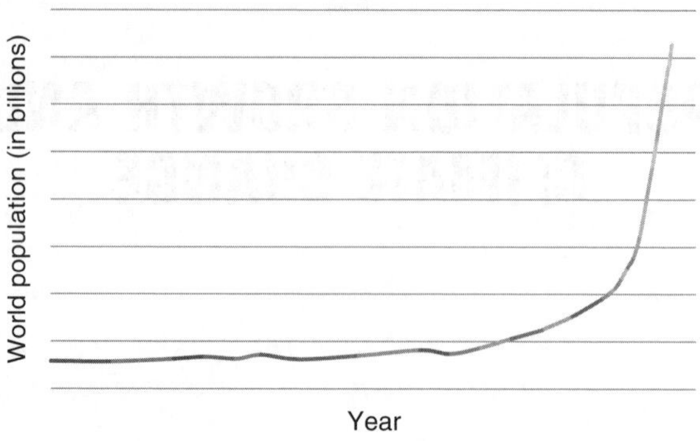

Figure 10.1 World population (in billions)

years before the Industrial Revolution, the concentration stayed at 275 ppm. The concentration of CO_2 in the atmosphere now stands at about 400 ppm. Scientists believe that by 2100 the concentration will be somewhere between 540 and 970 ppm.

10.5 Carbon dioxide is a **greenhouse gas**.[7] How warm it is on Earth depends on (i) how much energy radiated from the Sun comes here, and (ii) how much our planet emits energy outwards back to space through radiation. Because the Earth's atmosphere absorbs some of the outgoing radiation, not all energy escapes, which is why it is warm enough to live here. If the atmosphere didn't absorb some of the radiation, about 30% of the Sun's energy would be reflected back into space. This would make it, on average, around 19 degrees Celsius colder here.

10.6 Greenhouse gases like carbon dioxide, methane, ozone, and water vapor are called greenhouse gases because they absorb energy from the Sun's radiation before it's reflected back into space. These gases play the role of glass ceilings and walls in greenhouses. In a greenhouse, the glass prevents energy radiating back outside, which keeps the greenhouse warm. The more CO_2 there is in the atmosphere, the more of the Sun's radiation is captured by the atmosphere and thus the warmer the climate becomes. This greenhouse effect was first proposed by French physicist **Joseph Fourier** in 1824, and finally proved by **John Tyndall** in 1859.[8]

10.7 Because of the greenhouse effect, there is a historical **match**[9] between the concentration of CO_2 in the atmosphere and the average temperature on Earth. The average temperature was relatively stable after the previous **ice age**,[10] which ended about 10,000 years ago. This was when mankind learned to live in **civilizations**.[11] In these stable circumstances, we learned to farm, to make laws, and to govern ourselves democratically. We also began to develop new technologies and to industrialize. Since 1850, however, the average temperature has increased by almost 1 degree. More recently, it has increased at the rate of 1.5 degrees Celsius per century (Silver, 2012, p. 397).

When scientists forecast what will happen next, the key concept they 10.8
use is **climate sensitivity**.[12] It is the number of degrees by which the Earth's atmosphere would become warmer if the CO_2 concentration doubled from the pre-industrial level. The fourth Intergovernmental Panel of Climate Change (IPCC) estimated that this figure is **between 2 and 4.5 degrees Celsius**,[13] with a 60% likelihood.

Many people are worried about the consequences of population 10.9
growth and climate change. **These developments are believed to lead to famines and lack of clean water, extreme weather events such as floods and droughts, mass migrations, diseases, and wars and conflicts.**[14] The quality of life might thus turn out to be much lower for future generations.

The future is, of course, not yet set in stone. By having fewer children 10.10
and by emitting less greenhouse gas, we could keep the population size under control and avoid the worst climate change scenarios. Do we owe this to future generations? Are we under an obligation to help them to live well even if this requires sacrifices from us? What are these obligations? This chapter will introduce some of the most interesting recent philosophical work on these questions, which are some of the most pressing problems we face with regard to the future of mankind (for population ethics, see essays in Ryberg and Tännsjö, 2004; for climate change ethics, see essays in Gardiner *et al.*, 2010).

The Non-Identity Effect

Let's begin from a simple thought experiment. You might think that the 10.11
basic principle "**Do no harm!**"[15] captures our most important moral obligations. It says that you should never act in a way that makes other people worse off than they would have been otherwise. If you follow this basic principle, then intuitively you do the right thing.

This simple ethical rule is a **person-affecting principle** (Parfit, 1976). 10.12
When you apply the principle, you presuppose that other people exist. Whether or not you behave morally is then a matter of how you affect the

lives of those people. If you make them worse off by harming them, you act immorally. If your actions don't affect other people or if they make them better off, you are off the hook.

10.13 **Derek Parfit**[16] used the following example to show that the "Do no harm!" principle can't be the whole story of what you are required to do (Parfit, 1976). Consider Ann and Bea. Ann is one month pregnant and, unless she undergoes a simple treatment, her baby will become disabled later on. The baby's life would still be worth living, but perhaps not quite as good as it would be if Ann chose the treatment.

10.14 Bea, in contrast, is not pregnant yet, but she is considering having a child. If she becomes pregnant now, her child will have the same disability as Ann's child might come to have. If Bea waits three months, her child will not come to have the disability.

10.15 Most of us think that Ann should have the simple treatment and Bea should wait for three months. You should consider carefully whether you share this intuition, as it is important to note that not everyone does. If you share Parfit's intuition, then the problem is that person-affecting moral principles don't match that intuition. They can deal with the first case: if Ann doesn't take the treatment, the child she is carrying will be worse off. If Ann doesn't take the treatment, she will harm her child. If Ann is required not to harm others, she must not do this.

10.16 The problem is that Bea does not harm anyone if she doesn't wait three months. If Bea gets pregnant immediately, a specific person comes to exist in the future. If she waits instead, that person will never be born but rather a different person will come to exist instead. This is because your personal identity depends on when you are conceived (Parfit, 1976). If you had not been conceived roughly when you were conceived, then your parents could only have had a different child at a different time. She would have grown from a different egg and sperm cells and for this reason she would not have been you.

10.17 This means that if Bea doesn't wait, she will not harm anyone because harming someone requires making a specific person worse off than they would have been otherwise. If Bea's only moral obligation is to do no harm, then morality could not require her to wait. This is an absurd conclusion – we all think that she should wait just as much as Ann ought to take the treatment. This means that there must be additional moral obligations that are not based on person-affecting principles.

10.18 That you can affect the identities of who will come to exist in the future is called **the non-identity effect**.[17] This, together with the intuition that Bea should wait, shows that we are under moral obligations toward future people that are not person-affecting principles.

You could, for example, think that the utilitarian **principle of beneficence**[18] is one such principle. As you will recall from Chapter 4, it requires 10.19
you to maximize the amount of general well-being, and it doesn't matter whose well-being is in question. Let us apply this principle to Bea's case. When you make the decision about whether to wait or not from her perspective, you should consider two potential outcomes:

A. A disabled child with a slightly lower quality of life comes to exist.
B. A non-disabled child with a slightly better quality of life comes to exist.

If Bea is required to maximize the amount of well-being, then she clearly should bring about B by waiting three months.

We can draw the following three conclusions from this discussion: 10.20

1. Sometimes what we do affects which particular persons come to exist.
2. The case of Ann and Bea shows that acting morally cannot merely be a matter of following person-affecting principles like the "Do no harm!" principle.
3. Utilitarianism is not a person-affecting ethical principle and thus it has no problems with the non-identity effect.

Perhaps this means that we should understand our obligations toward future generations by relying on utilitarianism.

The Repugnant Conclusion

Even before Parfit's famous work on population ethics, many others too 10.21
had recognized that utilitarianism has **absurd consequences** in this context (**Sidgwick, 1907, p. 415**; **Broad, 1930, pp. 249–250**; Parfit, 1984, part 4).[19] However, Parfit has made it clearest that utilitarianism has the following **repugnant conclusion**:

> For any possible population of at least ten billion people, all with a very high quality of life, there must be some much larger imaginable population whose existence, if other things are equal, would be better, even though its members have lives that are barely worth living. (Parfit, 1984, p. 388)

Figure 10.2 Populations A and B (after Parfit, 1984, p. 385)

10.22 To understand this, consider the two possible future populations shown in Figure 10.2.

Here, the width of the rectangle represents how big the future generation is and the height of the rectangle the population's level of well-being. The wider the block the more people, and the higher the block the better their lives are. A is therefore a small population with a high quality of life. B is perhaps twice as big but the people in this population have a slightly lower quality of life.

10.23 Utilitarianism says that in this situation you ought to bring about the population B. If you sum up the total amount of well-being in B, the total will be higher than the total amount of well-being in A. Even if each individual in B has a slightly lower quality of life, there are just so many more people in B than in A.

10.24 Consider now the larger set of possible future populations in Figure 10.3. I have omitted the populations D to Y from this illustration. Each one of these populations has slightly more people than the previous population and, at the same time, everyone has a slightly lower quality of life. In this set of populations, from the utilitarian perspective:

- B is better than A because it has a higher total amount of well-being (each person has a slightly lower quality of life but this is compensated by there being more people).
- C is better than B for the same reason.
- D is better than C for the same reason.
- …
- Z is better than Y for the same reason.

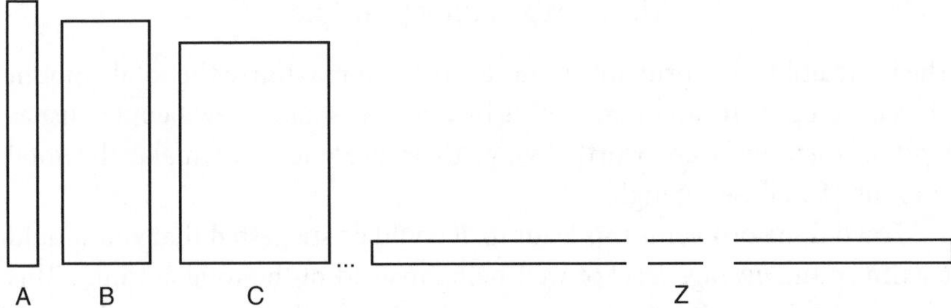

Figure 10.3 Populations A to Z (after Parfit, 1984, p. 388)

This means that if you are required to maximize the total amount of well-being, you must prefer B over A, C over B, D over C…and Z over Y. Consider the following illustration of the **principle of transitivity**.[20] If you think apples are better than oranges and oranges better than pears, then apples are better than pears. If this principle is valid more generally, then you also ought to prefer the huge population Z over the small population A.

In other words, even if the lives in Z are barely worth living, if you sum up the total amount of well-being in this scenario you'll get a higher total than in the other alternatives merely because so many people live in Z. Because of this, Z contains the greatest amount of general well-being. If morality requires you to maximize the total amount of well-being, then you should bring about Z. We should all, therefore, have as many children as we can! 10.25

Most people share Parfit's intuition that this consequence of utilitarianism is repugnant. We know that: 10.26

i. there must be a valid principle of beneficence which is not a person-affecting principle (or otherwise we could not explain why Bea ought to wait); and
ii. this principle of beneficence can't be the simple utilitarian principle because it leads to the repugnant conclusion.

A lot of philosophers have thus sought a principle of beneficence which could both explain why Bea should wait and avoid the repugnant conclusion. This has turned out to be a serious challenge. Let's look at some of the main alternatives.

The average utility principle

10.27 The basic utilitarian principle requires that you maximize the total amount of well-being. You can often do this by creating a lot of new people. Just as long as their lives are worth living, their presence will make the total amount of well-being higher.

10.28 To avoid the problems this leads to, it could be suggested that you should maximize the *average level* of well-being instead of the total amount. This often makes sense. If you want to create a great football team, you don't get as many players as you can. That would maximize the total amount of footballing ability in your team, but you wouldn't win any games. What you need is a small number of players who can all play very well. Perhaps we should think of populations in the same way.

10.29 Calculating the **average**[21] amount of well-being in a population is easy. Here's how you calculate the average height in a group: you first add up the heights of every member of the group; then you divide this sum by the number of people in the group. The **average height**[22] of men in the United States is 5 feet 10 inches, whereas the average height of women is 5 feet 5 inches. These figures were acquired by adding up the heights of American men and women and dividing these sums by the number of men and women, respectively.

10.30 In the same way, calculating the average level of well-being requires you to:

i. give a numeric value to everyone's level of well-being;
ii. add these values up; and
iii. finally, divide this sum by the number of people in the population.

The average utility principle then requires you to maximize the average level of well-being. This principle explains why Bea should wait before she gets pregnant. The average level of well-being will be higher if she has a non-disabled child later on than it would be if she had a disabled child immediately. The disabled child would not come to have an equally good life, which would lower the average level of well-being.

10.31 The average utility principle also avoids the repugnant conclusion. Consider the populations A to Z above. When you move from A to the populations B, C, D, and so forth, at every step the average level of well-being goes down. Because of this, the average utility principle requires you to bring about a small population with a high quality of life rather than a large population with a lower level of well-being.

Unfortunately, the average utility principle has unintuitive consequences in cases in which people's lives are not worth living (Parfit, 1984, p. 406). Imagine that you have to choose between two populations, where these are the last populations before human beings become extinct. Your first option is to bring about 10 people who will be in pain for 50 years and then die. The lives of these people will have no redeeming qualities. Your other alternative is to bring about a billion people who will each be in pain for 25 years and then die. Their lives do not have any redeeming qualities either. What should you do if you had no other options? 10.32

Most people think that you should choose the first option. The 10 people would have to suffer twice as long as anyone in the bigger population, but this would be all right because otherwise so many more people would be in pain. 10.33

The average utility principle gets this case wrong, because the average level of well-being is higher in the big population. If we give one year of suffering the value of negative one, then in the small population the average level of well-being is −50, whereas in the bigger population it is −25. If you are required to maximize the average level of well-being, then in this case you should bring about a billion people who all suffer terribly. If the average utility principle has this consequence, we should not accept it. 10.34

Critical-level utilitarianism*

The next alternative is called critical-level utilitarianism (Kavka, 1982). Let's start from Figure 10.4. Here, the blocks stand for individual people A to H and the height of the blocks represents how well off these individuals are. Given that all the blocks are above the zero line, everyone's life in this situation is worth living. The upper horizontal line in the graph thus represents a critical line set by critical-level utilitarianism. 10.35

Critical-level utilitarianism then tells you to maximize the amount of well-being above the critical level. To see how this works, compare the previous population to that in Figure 10.5. In this population, there's only one person, O, whose quality of life is above the critical level. In the previous population, five people had some amount of well-being above the critical level. Thus, if you ought to maximize the amount of well-being above the critical level, you should bring about the first population rather 10.36

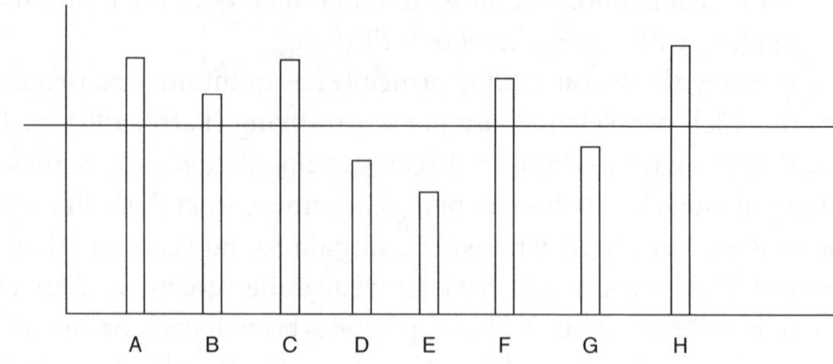

Figure 10.4 Individuals A to H

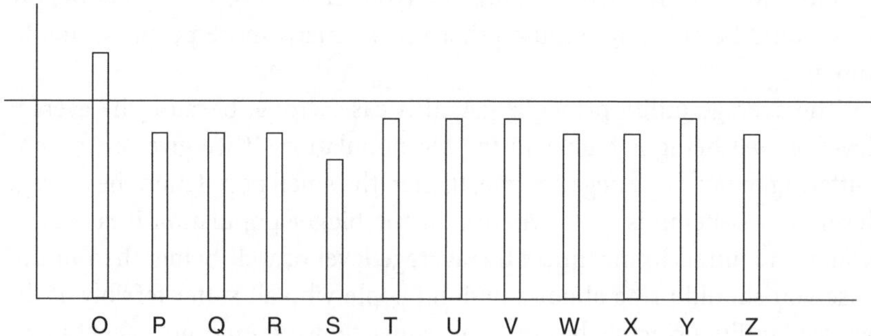

Figure 10.5 Individuals O to Z

than this second one. You should do this even if, in the second population, there are more people and well-being below the critical level. Critical-level utilitarianism is only interested in well-being above the line.

10.37 This view can avoid the problems of the previous views. It can explain why Bea ought to wait before she gets pregnant: by waiting she will create more well-being above the critical level. Critical-level utilitarianism can also avoid the repugnant conclusion.

10.38 If you compare the populations A to Z where these populations gradually get bigger in size and lower on well-being, at some point the level of well-being in the given population falls below the critical level. After this point, the new populations will no longer be better than the previous outcomes in terms of well-being above the critical level. Because of this, critical-level utilitarianism would not require you to create the huge population Z. According to this view, you should rather create the population between A and Z which maximizes the amount of well-being above the critical level.

The problem with this view is that setting the critical level is hard (Parfit, 1984, pp. 412–416; **Broome, 1992, p. 122**).[23] If you set it too low, you get the repugnant conclusion. In this situation, the best way to maximize the amount of well-being above the critical level is to create a vast number of people whose lives aren't that good even if they are just above the critical level. If you set the level too high, then adding people whose lives are fairly good but just below the critical level wouldn't do you any good. Given a choice between creating a population whose lives are worth living but are just below the critical level and creating no one at all, you might just as well create no one. After all, only well-being above the critical level counts, on this view. 10.39

These examples show how hard it is to find a principle of beneficence that does not have unintuitive consequences in some population cases. This has led to a whole cycle of more complicated principles and new counterexamples. 10.40

Variable value view and intuitions*

Some people have claimed that solving the previous problems requires more radical thinking. The previous views assumed that how much a new person with a certain level of well-being contributes to the value of the future outcome is always constant. Everyone matters equally no matter how many other people are around at the same time. How well off the other people are doesn't matter either. Creating a new person is always just as good. 10.41

As a defender of the **variable value view**, **Tom Hurka** has argued that we should give up this assumption (**Hurka, 1983**).[24] He thinks that how good it is to create a new person with a good life depends on how many people already exist. If only a few people exist, then it is important to have more people even if they will have a low level of well-being. In contrast, if a population is already big, then there is no point in having more people even if they would be fairly well off. The value of an individual can thus vary depending on how many other people exist. 10.42

Sophisticated views like this can be made to match our intuitions about different cases. Yet at some point these theories become so complicated that it's no longer clear what the point is. Ideally, you want to start from a simple, attractive ethical idea and then use it to decide how many people there 10.43

should be. In contrast, we are now beginning from our intuitions about the cases, and then we use these intuitions to formulate incredibly complicated moral principles. These principles therefore just capture what we already know. As a result, these principles are pretty pointless.

10.44 We should also consider the intuitions we are relying on. So far, we have evaluated different population principles by comparing them to our intuitions about different cases. Most people think that this is a good test for the principles. Yet there are also reasons to doubt that our intuitions about large populations are a good starting point. Most of us aren't good at imagining the consequences of the large numbers involved (Broome, 2004, p. 57). If you can't vividly imagine what it is like for a billion people to exist on a low level of well-being, then you can't make judgments about how bad the repugnant conclusion is.

10.45 **Torbjörn Tännsjö** has argued that when you think about these examples you tend to imagine what it would be like for you to live in a huge population (**Tännsjö, 2002**).[25] Because life would be bad for you, you'll judge that these outcomes are not desirable. Tännsjö thinks that this is not the right way to think about the question. According to him, moral deliberation should be more impartial and general. This means that if you are able to give up your personal biases and think about the numbers in question more impartially, it could be that the repugnant conclusion is something you should accept anyway.

Climate Change and Personal Obligations

10.46 The previous discussion shows that there is a lot of philosophical disagreement about population sizes. There is even more ethical controversy about climate change, but the philosophical aspects of climate change are simpler. **John Broome** has recently shown that it is fairly simple **what you ought to do as an individual about climate change** (Broome, **1992,** 2012).[26] This will be the topic in this section, whereas the next section will consider the more difficult question of what states should do about climate change. The final section will investigate how you should react to the uncertainty in climate change predictions.

10.47 When you think about what you should do about climate change as an individual, you only need to consider two things: you need to know certain basic facts about climate change and you need to rely on the basic "Do no harm!" principle. Luckily, this will not be too much trouble.

Let's use conservative estimates of the facts (Broome, 2012, pp. 74–75). 10.48
An average person from a wealthy country emits slightly over 10 metric tons of CO_2 per year. This means that over your lifetime you will emit roughly around 800 metric tons. As a consequence, your greenhouse gas contribution will raise the temperature on Earth half a billionth of a degree. Even if this is a tiny increase, you would be wrong to think that it makes no difference.

Consider the future people whose lives will be made worse by climate 10.49
change. As a result of the higher temperatures, **they will suffer from new diseases, heatstrokes, extreme weather events, mass migrations, lack of food and water, conflicts and wars.**[27] The half a billionth of a degree increase in the temperature for which you are personally responsible is just one tiny contributing factor to these harms. As a result, you are just one several billionth of a part responsible for each one of the serious harms in the future. You are thus responsible for a small portion of every future harm caused by the climate change.

You also need to take into account the huge number of future people 10.50
who will be harmed. As an individual, you harm billions of people a tiny bit. If we add these tiny harms together, you are all fully responsible for wiping out half a year of one healthy human life. Your personal lifetime CO_2 emissions therefore have the same effect as killing someone half a year before they would have died. It is therefore as wrong to emit 800 metric tons of CO_2 over your lifetime as it is to do just that.

This means that the "Do no harm!" principle requires you not to increase 10.51
the amount of CO_2 in the atmosphere. Many people find this conclusion absurd, because they think that this would require radical lifestyle changes from them. People imagine that you would have to stop using cars and planes, stop eating meat, and switch off the air-con in the summer and heating in the winter. If you had to do all of this, your life would be much worse.

Carbon offsetting

Fortunately, you wouldn't have to do any of that. Of course you should take 10.52
many small steps to **reduce your emissions.**[28] You should switch off lights when you can, eat less meat, and avoid unnecessary travel. Even if you take these steps, you would still emit a lot of CO_2. Luckily, there is a much easier way to avoid increasing the amount of greenhouse gases in the atmosphere over your lifetime. You can do this by **carbon offsetting**[29] your emissions (Broome, 2012, pp. 85–96).

10.53 The basic idea of offsetting is simple. You successfully offset your CO_2 emissions if for every unit of carbon dioxide you emit you take one unit away from the atmosphere. If you do this, your balance of greenhouse gas emissions and subtractions will amount to zero and you will therefore have no effect on the future temperatures and thus your actions will not harm anyone.

10.54 Commercial organizations can help you to offset your emissions for a small sum of money. It costs you roughly \$10 to offset a metric ton of CO_2, which means that it would cost you about \$8000 to offset your lifetime emissions. This sounds like a lot, but over a 40-year period it amounts to only \$16.67 per month. With this monthly contribution, you avoid harming other people by half a year of someone's life.

10.55 Should you do this? Imagine that you owned a car worth \$8000. When you are returning home, your neighbor's grandmother suddenly steps in front of your car. You know that she has only about half a year to live. You can either hit her or swerve, crashing into a tree which will wreck your car but not hurt you. In this case, you should avoid killing the grandmother even if this will cost you \$8000. You face a similar choice with respect to climate change. If you think that you should not kill the grandmother, then other things being equal you should also offset your CO_2 emissions.

10.56 The offsetting companies use the money to reduce CO_2 emissions around the world. Their projects usually take place in the developing world, where it is cheapest to diminish emissions by giving people more efficient stoves and by building dams, wind farms, and other sources of renewable energy. Even if you continue to emit CO_2 yourself, by offsetting you can thus avoid influencing the global temperature yourself and therefore it is relatively easy not to harm other people with your emissions.

Climate Change and Governments

10.57 There is an obvious problem with the previous conclusion. Even if you become CO_2-neutral yourself, most other people will continue to emit a lot of CO_2 without taking any away from the atmosphere. The amount of greenhouse gases in the atmosphere will therefore continue to increase and our planet will continue to get warmer. Your own CO_2 neutrality will only make a tiny dent to the global climate change process. Offsetting is not, therefore, a complete solution to the problem.

This doesn't mean that you shouldn't offset your own CO_2 emissions. It just means that something more must be done about climate change: mankind as a whole must reduce its CO_2 emissions radically. This is something that individuals can't do on their own. CO_2 emissions can be curbed to a sustainable level only if all the governments in the world decide to pursue this goal together. 10.58

This is where climate change ethics becomes more complicated. Let's look at theoretical problems first and then turn to the more practical challenges. When we discussed what you ought to do as an individual, we were able to rely on the simple "Do no harm!" principle. The problem is that, because of the non-identity effect discussed above, we can't use this same principle when we consider what governments should do (Broome, 2012, pp. 61–62). 10.59

If CO_2 emissions are to be reduced globally, this requires all countries to adopt new laws, which radically change how we all live. People wouldn't be allowed to use cars and planes as much as before, and they wouldn't be able to buy as many consumer goods and eat as much meat as before. Lives would be radically changed. Because of this, our children would not meet the same partners as they would have done otherwise. 10.60

This means that if new global rules are adopted to limit our emissions, different individuals will come to exist in the future. The good thing about this is that if all governments continue on the present path this won't harm anyone. What governments are doing now is not making anyone worse off, because the only other alternative for the governments is to create a totally different set of future people. This is true even if the current course of the governments will lead to low quality of life in the future. 10.61

This non-identity effect means that the "Do no harm!" principle can't require governments to do anything about the climate change. There is no corresponding problem when it comes to what you ought to do as an individual. If you offset your emissions, this can only affect who your children and their children will be. Given that other people continue to act in the same way, they will have the same children independently of what you do. This means that there are certain future people who will exist no matter what you do personally. You will harm these individuals unless you offset your greenhouse gas emissions. 10.62

Because of this, the principle that requires governments to do something about climate change can't be a person-affecting principle based on the notion of harm. Instead it must be some version of the principle of beneficence of the form "Do good!" If governments must do something about 10.63

climate change, they must be under an obligation to make the world a better place for their citizens – a place in which everyone's right to live well is respected. Fortunately, governments already recognize such a duty in many contexts: many governments try to see to it that their citizens are educated and healthy and have jobs so that they can live good lives.

10.64 If governments have a duty to guarantee that their citizens can live good lives, then they should agree to reduce CO_2 emissions globally to curb climate change. If governments pursued this goal together, more people would come to live happier lives in the future.

The discount rate*

10.65 As an individual you must therefore reduce your CO_2 emissions because of the "Do no harm!" principle, whereas governments should do this in order to follow the "Do good!" principle. This conclusion leads to two interesting philosophical problems. As you might have noticed, when you apply the "Do good!" principle you must first know what counts as good. This will have huge consequences for what governments ought to do about climate change.

10.66 When governments do good, they must weigh the costs and benefits of their options. If governments decide to reduce CO_2 emissions globally, there will be fewer extreme weather events, more people will have clean water and food, and fewer people have to migrate or die as a result of diseases and conflicts. Billions of people would enjoy these benefits over hundreds of years.

10.67 Reducing CO_2 emissions also has its costs. A lot of resources would have to be used for developing carbon-neutral technologies, which also have their risks. A massive investment in nuclear power could lead to disasters like the one that took place in **Fukushima**[30] in 2011. Material goods and traveling would also have to be made more expensive in order to curb emissions.

10.68 This means that we need some way of comparing the costs and benefits of different global climate policies. We can use well-being as a currency in these comparisons. Governments could then evaluate different policies by looking at how much well-being they produce and how this well-being is distributed. For this reason, governments will need to have some idea of what well-being consists in.

10.69 Governments face serious philosophical problems even before they take a stand on what well-being is. Consider how the harms and benefits in question are related temporally. Preventing the bad consequences of climate change requires acting immediately: our generation would have to reduce consumption and travel and invest in renewable forms of energy. We would also have to adapt to climate change by developing drought-resistant crops and by building levees in coastal areas. In contrast, the benefits of these actions will be enjoyed in the more distant future. This leads to the crucial question: **How does future well-being weigh against the sacrifices we need to make now?**[31]

In normal life, you care more about getting things now. Imagine that 10.70
you are offered a choice between getting a small chocolate bar now or getting a larger one a year later. This is a choice between one benefit now and a larger benefit later on. In these cases, most people choose to have the smaller benefit now. Sometimes this is because people act against their own better judgments, but most of us just believe that the current benefits matter more than the ones in the distant future. This is called **discounting the future.**

Economists talk about **the discount rate** of different commodities. If the 10.71
discount rate of apples is 4%, this means that an apple a year from now will have only 96% of its present value. With this discount rate of apples, you would be neutral between getting an apple now and getting approximately 1.0417 apples in a year's time. You would also be equally neutral between these two options and getting approximately 1.0851 apples in two years' time.

This is incredibly important because what governments should do 10.72
about climate change depends on what the correct discount rate for well-being is (**Sunstein and Weisbach, 2008**; Broome, 2012, ch. 8).[32] In other words, what discount rate is adopted has huge consequences for how good the outcomes of different policies are. If the correct discount rate is low, then the potential benefits in a hundred years' time will be just as important as the sacrifices we have to make now. If the correct discount rate is high instead, then the potential benefits in the distant future will not be as important and we can continue our CO_2 emissions as before.

In the climate change debates, the suggested discount rates have varied 10.73
from 1% to more than 5%. Because of this, different studies have come to very different conclusions about what governments should do now to prevent climate change. Low discount rates require governments to demand significant sacrifices from us now in order to help future generations, whereas higher discount rates let governments off the hook.

10.74 What the correct discount rate is, and how future well-being therefore compares to current well-being, is an ethical question. Our answer to it will have huge consequences for the future of mankind. The correct discount rate has been intensively debated in politics and economics, but so far moral philosophers have contributed less to these discussions. It is to be hoped that the next generations of ethicists will be more interested in these questions.

The social action problem

10.75 Finally, let's consider more practical problems which governments face with respect to climate change. Many people are frustrated by governments' inability to take action. We can now give an easy explanation for why governments are not doing more.

10.76 When it comes to climate change, governments face a prisoner's dilemma type of paradox of social action (see Chapter 3). Imagine that you are the President of **Kazakhstan.**[33] Would it be rational for you to curb the CO_2 emissions of your country? Your citizens would have to make significant sacrifices as a result, and if they didn't agree to make these sacrifices you would have to coerce them.

10.77 In this situation, you will have to consider the two following scenarios:

A. Other countries curb their emissions and climate change will be prevented.
B. Other countries do nothing and climate change takes place.

The problem is that in both A and B it is best for your country if you do nothing. Your citizens will always be better off if they can continue to emit. If other countries act, it makes no difference if your citizens keep on emitting CO_2. This is a win–win situation for you. Your citizens will not have to suffer the consequences of climate change or change their behavior.

10.78 If other countries fail to act, climate change will take place whatever your citizens do. In this scenario too, you should not make your country change its ways. It's better if you let your people continue to live in the same way, even if they will have to suffer some of the bad consequences of climate change.

10.79 This means that no matter what others do, your citizens will be better off if you let them freely emit greenhouse gases. The real problem is that all governments will think in the same way. This paradox is why governments are unwilling to reduce their emissions and why everyone will have to suffer the bad consequences of climate change. Every country will be worse off than they would be if a global climate agreement were reached. This problem can be solved only if governments decide to pursue good outcomes together.

Climate Change and Uncertainty

This chapter has so far assumed certain facts about climate change. The 10.80
people who disagree with these facts are called **climate change "skeptics."**[34] They say that climate change is not a fact but merely a theory. This is not a helpful way to think about things since well-supported theories are the best way to understand facts. In any case, climate change skeptics have denied:

i. that there is a correlation between CO_2 concentrations and global temperatures;
ii. that average temperatures have increased;
iii. that these increases will continue as predicted; and
iv. that climate change is man-made.

There is **almost no disagreement**[35] about these issues in the scientific 10.81
community, but scientists too are still uncertain about the exact consequences of vast CO_2 emissions. Furthermore, the climate models used by climate scientists are all probabilistic (Silver, 2012). The reports of the Intergovernmental Panel on Climate Change describe different **emission scenarios** and then make claims about the **likely effects** of these scenarios.[36]

If the likely range of temperature rise for a given emission scenario is 10.82
between 1.4 degrees Celsius and 3.9 degrees Celsius, this means that (according to the prediction) there is a 66% probability that future temperature increases will be within this range. This prediction also leaves room for a small possibility that the temperature will not change at all or that it will increase by 8 degrees. The IPCC reports also talk about what the likely consequences of the different temperatures will be.

Some people say that we shouldn't do anything about climate change 10.83
because we don't know for certain what will happen. This reaction is just silly, because no one follows this principle in normal life. Imagine that a

doctor tells you there is a 60% chance that you will get a painful disease and that you can probably avoid this by undergoing minor treatment. You probably won't think that you should do nothing in this case.

Maximizing expected value*

10.84 In the previous case, you would probably intuitively maximize **expected value** (see Chapter 4). You would first consider what possible outcomes your options have. If you choose not take the treatment, then you either get the painful disease or you don't. You would then consider how good or bad these outcomes would be and how likely it is that they will come about. The expected value of an option is the sum of the value of the different options multiplied by their likelihoods.

10.85 To see how this works, imagine that the likelihood of getting the disease is 0.8 if you don't take the treatment. Here the 0.8 probability means that there is an 80% chance that you will get the disease if you don't take the treatment. The harm of having the disease is minus 20 units of well-being, whereas if you don't get the disease you will get plus 10 units of well-being. The chance of getting the disease if you take the drug is only 0.1. The cost of taking the treatment is minus 3 units of well-being. In this case, you have two options, which both have two possible outcomes. This situation can be illustrated with the diagram shown in Figure 10.6. The expected value of taking the treatment and getting the disease is then $-23u \times 0.1$, which is $-2.3u$. Likewise, the expected value

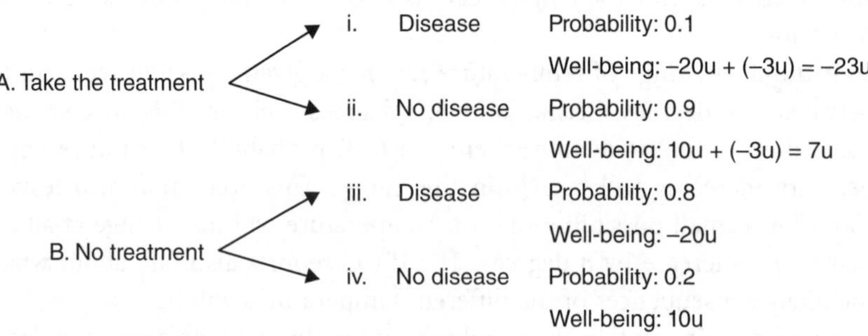

Figure 10.6 Expected value

of taking the treatment and not getting the disease is 7u × 0.9, which is 6.3u. The overall expected value of taking the treatment is then −2.3u + 6.3u, which is 4 units of well-being. In the same way, the expected value of not taking the treatment is (−20u*0.8) + (10u*.2), which is −14 units of well-being. In this example, you should therefore take the treatment because this would maximize expected value (4 units of well-being is more than −14 units).

If we use roughly this kind of reasoning in normal life, then we should react to uncertainty about climate change in the same way. Here too, we should start from what options we have. We can do nothing at all, and we have a range of options for how much to cut our emissions. For every option we have, the best scientific estimates specify different outcome scenarios and how likely these scenarios are. This enables us to calculate the expected value of different climate change policies. The rational reaction to climate change is to choose the climate policy that maximizes expected value. This is how you can take into account that there is still plenty of uncertainty about what will happen. 10.86

Of course, making policy decisions at the governmental level is still incredibly difficult, because of how much information is required. Fortunately, a lot of brilliant people are attempting to provide this information for our governments and us. Many of their predictions already have a good track record, and these predictions will become more accurate the more data is collected (Silver, 2012, pp. 397–398). More importantly, doing nothing is not a reasonable plan just because we are not fully certain about what will happen. Maximizing expected value is already a better way to react to uncertainty in the face of climate change. 10.87

Summary and Questions

This chapter has discussed two related global ethical problems: **population growth and climate change**.[37] When we consider actions that affect future generations, one problem is that what we do affects which individuals will come to live. As the example of Ann and Bea showed, in this situation you can't rely on person-affecting principles such as the "Do no harm!" principle. Instead you must use principles of beneficence according to which you must maximize the amount of well-being in the future no matter who will come to have it in their lives. 10.88

10.89 Unfortunately, this way of thinking leads to the repugnant conclusion according to which you should create as many people as you can just as long as their lives will be barely worth living. We saw how difficult it is to formulate an ethical principle that does not have unacceptable consequences like this. This means that a lot of important work still needs to be done in population ethics.

10.90 The second half of this chapter considered climate change. Many people believe that climate change is a serious threat to the well-being of future generations. Following John Broome, it is useful to consider separately what you should do as an individual about this and what governments should do on the international level. Because you should not harm other people, as an individual you should become carbon neutral. At the moment, you can do this easily by offsetting your emissions.

10.91 Offsetting your emissions doesn't, however, solve the climate change problem more generally. Only governments can solve this problem, by curbing greenhouse gas emissions globally. They should do this because governments are obliged to follow the "Do good!" principle by improving the lives of their citizens no matter who they happen to be. This leads to interesting philosophical questions about whether future well-being counts for less and about how governments should react to the uncertainty inherent in climate change predictions. The suggestion then was that doing nothing isn't a sensible option.

10.92 Based on the philosophical resources introduced in this chapter, consider the following questions:

1. What is the difference between person-affecting ethical principles and other principles? Try to imagine situations in which these two types of principles say different things.
2. What is the repugnant conclusion? Which versions of utilitarianism lead to this conclusion and which ones don't? Why not?
3. Why does John Broome think that we should offset our carbon dioxide emissions? Are there any problems with his argument?
4. Why aren't governments required to take action about climate change on the same grounds as individuals?
5. Does the well-being of future people matter less than our own well-being? Why?
6. This chapter suggested that maximizing expected value is the right reaction to uncertainty in the context of climate change. What complications does this ignore?

Annotated Bibliography

Broad, C.D. (1930) *Five Types of Ethical Theory*, full text available at http://www.ditext.com/broad/ftet/ftet.html, accessed March 12, 2014. Broad compares the ethical theories of Spinoza, Butler, Hume, Kant, and Sidgwick. The last chapter contains an interesting discussion of utilitarianism.

Broome, John (1992) *Counting the Costs of Climate Change* (Cambridge: White Horse Press), full text available at http://users.ox.ac.uk/~sfop0060/pdf/Counting%20the%20Cost%20of%20Global%20Warming.pdf, accessed March 12, 2014. Broome's earlier work on the ethics of climate change, in which he uses the tools of economics and moral philosophy to sketch how the costs and benefits of different climate change scenarios could be compared.

Broome, John (2004) *Weighing Lives* (Oxford: Oxford University Press). An insightful and sometimes technical book on how well-being should be measured, aggregated, and taken into account in public policy decisions.

Broome, John (2012) *Climate Matters: Ethics in a Warming World* (New York: W.W. Norton). A wonderfully clear and well-argued book on the ethics of climate change. Broome shows why we should think of our individual choices and the actions of governments in different ways. He also argues that we need both ethical sensitivity and the mathematical tools of economics to solve this problem.

Gardiner, Stephen, Simon Caney, Dale Jamieson, and Henry Shue (eds.) (2010) *Climate Change: Essential Readings* (Oxford: Oxford University Press). A comprehensive collection of some of the most important articles ever published on climate change ethics.

Hurka, Thomas (1983) "Value and Population Size," *Ethics*, *93*(3), 496–507, full text available at http://www.repugnant-conclusion.com/hurka-populationsize.pdf, accessed March 12, 2014. Hurka uses Moore's idea of organic wholes to make an important contribution to population ethics. According to him, the value of a human being can depend on how many people already exist.

Kavka, Gregory (1982) "The Paradox of Future Individuals," *Philosophy & Public Affairs*, *11*(2), 93–112, full text available at http://faculty.smu.edu/jkazez/pap/kavka.pdf, accessed March 12, 2014. An early attempt to deal with the non-identity problem and the repugnant conclusion it leads to. Kavka argues that we should avoid creating people who will come to live restricted lives, because by creating such lives we would not treat the future people as ends in themselves.

Parfit, Derek (1976) "Rights, Interests and Possible People," in Samuel Gorovitz *et al.* (eds.), *Moral Problems in Medicine* (Englewood Cliffs, NJ: Prentice Hall), pp. 369–375. Parfit's first discussion of population problems. He argued that R.M. Hare's utilitarian principles will have absurd consequences in medical contexts.

Parfit, Derek (1984) *Reasons and Persons*. See the bibliography of Chapter 1 above.

Ryberg, Jesper and Torbjörn Tännsjö (eds.) (2004) *The Repugnant Conclusion: Essays on Population Ethics* (Dordrecht: Kluwer). A collection of important articles on population ethics.

Sidgwick, Henry (1907) *The Methods of Ethics*. See the bibliography of Chapter 1 above.

Silver, Nate (2012) *The Signal and the Noise: The Art and Science of Prediction* (London: Penguin). A book on statistics and predictions for the general audience. The chapter on climate change contains a level-headed evaluation of the climate change data and predictions.

Sunstein, Cass and David Weisbach (2008) "Climate Change and Discounting the Future: A Guide for the Perplexed," *Harvard Law School Public Law and Legal Theory Research Paper*, 08-20, full text available at http://www.hks.harvard.edu/m-rcbg/cepr/Online%20Library/Papers/Weisbach_Sunstein_Climate_Future.pdf, accessed March 12, 2014. A helpful overview of discussions about the discount rate in the climate change debates, which includes an interesting discussion of whether this rate should be chosen on economic or ethical grounds.

Tännsjö, Torbjörn (2002) "Why We Ought to Accept the Repugnant Conclusion," *Utilitas*, *14*(3), 339–359, full text available at http://people.su.se/~guarr/FGkurs/TT%20On%20Why%20We%20Ought%20to%20Accept%20the%20Repugnant%20Conclusion.pdf, accessed March 12, 2014. An interesting attempt to argue that we should learn to live with the repugnant conclusion, because it follows from all acceptable ethical principles.

Online Resources

1 Wikipedia on world population: http://en.wikipedia.org/wiki/World_population.
2 Information about development of agriculture: https://genographic.nationalgeographic.com/development-of-agriculture/.
3 Nice illustration of this trend: http://www.youtube.com/watch?v=fTznEIZRkLg.
4 Another visualization: http://www.youtube.com/watch?v=4BbkQiQyaYc.
5 Al Gore with the famous graphs: http://www.youtube.com/watch?v=9tkDK2mZlOo, debate about the graph: http://www.newscientist.com/article/dn11646-climate-myths-the-hockey-stick-graph-has-been-proven-wrong.html and National Climatic Data Center's information page on global warming: http://www.ncdc.noaa.gov/cmb-faq/globalwarming.html.
6 Information of carbon dioxide: http://en.wikipedia.org/wiki/Carbon_dioxide.

7 Wikipedia on greenhouse gases: http://en.wikipedia.org/wiki/Greenhouse_gas.
8 The life and work of Joseph Fourier: http://en.wikipedia.org/wiki/Joseph_Fourier and John Tyndall: http://en.wikipedia.org/wiki/John_Tyndall.
9 A graph illustrating the correlation: http://www.brighton73.freeserve.co.uk/gw/paleo/400000yearslarge.gif.
10 On ice ages: http://en.wikipedia.org/wiki/Ice_age.
11 Civilizations: http://en.wikipedia.org/wiki/Civilization.
12 Explanation of climate sensitivity: http://en.wikipedia.org/wiki/Climate_sensitivity.
13 IPCC summary: http://www.ipcc.ch/publications_and_data/ar4/syr/en/mains2-3.html.
14 IPCC report summary for policy makers: http://www.ipcc.ch/pdf/assessment-report/ar4/wg2/ar4-wg2-spm.pdf.
15 Introduction to the often used principle: http://en.wikipedia.org/wiki/Primum_non_nocere.
16 Wikipedia on Parfit: http://en.wikipedia.org/wiki/Derek_Parfit.
17 An overview of the non-identity problem: http://plato.stanford.edu/entries/nonidentity-problem/.
18 Discussion of the principle: http://plato.stanford.edu/entries/principle-beneficence/.
19 Overview of the repugnant conclusion in population ethics: http://plato.stanford.edu/entries/repugnant-conclusion/, Sidgwick's early formulation of the thesis: http://archive.org/stream/methodsofethics00sidguoft#page/414/mode/2up, and Broad's 1930 formulation: http://www.ditext.com/broad/ftet/ftet6g.html.
20 Transitivity: http://www.britannica.com/EBchecked/topic/602836/transitive-law.
21 Information on calculating averages: http://en.wikipedia.org/wiki/Average.
22 Average height charts: http://www.disabled-world.com/artman/publish/height-chart.shtml.
23 Broome's *Counting the Costs of Climate Change*: http://users.ox.ac.uk/~sfop0060/pdf/Counting%20the%20Cost%20of%20Global%20Warming.pdf.
24 Hurka's homepage: http://homes.chass.utoronto.ca/~thurka/ and his "Value and Population Size": http://www.repugnant-conclusion.com/hurka-populationsize.pdf.
25 Tännsjö's homepage: http://people.su.se/~tanns/index_en.htm and his "Why We Ought to Accept the Repugnant Conclusion": http://people.su.se/~guarr/FGkurs/TT%20On%20Why%20We%20Ought%20to%20Accept%20the%20Repugnant%20Conclusion.pdf.
26 John Broome's homepage: http://users.ox.ac.uk/~sfop0060/, video of his 2012 Tanner Lectures on Climate Change: http://www.youtube.com/watch?v

=oSl_noHhhFI, and *Counting the Costs of Climate Change*: http://users.ox.ac.uk/~sfop0060/pdf/Counting%20the%20Cost%20of%20Global%20Warming.pdf.

27 Student guide to effects of climate change: http://www.epa.gov/climatestudents/impacts/effects/.

28 Top ten tips: http://bravenewclimate.com/2008/08/29/top-10-ways-to-reduce-your-co2-emissions-footprint/.

29 Information on carbon offsetting: http://en.wikipedia.org/wiki/Carbon_offset.

30 Wikipedia on the Fukushima disaster: http://en.wikipedia.org/wiki/Fukushima_Daiichi_nuclear_disaster.

31 Broome on how much we care about the future: http://users.ox.ac.uk/~sfop0060/pdf/The%20ethics%20of%20climate%20change.pdf.

32 "Climate Change and Discounting the Future: A Guide for the Perplexed": http://www.hks.harvard.edu/m-rcbg/cepr/Online%20Library/Papers/Weisbach_Sunstein_Climate_Future.pdf.

33 Information about Kazakhstan: http://en.wikipedia.org/wiki/Kazakhstan.

34 Wikipedia on the controversy: https://en.wikipedia.org/wiki/Global_warming_controversy.

35 NASA on scientific consensus: http://climate.nasa.gov/scientific-consensus.

36 IPCC on emission scenarios and their consequences: http://www.ipcc.ch/publications_and_data/ar4/syr/en/spms3.html.

37 On the connections between the problems: http://www.guardian.co.uk/environment/2013/jun/30/population-growth-wipe-out-life-earth.

GLOSSARY OF TERMS

act-consequentialism	A form of direct consequentialism according to which the rightness and wrongness of acts directly depends on the value of their consequences. An act is right on this view if and only if it has the best consequences of the options available for the agent.
actual duty	A notion in Ross's ethical theory which refers to what you ought to do, all things considered, once all the prima facie duties that are relevant in the situation have been taken into account.
actual value	Certain forms of consequentialism rank options in terms of how good their consequences are as a matter of fact – that is, according to how much actual value their consequences have. According to these views, an ordinary action that accidentally has bad consequences in a given situation is wrong in that situation.
agency condition	The thesis that says that only agents, and no other beings, can be morally responsible. Different agency conditions then set different standards for what it

This Is Ethics: An Introduction, First Edition. Jussi Suikkanen.

takes to be an agent. Minimally, agency requires having a conception of the world and an ability to pursue goals.

agent relativism The form of relativism that says that whether an agent's actions are right or wrong depends on the moral principles accepted in her own society.

amoralist A person who allegedly makes moral judgments but is not moved by them.

analytic A statement is said to be analytically true when it is true merely in virtue of the meanings of the words. For example, the sentence "vixen is a female fox" is often claimed to be true in this way because the word "vixen" just is synonymous with the words "female fox." There is much controversy in philosophy about this alleged category of truths.

appraisal relativism A form of relativism according to which whether your moral evaluation of someone's actions is correct depends on what moral principles are accepted in your society.

Argument from Motivation An argument which has the Humean Theory of Motivation and Moral Judgment Internalism as its premises and expressivism as its conclusion. It claims that because there is a necessary connection between moral judgments and motivation, moral judgments can't be beliefs.

attributability A quality which events have in virtue of being your actions. For example, the event of the door closing can be attributed to you as an action if you closed the door in order to achieve some goal.

average utility principle A version of utilitarianism according to which we should maximize the average amount of well-being in the world.

begging the question	In philosophy, you beg the question if you assume your conclusion as one of your premises in the argument to that conclusion.
capability approach	A theory of well-being defended by Amartya Sen and Martha Nussbaum. It is based on the idea that there are certain important and typical human functionings and that well-being consists of having the appropriate capabilities for taking part in these functionings successfully.
carbon offsetting	Actions in virtue of which you take away as much carbon dioxide from the atmosphere as you put there in the first place.
Categorical Imperative	According to Immanuel Kant, a fundamental moral obligation that is independent of our particular desires. In its most general form, it requires us to act on principles we can at the same time consistently will to be universal laws. Kant gave different formulations of the Categorical Imperative. The other well-known formulation states that we should treat humanity, in ourselves and others, always as an end in itself and never merely as a means.
causal responsibility	Causal responsibility for an outcome requires that your actions brought it about by causing it.
climate change skeptics	People who think that man-made global warming is merely a scientific hypothesis which is likely to be false.
climate sensitivity	How many degrees warmer the Earth's atmosphere would get if the amount of carbon dioxide in the Earth's atmosphere doubled from its pre-industrial level (which was about 275 ppm).

cognitive states	The word "cognitive" means anything to do with cognition, which is related to knowing and believing. The best example of a cognitive state is a belief. Distinguishing features of beliefs and cognitive states more broadly include that they aim at being true, that they are sensitive to evidence, and that they have the mind-to-world direction of fit.
compatibilism	The view according to which people can be morally responsible for their actions even if determinism is true.
compliance problem	A problem for contractarian ethical theories: even if there are principles which rational egoists would accept, it might still not be rational for you to comply with those principles as an egoist.
consequentialism	A family of ethical theories that are based on a value-theoretic element that allows you to rank options in terms of how good their consequences are, and a normative element that defines what is right and wrong in terms of the previous evaluative ranking.
constant valence	The idea that if a consideration is a reason for doing a certain action in one context then it must be a reason for doing that act in all contexts.
contractarianism	Ethical theories that attempt to capture what is right and wrong in terms of principles which rational egoists would accept.
contradiction in conception	A situation in which it is impossible to imagine a maxim to be a universal law. For example, it is inconceivable that everyone would be lying to one another all the time.
contradiction in will	When you can't will a maxim to be a universal law, because in the situation in

which that maxim is a universal law you could not pursue your goals effectively.

criterion of rightness — An understanding of an ethical theory according to which even if the theory describes what determines what is right and wrong, you don't need to use that theory in deliberation.

critical-level utilitarianism — A version of utilitarianism according to which we should maximize only the amount of general well-being above a certain critical threshold higher than what is required for having a life worth living.

deep attributability principle — The claim that you are morally responsible for an action only if doing that action is up to your real self.

deliberation procedure — An understanding of an ethical theory according to which you should use the ethical theory explicitly in deliberation to decide what you are to do.

deontic — Anything to do with obligations, duties, reasons, ought, and the like.

desire satisfaction theory — A theory of well-being according to which how well your life is going depends on how many of your desires are being satisfied. The more you get what you want, the higher your level of well-being is. A desire satisfaction theory of happiness would similarly say that the more you get what you want, the happier you thereby are.

determinism — The thesis that everything that happens in the universe is a consequence of the laws of nature and the state of the universe in its very beginning.

direct consequentialism — A version of consequentialism according to which the rightness and wrongness of acts depends directly on their consequences.

disabling condition	A feature of a situation which prevents something that usually is a reason for you from being a reason for you in that situation.
disagreement in planning	The explanation in terms of conflicting plans which expressivists give for how we can disagree when we make conflicting moral judgments. Such disagreements are to be understood with the model of how we disagree when we disagree where to go for dinner.
discount rate	By how much future goods are less valuable than current ones in a cost–benefit analysis.
discounting the future	Giving less weight to the interests of future people.
divine command theory	A theory in metaethics according to which what is right and wrong is determined by what God commands us to do.
embedding problem	An objection to expressivism according to which expressivists can't explain what moral words mean in more complicated sentences where they do not seem to express our planning attitudes.
epistemology	An area of philosophy that studies knowledge, justification, and evidence.
equivocation	Using a word in two different meanings in an argument.
ethical altruism	An ethical theory according to which right actions make the lives of everyone else go best.
ethical egoism	An ethical theory according to which you should always do whatever makes your own life go best.
Euthyphro dilemma	A classic objection to the divine command theory which can be traced to Plato's dialogue called "Euthyphro." According to the objection, the divine command

	theorists must accept either that actions are wrong because God forbids us to do them, or God forbids us to do them because they are wrong. Both of these options are then argued to be problematic for the divine command theory.
evaluative	Anything to do with value and goodness.
evolutionary biology	A subfield of biology which studies the evolutionary processes that lead to the development of different kinds of complex life on Earth.
expected value	Expected value of an action is roughly how good the consequences of an action can reasonably be expected to be. More precisely, the expected value of an option is calculated by first multiplying the value of the potential outcomes of the option by their likelihood, and then adding these products up.
expression	The non-causal relation which, according to expressivists, holds between moral utterances and moral judgments.
expressivism	A metaethical view according to which (i) the meaning of moral words is to be explained with the moral judgments they express, (ii) moral judgments are non-cognitive planning states, and (iii) moral properties are projections of our attitudes.
fitting fulfillment theory	Susan Wolf's theory of the meaning of life according to which your life is meaningful if you passionately pursue worthwhile projects. This view combines elements of both subjective and objective theories of the meaning of life.
flicker of freedom	A quick chance to do something else than what the person manipulating you wants you to do in a Frankfurt case. If the opponent can show that such

	alternatives always remain in the relevant cases, the cases fail both to undermine the freedom condition and to support compatibilism.
foundationalism	The view that you can have justified beliefs even if they are not justified by your other beliefs. Different versions of foundationalism disagree about what justifies these basic beliefs.
freedom principle	The claim that you are morally responsible for an action only if you could have done something else instead.
Frege–Geach problem	An objection to expressivism according to which expressivism can't explain the central logical properties of moral language, such as which sentences contradict each other and which inferences are valid.
generalism	The view according to which particularism is false. The content of generalism depends on how you understand particularism, but roughly it is the view that moral requirements can be captured with fairly simple principles, which we can learn and apply in practice.
global warming	The increase in Earth's average temperature during the last hundred years or so and its projected continuation.
greatest happiness principle	Jeremy Bentham's formulation of utilitarianism according to which you should maximize the greatest happiness of the greatest number.
greenhouse gas	A gas in the atmosphere that traps infrared radiation, thus warming up the atmosphere. Greenhouse gases include water vapor, methane, carbon dioxide, ozone, and other gases.
happiness	A quality of our lives we are all familiar with. Philosophers have attempted to

	capture what happiness is in terms of pleasures, whole life satisfaction, emotional dispositions, and well-being.
hedonism	The view that only pleasure and absence of pain can make your life go better.
Humean Theory of Motivation	A theory according to which there are two distinct kinds of mental states, beliefs and desires, which have different directions of fit. The theory also claims that both states are required to move us to act.
hypocrisy	What we accuse someone of when they say one thing and act in a completely different way.
imperfect duty	In the framework of Kantian ethics, a moral principle which merely tells you how you should aim to act. You have freedom to choose on what occasions you do so.
indeterminism	The opposite of determinism. It claims that the laws of nature and the original state of affairs of the universe leave many different possible futures open. Indeterminism entails that there are genuinely random events.
indirect consequentialism	A theory which first ranks rules, motives, or characters in terms of how good their consequences are, and then evaluates the rightness and wrongness of actions in terms of that ranking and whether the actions are compatible with the best rules, motives, or characters.
inferential justification	A situation in which your belief is justified (you believe it for a good reason) because it is supported by your other beliefs.
instrumental value	The type of value something has when it is an efficient means for getting something that has intrinsic value.

intrinsic value	The type of value an object has when that object is good for its own sake.
intuitionism	In normative ethics, the view that there are many different moral principles that do not have a single source. In metaethics, a theory of how we can know moral truths based on basic moral beliefs that can justify themselves.
Kantian ethics	A family of ethical theories that are based on the work of Immanuel Kant. These theories are based on different formulations of the Categorical Imperative: the idea that we should act on principles that we can at the same time consistently will to be universal laws.
life satisfaction theory	A theory of happiness according to which you are happy to the degree that you think that your life satisfies your life plan (and feel satisfaction from this thought).
maxim	A term in Kantian ethics referring to a subjective principle of action. It consists of a conception of the situation you are in, an action, and what you aim to achieve with that action in the situation you are in.
maximizing consequentialism	Forms of consequentialism according to which only actions that have the best consequences can be right.
meaning	A much debated concept in philosophy of language. A quality of words and sentences traditionally understood as what a competent speaker has in mind when she uses the word.
metaethics	The area of moral philosophy that studies mainly (i) the meaning of moral words, (ii) the nature of moral thought, and (iii) the nature of moral properties.

metaphysics	An area of philosophy which investigates what there is in the broadest sense.
mind-to-world direction of fit	A feature of beliefs: they aim at representing the world correctly. This feature of beliefs explains why they can be true or false.
moral judgment	The mental state you are in when you sincerely accept a moral sentence of the type "torture is wrong."
Moral Judgment Externalism	The denial of moral judgment internalism. It claims that the connection between moral judgments and motivation is only an accidental one.
Moral Judgment Internalism	The claim that there is a necessary connection between making a moral judgment and being motivated to act accordingly. If you make a moral judgment that acting in a certain way is right, then you will have some motivation to act in that way.
moral luck	A much debated topic in moral philosophy. The question is whether you and your actions' moral qualities can depend on factors that are beyond your own control.
moral realism	The theory in metaethics according to which moral properties and facts are independent of what we think.
moral responsibility	A person is morally responsible for their actions when it is appropriate to adopt reactive attitudes toward them.
natural properties	Properties which can be observed and studied scientifically and the having of which can also cause other things to happen.
naturalism	The view in metaethics according to which moral properties are natural properties.

non-cognitive states Non-cognitive states are all the mental states that are not beliefs or cognitive states more broadly. This category includes desires, sensations, feelings, many emotions, wishes, hopes, make-believe, and so on.

non-identity effect The fact that the time when a child is conceived can affect the identity of the person. If your mother had become pregnant a month earlier than she did, then the child your parents would have had would not have been you. Because of this effect, person-affecting principles seem unable to explain our duties toward future generations.

non-naturalism The view in metaethics according to which moral properties are of their own unique kind. These properties are very different from natural properties. They can't be empirically observed and they do not take part in causal connections.

normative ethics An area of moral philosophy which studies systematically which actions are right and wrong.

normativity According to non-naturalists, this is a unique feature of the moral properties that makes them different from natural properties. Normativity is often claimed to consist of a special authority to require actions from us.

objective list theory A theory of well-being according to which there is a set of goods such that having them in your life makes your life go better no matter what you think about those goods yourself.

Open Question Argument G.E. Moore's attempt to show that moral properties are not natural properties. It is based on the intuition that whatever natural properties we know actions to

	have, it is always a further question whether these actions are right or wrong.
ought implies can principle	A principle according to which morality can require you to do only what you are able to do.
particularism	A view in normative ethics which emphasizes the complexity of the moral reality we face and the idea that this reality can't be captured with any simple moral principles. Furthermore, according to this view, good moral agents do not need to rely on moral principles in moral deliberation.
perfect duty	In the framework of Kantian ethics, a moral principle which you must always comply with.
perfectionism	A version of consequentialism according to which we should maximize the amount of virtuous character traits in the society.
person-affecting principle	An ethical principle according to which whether an action is right or wrong depends only on whether it harms or benefits actual people. When we apply such a principle, we must ask whether our actions make real people better or worse off than they would have been otherwise.
pluralism	The view in normative ethics according to which there are many different moral principles or values that can't be derived from a single source (this view is also often called intuitionism in normative ethics).
practical reasons holism	The idea that, even if some consideration is a reason for you to do a certain act in one context, this same consideration need not be a reason for doing the same act in another context.

practical relevance	Non-naturalists' attempt to explain what the normativity of moral properties consists of. This is the idea that moral properties uniquely bear directly on what we are to do.
practical wisdom	A quality of a person who has all virtues.
prima facie duty	A notion in Ross's ethical theory which refers to an ethical principle that picks out a general quality of acts that makes acts right to some degree. The original meaning of the phrase is a "provisional" duty.
principle of beneficence	An ethical principle that guides you to help other people. A utilitarian version of this principle requires us to maximize the amount of general well-being in the world.
principle of transitivity	The principle according to which if A is better than B and B is better than C, then A is better than C.
projection	A model which expressivists use to understand moral properties. On this view, the properties of being right and wrong are projections of our attitudes in the same way as our culinary reactions color different foods with properties such as "yucky" and "yummy."
prudential value	The type of value something has when having that thing in your life makes your own life go better.
psychological altruism	The rather implausible view according to which we are always motivated to promote what we perceive to be in the interests of others.
psychological egoism	A thesis about human motivation: that we are all motivated to only pursue what we perceive to be in our interests.
reactive attitudes	These attitudes include blame, resentment, condemnation, praise,

respect, and love. We react to actions of others with these attitudes when we hold them responsible for what they do.

real self The part of an agent's psychological makeup that makes the person the very person she is. Philosophers disagree about what constitutes the person's real self: what the desires, plans, values, and beliefs are that make us who we are.

reference The object or a property which a word picks out from the world.

reflective self-evaluation What you do when you use your practical reason and values to determine whether you desire worthwhile things.

relativism A view in metaethics according to which the truth of moral evaluations depends on what moral code is accepted either in the speaker's society (appraisal relativism) or in the agent's society (agent relativism).

reporting The relationship which according to subjectivists holds between moral utterances and our attitudes.

repugnant conclusion The conclusion many principles of beneficence have according to which whatever large population with high quality of life you take, there will be always a much larger population with a very low quality of life such that its existence would be better.

rule-consequentialism A version of indirect consequentialism. On this view, an act is right if and only if it is authorized by the moral principles the general adoption of which has the best consequences.

satisficing consequentialism Forms of consequentialism according to which right actions are required to have only good enough consequences.

second-order desire	A desire to desire something. Likewise, a third-order desire would be a desire to desire to desire something. All these desires are higher-order desires.
Strong Internalism	The claim that when you make a genuine moral judgment, you must have at least some motivation to act accordingly.
subject–predicate sentence	A sentence of the form "X is F" where "X" stands for the subject and "F" is a predicate that describes X in some way. For example, the sentence "grass is green" has this form.
subjectivism	A metaethical view according to which by making moral claims we are talking about our own attitudes of approval and disapproval as individuals.
synthetic	The opposite of analytic. Thus, when a synthetic statement is true, it is not true merely in virtue of the meaning of the words used in the statement. For example, the statement "grass is green" is not true merely because of what the words "grass" and "green" mean but also because grass just happens to be green.
time-slice theory	A theory of an object that considers the object only as it is at a given time. A time-slice theory of moral responsibility, for example, claims that whether you are morally responsible at a given time depends only on your qualities at that moment.
true responsibility	A quality of a person in virtue of which she deserves to go to Heaven or Hell by God. This quality plays a central role in Galen Strawson's argument against moral responsibility.
universal law	A universal law is a more general version of a subjective principle of action. It states that whenever anyone is in a given

	type of situation, they are to act in a certain way in order to achieve a certain outcome.
universalization test	According to Kant, in order for your act to have moral worth, you must first test whether you can consistently will your maxim to be a universal law.
utilitarianism	The most basic form of consequentialism. It says that right actions maximize the amount of general happiness in the world.
valid argument	An argument which has the form such that if the premises are true then the conclusion also has to be true.
variable value view	A theory defended by Thomas Hurka which claims that how good it is that a given person exists depends on how many people already exist when the person is born.
Very Strong Internalism	The strongest form of Moral Judgment Internalism. It says that if you judge that you ought to do an act, you will do that act unless an external force stops you.
virtue	According to the Aristotelian virtue theory, virtues are character traits that are required for the activities that constitute living well. They consist of appropriate beliefs, motives, and emotions.
virtue ethics	A theory in normative ethics according to which we should use the character traits of a flourishing human being to understand right and wrong.
voluntarism	The view that moral standards must be created by an agent or a group of agents.
Weak Internalism	The thesis that when you make a genuine moral judgment, you will have at least some motivation to act accordingly, or else you are irrational.

weakness of will	Acting against your own better judgment. Thinking that you should really do something and then doing something completely different.
well-being	The level of how well your life is going. Having things that have prudential value increases your level of well-being by making your life go better.
world-to-mind direction of fit	A feature of plans and desires: their aim is to get the world to fit the plan or the desire. This explains why plans and desires move us to act.

INDEX

This Is Ethics: An Introduction, First Edition. Jussi Suikkanen.